John Candy

Also by Paul Myers

The Kids in the Hall: One Dumb Guy
A Wizard a True Star: Todd Rundgren in the Studio
It Ain't Easy: Long John Baldry and the Birth of the British Blues
Barenaked Ladies: Public Stunts, Private Stories

Paul Myers

Foreword by Dan Aykroyd

Published in Canada in 2025 and the USA in 2025
by House of Anansi Press Inc.
houseofanansi.com

House of Anansi Press is committed to protecting our natural environment. This book is made of material from well-managed FSC®-certified forests, recycled materials, and other controlled sources.

House of Anansi Press is a Global Certified Accessible™ (GCA by Benetech) publisher. The ebook version of this book meets stringent accessibility standards and is available to readers with print disabilities.

29 28 27 26 25   3 4 5 6 7

Library and Archives Canada Cataloguing in Publication

Title: John Candy : a life in comedy / Paul Myers ;
foreword by Dan Aykroyd.

Names: Myers, Paul, 1960- author | Aykroyd, Dan, writer of foreword

Description: Includes bibliographical references and index.

Identifiers: Canadiana (print) 20250164590 | Canadiana (ebook) 20250164604 | ISBN 9781487009526 (hardcover) | ISBN 9781487009533 (EPUB)

Subjects: LCSH: Candy, John. | LCSH: Comedians—Canada—Biography. | LCSH: Motion picture actors and actresses—Canada—Biography. | LCGFT: Biographies.

Classification: LCC PN2308.C36 M94 2025 | DDC 791.4302/8092—dc23

Jacket and text design: Alysia Shewchuk
Jacket photograph: Ron Galella, Ltd./Ron Galella Collection
via Getty Images

House of Anansi Press is grateful for the privilege to work on and create from the Traditional Territory of many Nations, including the Anishinabeg, the Wendat, and the Haudenosaunee, as well as the Treaty Lands of the Mississaugas of the Credit.

Canada Council for the Arts   Conseil des Arts du Canada

ONTARIO ARTS COUNCIL
CONSEIL DES ARTS DE L'ONTARIO
an Ontario government agency
un organisme du gouvernement de l'Ontario

With the participation of the Government of Canada
Avec la participation du gouvernement du Canada | Canada

We acknowledge for their financial support of our publishing program the Canada Council for the Arts, the Ontario Arts Council, and the Government of Canada.

Printed and bound in Canada

As with everything I make, this work is dedicated to my partner in life, laughs, and adventure, Liza Algar, who is both at my side and on my side. The feeling is mutual.

Contents

John Candy

Foreword

John Candy was as sweet as his name. Sweet, shot through with flavours of cinnamon, ginger, and capsicum. This particular blend of sweetnesses often enabled him to stand firm in the face of some directors whose choices for John's performances might have compromised the integrities of the characters he was portraying. He was sweet but far from weak.

John was a lovely, gentle, good man possessed of a brilliant creative fire, which was served well by his superb talents and skills as a comedian, dramatic actor, impressionist, writer, and originator.

He was beloved by his Second City and SCTV colleagues and by pretty much any professional group that had the privilege of working with him.

We did three pictures together, and apart from the rehearsing and on-camera work, the after-wrap hangs in his luxury motorhome were legendary. The best in refreshments, gourmet food, great music, and sometimes a variety of his non–show business friends. These long post-work parties had the Teamsters lobbying for overtime.

John loved fine things and was always beautifully turned out fashion-wise—a model from the Eaton's Department Store Men's Fine Furnishings catalogue.

When we first met, he was a Kleenex salesman with Kimberly-Clark, driving a company-owned brown four-door Pontiac sedan. He frequently wore tan cashmere blazers or tan and brown suits that seemed to match the car.

I was driving a Royal Mail truck then, so we were both just honest working men with a shared love of comedy greats, movies, music, and laughter.

There is a house in Toronto at 1063 Avenue Road. There should be a commemorative plaque on it. It was rented by John as a dwelling for his family, but the pre-Hollywood parties there were massive fun fests. We'd have Paul Shaffer playing piano, Dave Thomas, Martin Short, Rick Moranis, Andrea Martin, Gilda Radner, Catherine O'Hara, Eugene Levy, Joe Flaherty, Brian Doyle-Murray, all the talented *Godspell* performers, and whoever with Second City was passing through, singing and trying out material.

At the centre of it all was the master host, Johnny Toronto.

John loved his wife, Rose, his children, Jennifer and Chris, his Queen and country, his province, his city, his farm, his friends and colleagues, food and drink, the work of comedy masters, and life itself. He was self-effacing, somewhat shy, courteous, courtly, generous, and hospitable, with the mien of a Knight.

John leaves behind a substantial and beautiful work legacy. Those who knew him have memories of a lovable, wickedly magnetic, and charismatic human being.

He was the leader of our Canadian cohort, which earned international success in our field with him inspiring, supporting, and delighting his fellow performers all along the way. It's great that his work can be easily accessed today and that this book about him is now available to us all.

Dan Aykroyd

Prologue

I Like Me

By the time John Candy reported to the set of *Planes, Trains and Automobiles* in February of 1987, he had already logged plenty of miles during his career in comedy. Having first honed his improvisational comedy skills at the Second City theatre in Chicago, Candy had returned home to the Toronto Second City, evolving with that cast into one of the breakout stars of *Second City Television*. From there, he had eased into feature films with standout roles in a series of well-received comedies including *Splash* and *Stripes*.

But *Planes, Trains and Automobiles* was something new. This buddy comedy about an ill-fated road trip was what is commonly referred to in the business as a "star vehicle" for Candy and one of the biggest names in comedy at the time, Steve Martin.

Candy was working for John Hughes, the so-called Steven Spielberg of teen films, who was now ready to add grown-ups to his cinematic universe. Renowned for having a great ear for dialogue, Candy had been impressed with the way Hughes had written so much of his own voice into his film's character Del Griffith.

Hughes had rightfully earned a reputation in Hollywood for writing long screenplays, but when he loved his actors, as he did here, he was equally happy to let them ad lib. Candy and Martin initially basked in this freedom, which generated many hilarious moments that made it into Hughes's final cut—including the celebrated "those aren't pillows" sequence where the two actors awkwardly shared a comically cramped motel bed—but both actors grew concerned about what they felt were overindulgences on either side of the camera. As the eighty-five-day shoot dragged on, they agreed to curtail their open-ended riffing and honour Hughes's carefully written dialogue, including one of Candy's best monologues in the film, where his character Del erupts after being berated one too many times by Martin's Neal:

"You wanna hurt me? Go right ahead if it makes you feel any better. I'm an easy target. Yeah, you're right, I talk too much. I also listen too much. I could be a cold-hearted cynic like you... but I don't like to hurt people's feelings. Well, you think what you want about me; I'm not changing. I like... I like me. My wife likes me. My customers like me. I'm the real article. What you see is what you get."

In that moment, it was hard not to imagine that Hughes had somehow tapped deep into the soul of the *real* John Candy. It was true—whether they knew him or not, people *liked* John Candy, and those who knew him well even loved him deeply, as much for his inherent kindness as for his authenticity and integrity. Candy frequently played the jester, but he did not suffer fools and tolerated no disrespect toward himself or anyone else he saw being wronged. In a world where publicists routinely shield their star clients' dark sides from their adoring public, it is virtually impossible to find anyone with a bad word to say about him. Even among those with whom he had the occasional artistic or business disagreement, one would be hard-pressed to detect any lasting grudges.

He lived large, loved even larger, and the world loved him back in return. In her memoir, his *SCTV* co-star Andrea Martin described how everyone who came into Candy's orbit felt elevated by his presence. "He was a volcano of joy," she wrote. "It's no wonder the whole world still misses him. John ate, drank, and danced happiness."

One

Enter Laughing

On October 31, 1950, Sidney and Evangeline Candy of Newmarket, Ontario, took their new baby boy, John Franklin Candy, home from Newmarket General Hospital to meet his two-year-old brother, Jim. John was born on Halloween, and while it is tempting to presume that this accident of birth inspired a lifetime of dressing up in costume, nothing about the cute, drooling cherub that Sid and Van carefully swaddled in his crib particularly foretold of John Candy's evolution into one of the most highly regarded actors that Canada ever sent to the movie screens of the world.

The roots of the Candy family tree first extended into Canada when John's paternal grandfather, Charles, emigrated from Bristol, England, to Quebec in 1913. Seven years later, John's father, Sidney, was born in Toronto. After Candy's maternal grandmother, Jozefa Aker, left Ukraine to settle in Manitoba, she gave birth to six children, one of whom was John's mother.

Evangeline Aker met Sidney Candy and the two married in Toronto in 1946. Shortly after taking baby John home, they moved their family of four to nearby King City, where Sidney assumed a sales position at Champion Motors.

Then, at the alarmingly young age of thirty-five, Sidney Candy died suddenly from a heart attack, and Evangeline moved in with her parents and sister Frances to live in a modest postwar bungalow at 217 Woodville Avenue, in what was at the time the Toronto borough of East York.

Suddenly fatherless only three days shy of his fifth birthday, John Candy could barely comprehend what had just happened to him. Reacting like many children, he internalized the trauma in ways that his developing mind was not yet fully equipped to process. On the surface, however, young John presented as an outwardly happy kid, safe within the protective glow of a loving household.

"I was unhappy in the sense that I lost my father at a young age," Candy told *Oui* magazine's Robert Crane Jr. in 1982. "That certainly had an effect on me psychologically, I'm sure. But I had a good upbringing."

In fact, it would take a lifetime for Candy to come to terms with his father's sudden loss, which would manifest itself in later life as a constant low-level anxiety and even panic attacks. As late as 1992, in an interview with the American magazine *Parade*, Candy confessed that it was only after having kids of his own that he realized how much he missed his father, explaining, "I didn't have a role model."

While Candy would spend the remaining days of his childhood pondering the big questions of the universe, he and his seven-year-old brother were now the "men of the house" at a time when gender roles brought with them weighted expectations of responsibility and little time to wonder what might have been.

East York was a working-class community, and it was here that young John observed the common touch that would come to inform many of his characters. His Polish grandmother introduced him to the rich ethnic cuisine of her homeland: pierogis, bigos stew, schabowy (schnitzel), kaszanka (blood sausage), and plenty of cabbage rolls.

Evangeline raised her boys in a Catholic household, which meant enrolling John and Jim in Holy Cross Catholic School, across the street from Holy Cross Church, where John made a particularly cherubic altar boy. In their collective grief, the Candy family had to look out for each other, and everyone in the household played a part in keeping food on the table. Evangeline and her sister Frances worked in the toy section at Eaton's department store, where fellow sales associates knew them as "Van and Fran," while teenage John took various odd jobs as a delivery boy and restaurant worker.

These social interactions, both inside and outside the home, helped John feel less alone, and he discovered that it was easier to make friends if you could make them laugh. Those who knew him recall a dutiful, kind-hearted, and dependable friend with a big heart and low tolerance for injustice wherever it appeared, be it the schoolroom, the street, or the playing field.

Candy and his school friend Jonathan O'Mara would often seek refuge and solace by kicking back in the spring-loaded seats and cool darkness of the nearby Donlands cinema. There, for seventy-five cents each, they could take in a double feature and escape for a few stolen hours into the world of British and American cinema, sipping Coca-Cola and wolfing down hot buttered popcorn. Candy loved the movies so much that he eventually took a part-time usher's job at the Donlands, where he would memorize film dialogue and train his ear to pick up the nuances of foreign accents. He was taken by the physicality of comedic masters like Peter Sellers in *The Mouse That Roared* and the broad farce of Sidney James in the *Carry On* films. On the dramatic front, he looked up to actors like Gary Cooper in *High Noon* and Henry Fonda in *Mister Roberts.*

Like many children of his generation, Candy was also drawn to the television, which offered him a whole other global village of characters to study; from Jack Benny's deadpan "slow burn" takes, to Fred Gwynne's clumsy patriarch, Herman Munster, on *The Munsters* or the beloved animated moose and squirrel duo with the comic timing of seasoned vaudevillians, Bullwinkle and Rocky. Jackie Gleason provided a master class in physical comedy on the wildly successful sitcom *The Honeymooners*, and Candy took note of how a big man like Gleason could own his large frame with grace and dignity. And while he had no father at home, Candy could spend thirty minutes a day with a variety of idealized TV dads on *Leave It to Beaver* or *Ozzie and Harriet.*

"I was an avid Mouseketeer fan," Candy later recalled, "and I played soldiers and cowboys and played with my little cars."

Candy's Woodville Avenue backyard soon became an imaginary backlot, a safe space to re-enact his favourite scenes from the movies and television while wearing improvised costumes raided from the family closets.

Evangeline sent young John to Neil McNeil Catholic High School, a boys-only institution in the Beach area of East Toronto, which necessitated an hour-long commute, each way, by city bus. While initially shy at his new school, Candy soon won friends over with his secret weapon, a finely honed sense of humour.

He was elected treasurer of the Neil McNeil student council alongside O'Mara, who had also made the jump to McNeil and began to see in Candy a kind of intelligence that report cards could never reveal.

"John wasn't a great student," says O'Mara, "but he wasn't a bad one. I began to realize that anybody as witty as John had to have a lot going on in his head."

Candy and O'Mara shared a keen interest in music and were thrilled to sit on the Neil McNeil dance committee, where they booked some of the best bands that rolled through Toronto at the time, from American hitmakers like the Box Tops and the Left Banke, to homegrown heroes like Lighthouse and the Guess Who. Candy worked part-time at Towers department store and, after work, would head over to meet O'Mara as he cashed out at his job at the Becker's convenience store. Candy was already big for his age, and O'Mara remembers him as an excellent bodyguard for his evening walk to the bank's night deposit box.

"Then we'd just go out cruising," O'Mara recalls. "A lot of those times we didn't have girlfriends, so we would drive around for hours, just talking."

After saving up money from various odd jobs, Candy bought himself a used Chevrolet, which he nicknamed the "White Knight." At home, this meant he was expected to chauffeur Van and Fran to the grocery store or their regular bingo nights. But the car also meant freedom, and he and O'Mara could take long-distance joy rides south of the border to Buffalo, New York, for some underage drinking and hot chicken wings. Cruising in the White Knight with the radio blasting, the two boys shared their deepest dreams and insecurities, while musing aloud on the state of the world. Mostly, the conversation turned to what they were going to do with the rest of their lives. And often during their long drives, Candy would confess that his body issues undermined his self-esteem, while O'Mara did his best to reassure him that he was well liked.

"[As a teenager] John was a big guy," says O'Mara, "but not really a 'fat guy.' He just looked like a football player, and nobody that I know of at our school ever said anything to him about his weight. Everybody liked John very much, so they didn't want to hurt him. His weight didn't define him for us; he was just this jovial, sweet guy that you could rely on for pretty much anything."

According to O'Mara, it was on these night drives that the unguarded Candy would share his various anxieties, such as his dread of any sports in which he'd be obliged to take off his shirt. There was one sport, however, where his height and heavy frame proved to be an asset. Already an enthusiastic fan of the Toronto Argonauts of the Canadian Football League, Candy would often sneak into home games at CNE Stadium on Lakeshore Boulevard, and Evangeline would occasionally bring home Argos tickets that she had won through a promotional scheme with the local Dominion supermarket. Candy's commanding physical presence made him a natural to play left tackle on the offensive line for the Neil McNeil football team. Nicknamed "the Pink Panther" in the school yearbook, Candy cut an imposing figure on the field, and few could get by him. He was bitten by football fever, and the controlled brutality of football gave him a socially acceptable outlet for his adolescent anger and frustrations. Tragically, after guiding McNeil to one championship season, a serious knee injury dashed his gridiron dreams forever.

In a 1986 interview with Brian Linehan for his *City Lights* television program, Candy was still reliving the injury. "Not one day in the pro ranks did I make it," he told Linehan, "only I've got the arthritis to prove it now though."

And in a 1991 appearance on CBC Radio's *Morningside*, Candy was still lamenting his lost football years with host Peter Gzowski: "I was okay, but I hurt my knees so badly and that was the end of it ... let's talk war wounds, shall we?"

An athlete's life may not have been in the cards for him, but as a fan of the Toronto Argonauts, Candy would remain a loyal supporter of the Double Blue for the rest of his life.

High school life wasn't all dour introspection, however, and Candy's comedic instincts became evident as he perfected impressions of the famous, such as comedian Jonathan Winters, as well as McNeil's own Father Fitzgerald. With his football dreams sidelined, he was in search of a new after-school activity when he chanced upon the school's theatre department. There, on the stage and under the guidance of drama teacher Ernie Brown, he basked in the heightened reality of the spotlight.

"Everything was amplified when he got onstage," says O'Mara. "He was also really funny. I think a lot of these big fellas he admired, like Jackie Gleason and Charles Laughton, had also used being jolly as a coping mechanism to deflect criticism."

While Candy was fascinated with drama, getting big laughs onstage felt to him like a magic act. Once he heard the roar of laughter from an audience, he couldn't wait to do it again. Comedic skill was also a handy way to counter the loneliness he felt at not having a girlfriend. He found it easier to win a smile from the girls in school than to get a date with them.

When he was struggling, Candy would often find himself in room 310 to confide in a teacher at McNeil named Ted Schmidt. More than a guidance counsellor, Schmidt was a critical thinker and self-described "social justice Catholic" who was also the school's basketball coach and had a knack for connecting with the students. Candy was fond of his confrontational style, which combined spiritual guidance with a sardonic sense of humour.

According to O'Mara, Candy became so "tormented" by his body image that, late into his high school years, he concocted a scheme to drive to the United States and enlist with the US Marine Corps. Candy's logic was that the rigorous Marines training camp might whip him into shape, which would go a long way toward bolstering his self-esteem. But when Candy entered Schmidt's office to inform him of his dangerous intentions, his trusted counsellor actively attempted to dissuade him. Beyond the obvious fact of Candy's Canadian citizenship, Schmidt impressed upon him that there were scores of American draft dodgers fleeing the US precisely to avoid the conflict in Southeast Asia. But Candy's mind was made up, so he and his dutiful friend O'Mara hopped into the White Knight for one last road trip to Niagara Falls, before continuing to the Marines recruiting centre at Parris Island, South Carolina. Once there, he was promptly rejected due to his ravaged knee. Candy was dejected, but on the long drive home, the two movie buffs steered the White Knight into Buffalo and took in a showing of the recent Steve McQueen car chase thriller, *Bullitt*. The movies had always provided an escape, while for once his knee injury may well have saved his life.

"He was very disappointed," says O'Mara, "but hey, Vietnam's loss was Hollywood's gain, and the world got a movie star instead of a soldier."

Although he didn't realize it at the time, Candy's time at Neil McNeil had been positive and formative. In 2008, the Catholic diocese publication *Spiritan* commemorated McNeil's fiftieth anniversary in a special issue that bears a posthumous quote from Candy, crediting his success in later life to "the values of discipline and respect for others that I was taught at Neil."

Yet when his time was up at McNeil, Candy's only plan was to continue his education until something better materialized. After enrolling in Journalism at Scarborough's Centennial College, he lost interest in that too. But his transformative experiences on the stages of Neil McNeil had stayed with him, and in Candy's second year at Centennial, he followed his bliss into the drama department, before deciding to drop out of college altogether and pursue acting full-time. Candy knew he belonged onstage, where he could be whoever he wanted to be for however long he was there. He had always loved the movies, so why not become one of the actors up on the big screen? Nothing was guaranteed, of course, but by the age of nineteen, John Candy knew one thing for sure: He was willing to do whatever it took to find out.

Two

An Actor Prepares

Candy met talent agent Catherine McCartney literally by accident. Striking up an awkward conversation after nearly knocking her over in line at the Eaton's cafeteria, he discovered that her talent office just happened to be across the street, next to the Fran's Restaurant where he sometimes dined. McCartney later saw him at Fran's and invited him up to her office, where he shyly confessed to her that he had been taking acting classes with an eye toward becoming a professional actor. Charmed by Candy's baby face and disarming wit, McCartney was eager to help him get a foot in the door. In 1970, she happened to be casting for a television commercial in which a high school football player would expound on the virtues of Colgate toothpaste. She knew just who to send out on the audition.

Candy had played this character in real life, and after passing the cursory audition, he found himself walking across a studio floor in full football padding, to act across a locker room set from the Canadian-born icon of American television Art Linkletter, whom Candy recognized from his 1960s television program *People Are Funny.*

"I did anything I could," Candy later told David Letterman on his *Late Night* talk show. "Art was talking about the protection in the front of your mouth much like my football helmet protects my head. My one big line was 'Oh sure, Casanova!' [We did] about a hundred takes of that."

That day on the set, Candy immediately felt at home and discovered an instant and easy rapport with the film crew, breaking up a long day with well-placed laughs between takes. The Colgate spot gave him confidence to ask McCartney to send him out for more commercials, and he booked a few. One was for Molson Golden Ale, and Candy was thrilled to see it running constantly during the CBC's *Hockey Night in Canada* broadcasts, where all of his old Neil McNeil pals were sure to see it.

Meeting frequently in McCartney's talent office, McCartney and Candy chatted about life, the universe, and everything, bonding over the sad coincidence of them both having lost their fathers at a young age.

"John had a quality of vulnerability," McCartney later told journalist Martin Knelman. "He was young and awfully cute. John had the ability to make people feel special even if he had only known them a short time. Once he became your friend, he was always there for you, to listen and provide a shoulder to cry on."

McCartney now assumed the role of trusted counsellor and confidant. But more to the point, McCartney was an agent, and as Candy dared to dream aloud of fame and fortune, she was ready to guide him where he needed to go. Meanwhile, Candy continued to pursue work on the stage, taking on a supporting role in a Bill Glassco production of David Freeman's savagely sardonic play *Creeps* at Toronto's Tarragon Theatre, and other small roles. Candy was only earning forty dollars a week, but he was now a professional working stage actor, happy to be paid at all.

For the time being, Candy split his time between acting and a series of aimless day jobs. These included selling paper products door to door for Perkins Paper out of the back of his beat-up brown Pontiac, and continuing to maintain his post at Eaton's. It was there, in 1972, that fate once again crossed the threshold to meet him, in the form of a young actor named Valri Bromfield.

"I went into Eaton's to buy something and there was John," says Bromfield. "He was so sweet and nice and funny. If somebody makes me laugh, I'll just stand there and laugh, it's like an addiction. And it's deadly because you don't care about anything else. Building on fire? 'Oh, that was funny.' John was like that. Everything he did, he just kept tripping over great, great lines, the next one came, and he was funny and we fed each other. He just seemed glowing and brilliant to me."

Bromfield and her comedy partner Dan Aykroyd had recently moved to Toronto from Ottawa, where they had created a local television sketch comedy program called *Change for a Quarter*. They had shown tapes of the program to Toronto-born writer and performer Lorne Michaels, who had just left a CBC television sketch program of his own, *The Hart and Lorne Terrific Hour*, with Hart Pomerantz. While that series had only aired for one season in 1970, Michaels was clearly going places, and his encouragement was all that Aykroyd and Bromfield needed to make the move to Toronto. There, they became regular performers at late-night venues around the city, such as the Platform, where a young entrepreneur named Andrew Alexander was the talent booker, and at the Global Village theatre, where an unknown Gilda Radner worked the box office. Bromfield had also been performing for children with the Caravan Theatre troupe, staging plays in hospitals, schools, and public parks, and a few indoor venues such as Toronto's Poor Alex Theatre, funded by a modest arts grant from the federal government. After meeting Candy, Bromfield introduced him to the Caravan's director, Stephen Katz.

"Stephen had said he needed a big guy to play a king and a bunch of other parts," says Bromfield, "so I just told John, 'You know what? You should quit your day job,' which paid real money, 'and come make nothing with us. We all squeeze into one car and go do children's theatre. It'll be fun!'"

To Bromfield's surprise, Candy agreed to jump into his battered Pontiac and meet with Katz, who hired him on the spot. Candy cut an imposing figure and showed impressive range, handling roles great and small with equal finesse.

"John was just fabulous as this very stately king, and children just loved him," says Bromfield. "He'd try to break us up onstage or make us forget our lines, and we'd sneak in all this double-entendre stuff. We had a lot of fun, and the fun never left us."

Bromfield had been telling Aykroyd about Candy for weeks by the time she finally made the introductions one afternoon at her place on Yonge Street.

"I had been walking with my friend Marcus O'Hara," says Aykroyd, "and Valri yelled at me from a building she was living in. I went up to her apartment, where I met John Candy for the first time. He had that big brown Pontiac, and he was always beautifully turned out so elegantly, a real clothes horse. He loved smart blazers and nice slacks, shoes, and shirts."

By now, Aykroyd trusted Bromfield's judgment about the people she brought into their ever-widening social circle within the relatively insular Toronto scene, and a shockingly high ratio of their talented new acquaintances seemed destined for bigger things. Many of them, including Radner, who had just arrived from Detroit, had been introduced to the circle through Marcus O'Hara, a social connector and the brother of Catherine and Mary Margaret O'Hara.

"We were all hanging out," says Aykroyd, "but Candy and I were in other careers when we met. I knew he had done theatre in high school, but he was right there in the working world; I was a mailman, he was a paper salesman."

By Candy's own admission, he had been a terrible salesman, routinely ranked last among his fellow hustlers. "I had a trunk that was filled with Halloween, Valentine's Day, Easter, happy birthday greetings from the Disney characters," Candy later explained to *City Lights* host Brian Linehan. "While I was rehearsing... I was supposed to be on the road, and they finally caught up to me and fired me."

He took his boss's parting shot, that he "never should have hired an actor," as an unintended confirmation of his true calling, and vowed he would never work as a salesman again.

"I finally realized I'm not doing anything else," Candy told Linehan. "I'm gonna stick with acting."

While a natural comic actor, Candy made no secret of his desire to also tackle a dramatic role like Willy Loman in Arthur Miller's *Death of a Salesman*, but for now he was content to do whatever theatre work he was offered, which included joining James Iwasuk's children's theatre troupe, the Jolly Jesters, to bring *Rumpelstiltskin* and *Treasure Island* to Toronto-area schools.

Still living at his childhood home in East York, Candy took on additional responsibilities for the Jesters, at turns stage managing, loading all the props and backdrops into a rented cube van, and driving the cast all over Metropolitan Toronto for the measly wage of sixty-five dollars per week.

IN THE FALL OF 1972, Katz tapped Candy to return to the Tarragon Theatre in Sheldon Rosen's adaptation of Carlo Gozzi's eighteenth-century Italian comedy *The Stag King*, about a king who awakens in an enchanted forest with the body of a stag. Candy was working constantly, but he wasn't getting rich, owing as much to the limited wages as to his burgeoning taste for the finer things.

"I've always lived beyond my means," Candy later confessed to the CBC's Peter Gzowski. "I always had an apartment that was great. I never did without. I probably had more fun then, but I don't look at the zeroes, I mean they're there, uh, my accountant is still always screaming at me 'John, for god's sakes!' you know, I probably lend too much money to people."

Increasingly, Candy found himself socializing with the network of fellow aspiring actors he was meeting through Aykroyd, Bromfield, and O'Hara. In the 1970s, the Toronto bars still closed at midnight, and so, to accommodate their fellow bohemian night owls, Aykroyd and O'Hara launched their notorious speakeasy at 505 Queen Street East. The 505, as it was known, was a late-night refuge for all who worked late, not just actors and musicians but streetcar drivers, restaurant and bar workers, and nurses and doctors who convened there to loosen up after their night shifts, far from the prying eyes of the parochial liquor board laws of Toronto the Good. Legendarily, the 505 was also where Aykroyd would later meet John Belushi and dream up the Blues Brothers act after grooving to the Downchild Blues Band until the sun came up.

"The 505 was initially a storefront place that I rented," says Bromfield. "It was two doors down from a café where a guy made pies at four in the morning, and Marcus came and lived with me in that house. Then Danny took it over and turned it into an off-licence."

"It was a great environment," says Aykroyd. "There should be a plaque on that building because all of the comedy stars and music stars came through there. Also, there should be a plaque at 1063 Avenue Road."

1063 Avenue Road was a rented house in the Eglinton-Lawrence neighbourhood of Toronto that would later come to play an important role in exportable Canadian culture. The Victorian detached brick house was initially the residence of aspiring actor friends Eugene Levy, Martin Short, and Dave Thomas, all of whom had met at as students at McMaster University in Hamilton, Ontario, and were now part of the young Toronto cast of the post-hippie stage musical *Godspell*, which had become something of a phenomenon in local theatre circles.

Godspell, composed by Stephen Schwartz with a book by John-Michael Tebelak, had opened off-Broadway at the Cherry Lane Theatre in May 1971, and had produced a Billboard Top 20 single in "Day by Day" in the summer of 1972. That same year, a Toronto production opened to rave reviews and launched the careers of many of its cast members, including Victor Garber, Paul Shaffer, Howard Shore, Gerry Salsberg, Eugene Levy, Andrea Martin, Gilda Radner, Martin Short, and Dave Thomas.

Levy, Martin, Radner, Short, and Thomas were frequently among the revellers at the house on Avenue Road, along with Aykroyd and Bromfield, who soon introduced Candy to the clique. By this time, Candy was at last in a serious relationship. He had met a young student at the Ontario College of Art by the name of Rosemary Hobor. While the two had met casually in 1969, they were a serious item by the time they walked through the door together at 1063 Avenue Road for what came to be known as the weekly Friday Night Services.

According to Dave Thomas, the sheer brilliance of the talent involved sometimes fostered a competitive atmosphere.

"It was a social scene," says Thomas, "with all these people connecting on their similar sense of comedy and making each other laugh. But sometimes it was also kind of scary because there was always a question of 'Am I actually good enough to be in the company of these people?' because they were really good."

A typical night at the Friday Night Services included performing songs and improvised skits. And everyone was obliged to take a turn at a popular game at 1063 that involved riffing along with an Albert Brooks comedy album called *Comedy Minus One*.

"Albert had written scripts in the liner notes," says Thomas, "and you would put on the album and read along with the scripts. Albert would say a line [on the record] and then it was your cue to do the next line. At the start of the bit, Albert gave you plenty of time to say your dialogue, then the pace picked up and you had no time at all. It was a fun game for us, and it created an opportunity for us to perform for each other."

While Catherine O'Hara didn't consider herself "deep in the circle," she also felt welcomed by the *Godspell* crowd at 1063.

"It was really fun," says O'Hara. "Andrea and Marty had done a lot of stage in Toronto, musicals. It was a really ridiculously talented crowd, and it was really exciting to be around them and to watch them with each other, and they're all lovely people. The *Comedy Minus One* game became a kind of all-in-good-fun initiation ritual for first-timers. Somebody would put on the album and go, 'Hey you. First time here? Why don't you come on and try this album?' It was parlour games galore, and to this day, I still love the parlour games."

Soon, Candy was taking a turn with the Brooks album, and in no time, he became a beloved regular at the Friday Night Services. In a 1989 feature for *The New Yorker,* writer James Kaplan summed up the talent pool surrounding the Toronto cast of *Godspell* as "one of those artistic nexuses that crop up now and then, like Paris in the twenties, Los Angeles in the thirties, London just before the First World War."

As Paul Shaffer tickled the keys of the house piano, Martin Short worked out his generic lounge singer character, which later became his standing schtick on David Letterman's late-night shows when Shaffer was the bandleader.

"We'd have parties, and everyone would just get up," says Short. "Paul would play, I'd sing, Gilda would sing. And we'd all just do songs from *Godspell.*"

Short, who met Candy for the first time backstage after a *Godspell* performance, recalls that Candy made it known that he had a low tolerance for the constant singing of *Godspell* songs at 1063.

"John thought it was insane," says Short. "We were singing it all day, then singing it at night. I think it seemed obsessive to him. I just remember that we would all party together, and it was a very cool scene in Toronto then. And you must remember, no one particularly thought they'd ever become successful outside of Toronto. It wasn't like people were saying, 'Someday we're going to be in the movies' or something."

By her own description, 1063 regular Jayne Eastwood was "already semi-famous in Toronto" as one of the stars of Donald Shebib's influential 1970 Canadian independent film, *Goin' Down the Road*, when she began showing up at what she calls "the best parties ever."

"I remember that's where Eugene [Levy] and [his wife] Deb [Divine] first hooked up," says Eastwood, "and John and Rose were there all the time. I've never laughed so hard in my life. I don't think any of us knew how famous we were going to become."

Meanwhile, down on Queen Street, Aykroyd and Bromfield were excited about auditioning for an improvisational theatre company founded in Chicago that was about to open a Toronto branch. It was called the Second City, and it would soon change everything.

Three

Johnny Toronto Meets the Second City

The Second City theatre first opened its doors in Chicago in 1959 with an improvisatory comedy method developed by a group of University of Chicago students that included David Shepherd and Paul Sills, based on *commedia dell'arte* and the improvisational theatre games created by Sills's mother, Viola Spolin. Its initial troupe, the Compass Players, had formed in the summer of 1955, significantly launching the careers of Mike Nichols and Elaine May. Four years later, the Second City became a Chicago improv institution known for its satirical skits and social commentary, which jumpstarted the careers of Alan Alda, Jerry Stiller, Anne Meara, Alan Arkin, David Steinberg, Joan Rivers, and countless other comedy icons.

After conquering Broadway in 1961, a touring revue of the show hit Toronto for a critically acclaimed run at the Royal Alexandra Theatre in 1966, inspiring Toronto theatre critic

Nathan Cohen to muse in the *Toronto Star*: "What a wonderful gift it would be to have a permanent Second City here." In 1973, Cohen got his wish when Second City announced its intention to launch a Toronto troupe. Auditions for the inaugural Toronto cast were presided over by the Chicago company's producers Bernard Sahlins and Joyce Sloane, plus Del Close, the legendary comedy guru who had once compared stage improvisation to a fireworks display: "It's the more ephemeral of art forms—once it's gone, it's gone, baby."

Additionally, Sahlins delegated two members of the Chicago cast, Brian Doyle-Murray and Joe Flaherty, to come up to Toronto and help preside over the auditions, which were held at a tiny church in the Yorkville neighbourhood. While it was an open call audition, Sahlins also drew from a short list of actors from the local stage community and made sure that the Chicago contingent took in a performance of *Godspell*, which was still selling out shows and earning solid reviews.

"We really enjoyed *Godspell* and the people in it," says Flaherty, "so it was like striking gold. Still, we had no clue if anybody in Canada could do improv comedy."

At the auditions, Flaherty was pleasantly surprised to learn that these Canadians, such as Dan Aykroyd and Valri Bromfield, actually *could* improvise.

"We were all kinds of ready to take the risk and make the transition to doing improv, which we loved," says Aykroyd. "So on our way to the audition, we had invited our pal John to come along with us."

Flaherty was sufficiently impressed with Aykroyd and Bromfield that he took their recommendation to heart and agreed to take a look at "this big-boned, long-haired young guy.

I don't know how old he was, but he sure seemed a lot younger than the rest of us."

Candy would later insist that he had only come along that day to lend moral support to his friends and that his name had been added to the audition list without his consent. But when called, Candy reluctantly stepped up, with little or no idea of what he would do.

"I said 'Aw, I'll kill you. I'll kill you for doing this to me,'" Candy told Sheldon Patinkin for his account of those years, *The Second City: Backstage at the World's Greatest Comedy Theater.* "I was scared. They said 'Go up on stage there. This is a department store exercise. You have to do this game. That's all we want from you.' Sweat was all over me."

As it happened, Candy was a natural. Despite having none of the flashy song and dance skills of his *Godspell* peers, and with no standup comedy experience to fall back on, Candy remained genuine and charismatic in the face of mayhem. According to Flaherty, no matter who else was onstage, all eyes stayed on this everyman teddy bear to see how he would react.

"At Second City we used to teach 'give and take,'" says Flaherty. "But some actors are all take and no give, especially if they're auditioning. We asked John to do an improv opposite this motormouth guy. Now, normally this would end up with two people fighting for focus, but John just kind of sat there and listened to the guy, and his subtle reactions were perfect. He'd shrug, or he'd smile and just nod his head, which is absolutely the right thing to do when you're in a scene with a motormouth like that. John was the one that impressed us by not saying anything, just being right there in the scene and advancing the action."

Candy fared even better in a theatre game developed by Del Close called "Five Through the Door," in which an actor enters through the door onstage as one character, exits quickly, and then, without thinking, re-enters the stage four times more as subsequent characters in rapid succession.

By the time the Second City auditions had ended, a partial consensus had been reached about who would make the cut. Aykroyd, Bromfield, Radner, Jayne Eastwood, and Gerry Salsberg had all made an impression, but the jury was still out on Candy and Levy. According to Flaherty, Sahlins liked Levy but felt he was "too low-key" for the comedy troupe, while Candy was simply too young and inexperienced. Close, however, felt that Candy was worthy of further development.

"Del said, 'Look, if you don't want Candy, I'd like him,'" says Flaherty. "He told Bernie, 'I'm going to take him down to Chicago.'"

In less than forty-eight hours, the Second City had its first Toronto cast, and Del Close was returning to Chicago with John Candy under his metaphorical wing.

"They were probably more excited about discovering John that day," says Aykroyd, "than they were about hiring Valri and me."

Toronto's first Second City cast would come to include Flaherty and Doyle-Murray from Chicago, along with Bromfield, Aykroyd, and three of the *Godspell* kids—Eastwood, Radner, and Salsberg—plus musical director Fred Kaz from the Chicago theatre.

Sloane called Candy with the mixed news that while he had failed to make the Toronto cast, Del Close, no less, had personally requested that he come to Chicago, should he care to relocate.

"It took me about five seconds to get my mouth open," Candy later recalled. "They said 'You'll be there for a couple of weeks.' I ended up living there for about a year and half."

To assist in the launch of the Toronto Second City, Sloane and Sahlins had enlisted the help of Andrew Alexander, who found them a cramped 250-seat black box cabaret space on Adelaide Street East. They had no liquor licence or air conditioning, but Toronto's Second City officially opened in June 1973 with a revue entitled *Tippecanoe and Déjà Vu*. As Flaherty remembers it, this was one of the city's hottest summers on record, making for a miserable experience for the cast, the audience, and the staff.

"We had a really strong cast," says Flaherty, "but we'd come out there every night with only five and six people out there, so it was depressing."

Admission to the so-called improv set, performed as an encore each night after the written show, was free to anyone walking in off the street, and it was here that the Toronto Second City began to find its niche, as young and broke college students embraced its high-risk, low-cost comedy.

"They'd go crazy over everything we did," says Flaherty. "Suddenly we were a hot commodity in Toronto."

As Toronto audiences fell in love with the Second City, Flaherty, a son of Pittsburgh who had relocated to Chicago, fell in love with Toronto. "Chicago," says Flaherty, was "rife with crime at the time. Toronto, by comparison, was like a breath of fresh air. I was so happy to get the hell out of Chicago, and Toronto was like heaven."

Leaving behind his girlfriend, Rose, with whom he would maintain a long-distance relationship for the time being, Candy had flown into Flaherty's vision of hell a little wide-eyed but cautiously optimistic. Having never travelled beyond the confines of Metropolitan Toronto, Chicago's newest resident was as impressed by the city's elevated trains as he was by its vibrant cultural scene, which ran the gamut from authentic blues joints to a legitimate theatre. Having grown up watching tales of Chicago gangsters on TV's *The Untouchables*, he was ill-prepared for what was now a bustling metropolis on Lake Michigan. Big-shouldered Chicago, America's "second city," was to become for Candy what Hamburg, Germany, had been to the Beatles: a harsh and gritty proving ground where he could log his "ten thousand hours" of stage time and sharpen his skills. Under Close's direction, Candy was thrust into a cast that included fellow newcomer Bill Murray. In the weeks before his onstage debut, Candy took in the show from the audience and immediately felt intimidated by the cast's quick-witted pace.

"I thought, I'll never be able to fit in," Candy later told Patrick Goldstein in the *Los Angeles Times*. "I can never do this. Then Del Close leaned over to me as I was watching and said, 'You'll be doing this Wednesday night...' I was so nervous that on my first night while the stage was dark between sketches, I ran smack into one of the guys and hit him so hard I split my lip. And I had to introduce the next sketch—our V.D. sketch. Blood was running down the side of my mouth as I talked. Everyone started laughing. I guess they just thought it was part of the act."

Despite his size, Candy felt daunted by Murray's rapid-fire approach to scene work, yet the truth was they were both just learning the ropes.

"We were both terrible," Murray later recalled on *The Tonight Show Starring Jimmy Fallon*. "We were both lousy, and no one would [do scenes] with us. So it was just Candy and I looking at each other like, 'I guess it's us again,' you know? But it worked out okay for us, eventually."

Early in his Chicago run, Joe Flaherty paid Candy a visit and found him "feeling a little lost in this pretty high-powered cast. It wasn't really working out."

Andrew Alexander, who had by this time taken a job in Chicago at the nearby Ivanhoe Theater, recalls popping into the Second City to check on Candy's progress.

"I really got to know him there," says Alexander. "His confidence was a little fragile in those early days and he used to just sort of disappear onstage, but I saw him evolve while he was there. I think it was partly that he was learning the technique but also just doing those improv sets every night; you could see it change from week to week. John was extremely friendly, so he made a lot of friends really fast. He was just a sweet young man, and his generosity was already evident."

Second City's Sheldon Patinkin also spent a lot of time with Candy, bolstering his stage confidence and encouraging him to keep trying. "It was better that [John] tried," Patinkin told writer Tracey J. Morgan. "All because we really believed in how good he was and *could* be."

According to an uncredited transcript of a conversation overheard at Second City circa 1973, kept by Sloane and published in Patinkin's book, Candy remarked, "I think we're vicious at times, too, though 'vicious' doesn't mean we hate the person. It just means everyone's up for grabs, and we should expose as much as we know."

Over time, Candy gained enough knowledge and confidence to dominate a scene when he wanted to. The title of Candy's inaugural revue, *Phase 46, or Watergate Tomorrow, Comedy Tonight,* reflected the nature of the humour onstage. While Richard Nixon's high crimes and misdemeanours may have been the headlines of the day, political satire was put on the back (or side) burner in favour of character-driven scenes where funny was just funny, topicality be damned.

Initially, Candy moved into Flaherty's old apartment on Crilly Court, in the heart of Chicago's Old Town, not far from the Second City theatre on North Wells. His neighbour was Bill Murray and the two became increasingly close. Just as 1063 Avenue Road had been crucial to the social fabric of Candy's Toronto scene, Crilly Court became a place for the Chicago cast and their friends to smoke the odd joint, drink until all hours of the morning, and talk about movies. Candy had always loved film and had developed an encyclopedic knowledge of cinematic history that was recognized by his castmates. Murray, meanwhile, knew all the ins and outs of life in the Windy City and proved to be a useful guide on pub crawls through dodgy after-hours clubs, or to quirky Chicagoland sites like the original McDonald's hamburger stand.

"He took me all over the city, showed me every landmark," Candy later recalled. "We went to every weird, seedy area imaginable. He'd always say, 'This is my town, and this can be your town too.' When we'd go to Wrigley Field, he knew every Cubs player that had ever lived. In fact, I had my first case of sunstroke seeing a Cubs game."

Aykroyd and Bromfield also paid Candy a visit to check on his progress, and were relieved to find him holding court at Crilly, comfortably settling into life in Sweet Home Chicago.

"John and Billy were our guides to the city," says Aykroyd, "so it was pretty exciting. Wherever John lived, he was always set up nicely, and in Chicago it was no different. He'd found a nice spot there, with a bar, a big TV, comfortable chairs, and of course he was always the consummate host."

When Rose Hobor eventually came down from Toronto, the two rented some furniture and made a cozy nest at Crilly Court. They had barely settled in when Sahlins summoned Candy to return to Toronto at the end of 1973.

"He was having such a good time in Chicago," Sahlins later remarked, "he really didn't want to go home. But once he got [back to Toronto], he fell in with an excellent cast and found himself in a company that was just right for him."

Not only would Candy's homecoming reunite him with some of the old gang from the Friday Night Services, but each of his castmates had the talent to spur one another on to greater things. There's an old saying that one should never yell "Fire!" in a crowded theatre, but for the Toronto Second City, moving into a new theatre space inside an old fire hall would transform it from a failing cabaret into a blazingly creative hothouse.

This was John Candy's time to shine.

Four

Turning Up the Heat

While Candy was away, the Toronto Second City had opened with neither a liquor licence nor air conditioning, but the popularity of its nightly improv set had proved to be its saving grace.

"The crowds were so happy to be there," says Catherine O'Hara, who started as a waitress, along with her sister, singer Mary Margaret O'Hara, slinging crepes for comedy fans. "And the cast was just amazing, so it was a lovely, fun place to work."

Also taking in the show from the audience were a few of the 1063 regulars who hadn't gone out to the auditions, including Eugene Levy, Martin Short, and Dave Thomas. Just as O'Hara had, they liked what they saw, even if they were slightly jealous that they couldn't join the fun.

In the heady times after Canada's 1967 Centennial year, a patriotic fervour had gripped the cultural conversation, and a kind of nationalistic favouritism for homegrown talent began to make some of the Americans in the cast, such as Joe Flaherty and Brian Doyle-Murray, feel unwelcome. While Gilda Radner didn't share this feeling, Doyle-Murray and Flaherty returned to the US, and Eugene Levy joined the cast.

The Second City had barely reshuffled its players when its Adelaide Street theatre was unexpectedly shut down for running a cabaret without a liquor licence. Andrew Alexander, back from Chicago, re-entered the picture, convincing Sloane and Sahlins to let him assume control of the entire Toronto operation, including its massive debts, for the sum of two Canadian dollars. After borrowing $7,000, Alexander moved the Second City into an abandoned fire hall located at 110 Lombard Street.

What became known as the Old Fire Hall theatre featured a ground-floor stage complex with an upstairs dining room in what used to be the firemen's quarters. The new Second City could offer dinner theatre package deals, a necessary requirement to obtain a liquor licence. This business model, combined with an aggressive marketing plan to attract block bookings for parties and business conventions, would prove to be a vital way to keep the theatre alive. Significantly, Alexander also summoned Flaherty back from Pittsburgh, and John Candy home from Chicago to join Levy, Radner, and Bromfield.

Flaherty and Candy drove up to Toronto together in a converted bread truck stuffed with their belongings. As they rounded Lake Ontario on the Queen Elizabeth Way, they kicked around sketch ideas and shared their visions of what they could accomplish with the revitalized Toronto cast.

"We had a lot of fun on the drive up," says Flaherty. "We worked out this whole *Bull Durham* baseball thing, where John would be the rookie who wanted to prove himself in the big leagues and I was this grizzled veteran who showed him the ropes."

It wasn't far from the truth of their relationship, and when they arrived in Toronto, Candy invited Flaherty to stay with him at his mother's home in East York until he found a place of his own.

The inaugural Second City revue at the Old Fire Hall, *Hello Dali*, co-directed by Flaherty and Sahlins, opened in February 1974; eventually Dan Aykroyd replaced Flaherty, and newcomer Rosemary Radcliffe replaced Bromfield. According to Flaherty, who remained as the director, there wasn't even a proper stage in the beginning and the cast and crew pitched in to build one from scratch. Similarly, the cast used guerrilla marketing tactics to drum up an audience from local bars and clubs.

"God, that was fun, getting that show together," says Flaherty. "Gilda would go down the street to the [Toronto watering hole] Jarvis House. She'd say 'We've got a comedy show! Come on and watch us at the Old Fire Hall!'"

Candy was triumphant at the new Second City, emboldened by his time in Chicago, and thrilled to be making good on Del Close's early belief in him.

"Of all the people I've worked with," says Flaherty, "John improved the most as an actor. He grew by leaps and bounds, constantly getting better. I remember walking down Yonge Street with him, and I said, 'John, you ought to do a TV show where you play a private eye. You could call yourself Johnny Toronto. He said, 'Yeah, I like that.' And that's how he got the nickname 'Johnny Toronto.'"

Upon his return to the Second City, Aykroyd was impressed with Candy's evolution into "a bold and wild chance-taker."

"There was great volume in the voices of all the characters he tried out," recalls Aykroyd. "He was not afraid to take it over the top, but he could be subtle too. We did a scene called 'Freaks,' where we were two hippies just sitting on a bench, with not much going on in their lives. It was such a gentle, loving piece. People loved it."

As the cast gelled at the Old Fire Hall, they gave birth to a deep bench of characters that would later be immortalized on television. Candy used his size to great effect, and while he was an unlikely choice to play Toronto Maple Leafs hockey star Darryl Sittler, he would routinely bring down the house with a scene ("Weetabix," later remounted on *SCTV* as "Cornabix") in which a hapless, and toothless, hockey player attempts to film a cereal commercial. But he also got big laughs portraying Toronto's then-mayor David Crombie, a well-liked but diminutive politician whom the press had affectionately nicknamed "the tiny perfect mayor."

"John wasn't tiny *or* perfect," says Flaherty, "which made it funnier."

As Crombie, Candy would sing "The Mayor's Song," slurring the words for comic effect. Most nights it was part of the bit, other times not so much. One night, Flaherty told Levy that Candy seemed particularly inebriated during his Crombie song, but the two agreed that he typically had it under control.

"Sure," says Flaherty, "John would sometimes imbibe during performances, but he wouldn't get loaded until the improvs. He wasn't alone, though; you could be looser in that set, so we all had a lot of fun."

Allan Guttman, who had replaced Fred Kaz as the musical director, recalls that while Candy and Radner were "the two nicest people in the cast," he also sensed a "deep emotional hole" inside Candy, even then.

"Humility was a big part of his comedy," says Guttman, "and his genuine personality was always part of any scene or character. Still, the audience always felt safe in John's hands, which I think was one of his greatest gifts."

Having failed her audition back when the theatre was still on Adelaide Street, Catherine O'Hara tried again. This time she auditioned for Candy, who picked her for the new Second City Touring Company.

"John, God bless him, gave us our start," says O'Hara. "The Touring Company would only have about ten people in the audience, mind you, but it didn't matter. Joe finally made me the understudy for Gilda and Rosemary Radcliffe, then Gilda went off to do the *National Lampoon* road show, which meant I got to be in the full Second City cast, all thanks to John."

Flaherty was impressed with the chemistry between Candy and O'Hara, both comic geniuses in their own right, in a scene called "Cadets."

"They play two actors hired by the Toronto police force to simulate a dangerous domestic disturbance for these police cadets," remembers Flaherty. "They come out, take a bow, then go into this loud and physical marital row. It was mayhem, and the audience just went wild. It was so extreme that it became one of my favourite John and Catherine scenes ever."

At one point in 1974, the Toronto and Chicago casts of the Second City swapped cities. On their first night in the Windy City, they were joined onstage by Tino Insana, Betty Thomas, and John Belushi, who had recently left the Chicago cast. On another night, Levy found himself dealing with a drunken audience member who approached the stage, maniacally ranting about having lost her shoes. Fearing for his safety, Levy breathed a sigh of relief when, out of nowhere, Candy's large frame appeared; Candy excitedly gave the woman the good news that her shoes had been located and they were safe backstage, then promptly escorted the patron out the back door of the theatre. The show could go on.

Back in Toronto, Candy and the cast began to forge a uniquely Canadian vision of the Second City theatre philosophy. This comedy was sillier and slightly less cerebral than the Chicago way, and better suited, in Flaherty's words, "to go over in a room full of Canadian beer drinkers."

In a sketch called "I'm Gonna Be All Right, You Creep, Leaving Home and All, Eh," a.k.a. "The Canadian Play," Candy portrayed a hockey player in a loving parody of the prevailing national identity crisis of the times. Toronto audiences ate up all the local references.

THE OLD FIRE HALL was now a bona fide Canadian playhouse, which is why, in hindsight, exporting the company's comedy style to a strip mall in Pasadena, California, was doomed to fail.

In 1975, Candy, Flaherty, and Levy were sent down from Toronto to start the Pasadena Second City, along with Chicago cast members Betty Thomas and Deborah Harmon and future *SCTV* writer Doug Steckler. Chicago's David Rasche (a future star of HBO's *Succession*) would join them later.

Aykroyd had recently auditioned for a new weekly live television variety series that his old friend from the CBC, Lorne Michaels, was putting together for NBC in New York. Having assumed that he hadn't got the series, Aykroyd opted to drive down to Pasadena with Candy. Both actors had always enjoyed a good road trip and were more than happy to get the motor running on Candy's new 1973 Mercury Cougar and head out on the highway like a pair of comedy outlaws. With the pedal to the metal and the car stereo blasting, Aykroyd and Candy stopped only for gas, food, or the call of nature. In truth, they hadn't really known each other very long, but by the time they arrived in Pasadena, thirty-eight hours later, the two had cemented what would become a lifelong friendship.

"This was at a time when you could be waved through the border with no questions," says Aykroyd. "Nobody cared about anything. We were listening to music on eight-track, lots of country, some heavy metal, Cream, Zeppelin, but also radio comedy stuff like Bob and Ray, and tuning in the radio late at night. The conversations we shared were deep, talking about the possibilities of what we were going to do, how we were going to polish the pieces that we already had into scenes, so when we arrived, we were confident that we had some good material to bring to the party."

Aykroyd had barely parked the car in Pasadena when Michaels called him back to New York for further in-studio camera auditions for what would eventually become *Saturday Night Live*. Meanwhile, Flaherty, Candy, and Levy set about launching Second City's new theatre, located, to their dismay, in a strip mall far from Hollywood. Los Angeles audiences stayed away in droves, Second City Pasadena ultimately closed its doors, and the trio came home to new cast members Martin Short and Dave Thomas, who were finally treading the boards at the Old Fire Hall, alongside Andrea Martin and Catherine O'Hara.

"They were just so good," says Thomas. "John's return marked the beginning of my most concentrated experience working onstage with him. We really hit it off and we ended up doing a lot of stuff together. John was a big kid, and I related to that because I was a big kid too. The scenes we did together were always a lot of fun."

The Second City stage had no sets or curtains, and scene breaks were often marked by the stage and houselights simply going dark (known as a "blackout"). The back wall had only two doors plus café-style bentwood chairs for each member of the cast to sit on, if needed. Few if any props were used, so the actors simply mimed holding objects, accepting a shared reality of what was *supposed* to be at hand.

"You would look at each other as a scene was about to begin," says Thomas, "and say something like 'Put away that gun, Bob. It's not gonna do you any good.' Now, the other guy immediately *has* to mime a gun. You can't *deny* [the other actor's] scene choice, he has a gun now, and there's a story there to discover, which heightens the scene."

Frequently, certain audience members, having just had dinner and drinks in the upstairs dining room, were drunk by the time they were seated in the theatre. Heckling was a constant problem, and on some nights, onstage safety became a concern.

"John and I were in the middle of a scene," says Thomas, "when suddenly somebody threw a glass toward the stage, and it just smashed on the back wall. We really had to dodge shards of glass."

Thomas fled backstage, leaving Candy alone onstage until Thomas re-emerged at the back of the house posing as a Toronto police officer, wearing a blue parka and a policeman's cap hastily pulled from the theatre's limited selection of props and wardrobe.

"At first, John didn't even know it was me," says Thomas, "and he couldn't believe how fast the cops got there. I screamed, 'Who threw that glass?' and people in the audience pointed at this woman. So, I just said, 'You! Out!' and she gets up and starts walking towards me. John grabs her by the lapels and walks her past the bar and out to the little walkway behind the stage, opens the exit door and sends her out into the alley behind the theatre. John and I went back onstage and told the audience what just happened, and they were all laughing their asses off and applauding."

O'Hara says that she always felt safe standing onstage next to John Candy. "When you're improvising with people, you just want to feel creatively safe," says O'Hara, "and that you're treated like you have a right to be there. You depend on each other to raise each other's game, and you're always open to whatever direction another cast member leads the scene. A lot of people compare it to jazz improvising, where you're just riffing off each other, but with the goal of creating something that makes sense too. And of course, you hope it's also funny."

She remembers Candy as an "open and generous" improviser, recalling a scene they had pulled out of thin air that was based on the audience suggestion of "mosquitoes in cottage country."

"We were going to slap each other," says O'Hara, "because of all the mosquitoes. Back then, I didn't know what a 'stage slap' was, so I just *really* slapped John, and hard. Later, when we came backstage, he said, 'Um, have you ever heard of a stage slap?' And he did a little fake punch in the air, shaking his fist like, 'Why, I oughta—if you wasn't a dame!' And I said, 'Oh John, I'm so sorry. I'm so sorry.' But he was like, 'It's okay, whatever.'"

Thomas recalls that, walking out on a stage with Candy, "half your work was done, because the audience already liked you because they loved him. All you had to do from that point was to try to deliver some funny material and not fuck it up."

In character, Candy could be a fearless performer, but during one improv set, when Thomas suggested that the two of them go out and improvise as themselves, a different, more vulnerable side of Candy revealed itself. He had reluctantly agreed to do the scene, but when they retreated backstage, Thomas remembers Candy becoming angry with him. For Thomas, the outburst was a fleeting first glimpse into an inner turmoil that he had never seen in Candy. To be fair, at that moment, neither of them had the tools to recognize or understand the complexities of Candy's psychological wiring.

"I was a little surprised," says Thomas, "because I thought if anyone had a persona that they should be comfortable with, it was this big, chubby, lovable guy that the audience loves instantly. I mean, it's John Candy, so of course you love him."

A communal sense of the ensemble, and a strong reliance on teamwork, elevated the entire cast to better work. To Aykroyd, the Second City was like a comedy university, and the skills each actor perfected there would enable them to thrive in all of their future endeavours.

"That discipline taught us to listen to the other players," says Aykroyd. "You make everyone else look good, and that way, you're in service of the group and in collaboration with these brilliant talents and minds like John Candy. It was such a pleasure to be able to share those nights of laughter with him and the audiences at the Second City, on top of all the socializing, laughter, and fun."

The Second City was finally a hit in Toronto, but on the horizon, a new threat was coming from the US. Ironically it came from a friend and fellow Torontonian, Lorne Michaels, who had lured away Aykroyd and Radner to work for him at NBC's *Saturday Night* in New York. While Andrew Alexander was happy for Michaels as his show transformed the face of American TV comedy, he was also concerned about the effects of the talent drain on Second City. Alexander and Sahlins began to seriously look into a way to take their own stars to television without losing them to Michaels. Their solution was to brainstorm an imaginary network that would allow Candy and his fellow Second City graduate class to extend their comedy reach beyond the blackouts and bentwood chairs of the Old Fire Hall. Together, they were about to make television history of their own.

Five

From Stage to Screen

NBC's *Saturday Night* premiered on October 11, 1975, with a cast that included Second Citizens Dan Aykroyd, Gilda Radner, and John Belushi, along with Garrett Morris, Laraine Newman, Jane Curtin, and Chevy Chase. By its second season, *Saturday Night Live*, as it came to be known, had made an overnight star of Chase, who abruptly departed to try his luck in Hollywood. In his place, Candy's old neighbour Bill Murray became an essential member of SNL's Not Ready for Prime Time Players. All of them were gifted young comedians trained in the kind of improv comedy that Candy and his cast were still practising six nights a week at the Old Fire Hall in Toronto.

Onstage, the Toronto cast were a hit. Meanwhile, in the front office, the Second City was constantly struggling to keep the lights on. By the end of 1976, with SNL already raiding their talent pool, Andrew Alexander and Bernard Sahlins wondered if the exposure and reach of television might just elevate the

Second City brand beyond its precarious dinner theatre business model, and in the process, give his players a reason to resist the lure of Lorne Michaels or any other upstart American network now jumping on the bandwagon. They immediately set about visualizing what would become *Second City Television*.

Some of the cast had already made tentative steps into the world of film and television, among them Andrea Martin and Eugene Levy, who had both appeared in Ivan Reitman's earliest films, *Foxy Lady* and *Cannibal Girls*, but it was John Candy who had been working more than any of them. Besides his television commercials and work as an extra in the 1971 hockey drama *Face-Off*, Candy had taken minor roles in Paul Bogart's *Class of '44* and had spun off his role in John Trent's 1975 sex farce *It Seemed Like a Good Idea at the Time* with a starring role (alongside Lawrence Dane) in Trent's 1976 follow-up, *Find the Lady*. Candy's experiences in children's theatre had come in handy when he was cast in Trevor Evans's CBC kids' program *Dr. Zonk and the Zunkins*, and Candy (working alongside Gilda Radner and Rosemary Radcliffe) was excited to be earning a reported $200 a day on the series, in stark contrast to the estimated $160 a week he was pulling in at Second City. *Zunkins* led to a subsequent role on Evans's next sitcom for kids, *Coming Up Rosie*, this time alongside Catherine O'Hara and Dan Aykroyd, who was as surprised as anyone to find himself working on a kids' show.

"I never saw that coming," says Aykroyd. "I don't think Candy did either, but we had a lot of fun. It was whimsical, it was gentle, it was for kids."

Additionally, Candy had taken a small role in the 1972 TV program *Cucumber* (with Martin Short) and stretched his dramatic muscles guest-starring in two episodes of the Canadian medical crime series *Police Surgeon* (a.k.a. *Dr. Simon Locke*). He and Lawrence Dane had appeared in director Martyn Burke's thriller *The Clown Murders*, which has since gained the dubious distinction of being named one of director Quentin Tarantino's favourite "killer clown" films. From job to job, Candy earned a reputation for personal charm mixed with an intense devotion to craft that made him an attractive hire in film and television.

But there were two jobs in the year leading up to *SCTV* that most prepared Candy for television comedy. He was a regular player on *90 Minutes Live*, a CBC television talk and variety show hosted by radio's Peter Gzowski, in which Candy performed short comedic segments, sometimes joined by Valri Bromfield or Jayne Eastwood or a precocious radio comedian named Rick Moranis. And Candy enjoyed even greater visibility as a member of the ensemble cast of a CTV variety series hosted by the Winnipeg-born comedian, and former Second City Chicago player, David Steinberg, who had gained fame in the late 1960s on CBS television's notorious *Smothers Brothers Comedy Hour*. In 1976, CTV had teased him back to Canada to make *The David Steinberg Show*. Modelled on comedian Jack Benny's television program from the 1950s, Steinberg played himself as the host of a variety show, with backstage sketches featuring the show's repertory cast, which included Bill Saluga, Trudy Young, and a selection of comedians recruited from the Toronto Second City, including Candy, Dave Thomas, Joe Flaherty, Martin Short, and occasionally Andrea Martin.

"I would always drop in to the Old Fire Hall to see what was happening," says Steinberg. "They had an amazing cast who were all great performers. The first time I saw John he was already the best and just as funny as anyone I'd ever seen."

On Candy's first day reporting to the set, Steinberg was charmed by his impression of Jackie Gleason, and from there, a long and lasting friendship grew between them. While there was what Steinberg refers to as "a mild learning curve" as his cast adjusted to working in television, Candy "came to us fully formed."

"John was already great," says Steinberg, "and as our friendship bloomed, we would be together all the time, working out ideas and improvising. We all shared that old Chicago rule, which is to always play from the top of your intelligence, so we all spoke the same language and wanted the same version of comedy. It was a very unstructured and creative atmosphere. We would just laugh all the time, and somehow it paid off for us. Our only concern was 'What is the funniest way that we could approach this? And could we do that?'"

Candy was especially happy to be making television with Martin Short, and the two would play well together, onscreen and off. And although Short later revealed that Candy had unintentionally broken two of his ribs while tossing around a football on the set, they were young and flexible and seemingly invincible.

"This was a close-knit group back then," says Short. "We were all buddies, and we all hung out constantly. Everyone was just happy to be out of university and getting paid for doing something they adored doing. It was quite a unique experience."

The David Steinberg Show not only introduced Candy to the daily grind of making a weekly television program, it was also the beginning of a fruitful collaboration with the show's costume designer, Juul Haalmeyer.

"It was my first time working on TV," says Haalmeyer, "and it was a son of a bitch to pull together every week, but this is where

I first met John, Marty [Short], and Dave [Thomas], mostly out on the set, because we never had time to do proper fittings for anybody and no time for small talk."

Having previously created costumes for full-figured opera singers, Haalmeyer didn't flinch when putting together plus-size outfits for Candy. He was, however, impressed with the size of Candy's personality.

"I loved John from the moment I met him," says Haalmeyer. "Everybody was always equal to John, which was the way with all the Second City people; I've never met one malicious person that came out of there."

Finally, in 1976, Candy was part of a large ensemble cast in a low-budget satirical comedy film, *Tunnel Vision*, along with Flaherty and Saluga from the *Steinberg* show, Bill Murray, Doug Steckler, Betty Thomas, and emerging *SNL* stars Chevy Chase, Laraine Newman, Tom Davis, and Al Franken. A loose aggregation of short comic sketches, *Tunnel Vision*'s premise was that these disparate countercultural vignettes were all part of a day's programming on America's first totally uncensored television network. Set in the not-too-distant future, 1985, the network premise enabled a number of commercial parodies, shorts, and fictional movie and television trailers, including one for a police procedural series called *Get Head*, in which Candy appeared as the severed head of a decapitated detective. Conceptually, *Tunnel Vision* was not far off from what would become *Second City Television* the following year. While not half as cynical, *SCTV* would provide a loose framework for an aggregation of commercial parodies, sketches, fictional variety shows and movie trailers, all beamed to the world from the show's imaginary studios in beautiful, fictional, Melonville.

Six

SCTV Is On the Air!

Television as you've never seen it before!

If SNL was the great leap forward, SCTV was the great leap sideways. It was also Andrew Alexander and Bernard Sahlins's attempt to curtail the defection of Second City's mostly Canadian talent pool to SNL and any other American-based comedy upstarts like ABC's *Fridays*.

"We had what we felt was a new genre of comedy," says Alexander, "and they were going to grab our people. Being from Chicago, Bernie [Sahlins] was eager to get us on American television, but we agreed that it might be easier to do it in Canada."

Del Close, Harold Ramis, and Sheldon Patinkin were invited up from Second City Chicago to join a think tank that included Joe Flaherty, Dave Thomas, and Eugene Levy. Together they brainstormed their vision for SCTV, purportedly "the world's smallest television broadcasting company," presenting "an entire broadcast day in a half-hour." The open-ended concept made room for numerous short sketches that could utilize a rotating cast of imaginative characters working at the fictional network's decidedly low-budget facility in "Melonville." The premise wasn't far from reality, and the initial season of *SCTV* was produced on a shoestring budget at the Don Mills studios of the fledgling Global Television Network, with supplemental financing from a US syndication deal with Rhodes Productions, who had had great success syndicating the American sitcom *Mary Hartman, Mary Hartman*.

The stage was now set for John Candy, Catherine O'Hara, Eugene Levy, Andrea Martin, Dave Thomas, and Joe Flaherty to translate the comedy they had developed onstage into a real-life television show. Harold Ramis, the most experienced scriptwriter within Second City at the time, stayed on as head writer (and occasional performer) to help with the transition.

"We were hired for 250 bucks a week to write and perform in this television show," says Flaherty, "which we all loved doing. Still, I don't know what Andrew and Bernie were thinking about us competing with *Saturday Night Live*."

Since many of the stage scenes had been developed collaboratively through group improvisations, there was some disagreement within the ranks as to what constituted "writing" for television. Ramis, for one, believed that while Candy was an inventive and funny improviser, his undisciplined methods didn't quite live up to his own definition of the term.

"You'd sit at a table and John Candy would pull a napkin out of his pocket from a bar the night before," Ramis later told one interviewer. "He'd unfold it, and it had an idea, but it was like 'Davy Crockett hat.' You'd try to piece that together for John. He would just keep throwing things in until the scene grew and grew."

According to Thomas, Candy was deeply humiliated by Ramis's "cocktail napkin" quote. "I don't think that Harold understood John's process," says Thomas. "John just didn't have the patience to sit down and engage himself in formal script-writing. You had to recognize that and help him. Writing a script with John was like trying to keep a rabbit in a cage, he'd keep trying to leave."

But when the paycheques were handed out, Candy was especially angered to discover that he, along with Martin and O'Hara, was being paid less than the rest of the cast, who were considered "writer/performers."

"We were all sitting around one day when we got our cheques," says Thomas, "and John playfully asked me, 'What did you get?' So I tossed him mine and said, 'See for yourself.' John looked at it and got quiet. I didn't realize until that moment that he wasn't making the same amount as me."

Candy stormed into Alexander's office to confront him on the pay inequity. "John always thought I was cheaping out," says Alexander, "but Harold and Bernie had indicated to me that John wasn't contributing as much to the writing. But it obviously upset him, which I totally understood. He was always looking out for any unequal treatment."

Candy also stood up for Martin and O'Hara, the only two women in the cast, who he felt were being undervalued for their contributions to the writing.

"Andrea and I were not paid as writers," says O'Hara, "which was bullshit, because all of us had written this, right? I never knew at the time, though, isn't that funny? At least John got them back, because by the end of the series, he brought in his own lawyer and was getting more than anyone else. He fought for his rights. Then he would tell the rest of us what he was doing so that we could fight for our rights, too. John stood up for everyone."

Second City Television debuted on September 21, 1976, airing on Global on Tuesdays at 7:30 p.m. In an odd coincidence, CTV debuted *The David Steinberg Show* that same week, creating an unusually high television visibility for both Candy and Flaherty.

Whatever Candy may have lacked in discipline as a writer, he more than made up for in brilliant ideas, and Thomas credits Candy for devising *Second City Television*'s iconic opening sequence in which the cast threw television sets off the balcony of a high-rise apartment building.

"That one idea," says Thomas, "did a lot to increase awareness of *Second City*. It got us real serious press, and it was all John's idea."

Having fought for his own wages, Candy, who had always enjoyed a good relationship with those who worked behind the camera, became "apoplectic" when he learned that the crew was being fed reheated takeout chicken while working on set.

"John punched a hole in the wall at Global [studios]," says Alexander. "I think he held onto that [anger] for quite a while."

It is not hard to imagine such backstage grievances informing one of Candy's most popular creations for *SCTV*, Melonville's vainglorious yet lovable loser, Johnny LaRue—a character who papered over Candy's own innate sweetness with a layer of extreme vanity, transparent insecurities, and an endless appetite for indulgence. Candy readily acknowledged that LaRue was an exaggeration of the petty tyrant he was mindful not to become in real life.

"Hell, we all have a bit of LaRue in us," Candy admitted to Robert Crane Jr. in *Penthouse* magazine. "We all like to have a good time, to party. That's why I created him. Here's a guy who has everything: beautiful women, good times, limousines. LaRue is the enjoyable times, the no-no's in all of us."

Noting the real Candy's preference for the finer things, Flaherty would sometimes alternate between nicknames for him; "Johnny Toronto" was often switched to "Johnny Deluxe."

"Johnny Deluxe would always want to be put up in the biggest suite at the best hotel or get the biggest per diem," says Flaherty. "All that stuff befitting his big personality. Now LaRue expanded on that idea and magnified it. John really liked playing that part and expanded it. In that first season, LaRue answered to Harold's station manager character Moe Greene. After Harold left, I took over as the new station manager, Guy Caballero."

Candy's exaggerated alter ego performed a variety of different functions at the fictional television station, including hosting "Street Beef" man-on-the-street segments, and reviews of local restaurants. In the *SCTV* pilot, he was presented as a struggling producer whose career at the station was in jeopardy.

"We had this whole backstage storyline where LaRue thought he was going to get fired," says Flaherty. "This culminated in him being carried out on a stretcher. That episode ended up running an hour overtime, so we decided to keep the sketches and only leave in bits of the LaRue stuff as a running gag throughout the show."

O'Hara cast Candy in a scene about a high school television quiz show called *Hi Q*.

"John's bit was pressing the buzzer too early," says O'Hara, "then saying, 'What? What? I didn't press the buzzer. What do you mean? What?' He was so hilarious in *Hi Q*, and we did it again later as *Night School Hi Q*."

O'Hara was always impressed with Candy's ability to capture the true spirit of any character he played, such as a hockey player in the *SCTV* adaptation of the breakfast cereal commercial parody that aired as "Cornabix." "John had done the scene onstage, which probably gave everybody the confidence that John could pull it off," says O'Hara. "At Second City, we didn't have to actually look like anybody onstage, and we didn't have hair and makeup experts that we would get later on television. I believe that made us try harder to capture a character's essence."

Ramis had cast Candy in the title role in *SCTV*'s *Dialing for Dollars* presentation of *Ben-Hur*, entirely on the premise that a "fat Ben-Hur" would be funny, but Candy gave it an added dimension by playing the scene as Curly of the Three Stooges, elevating the sketch beyond its initial premise as a mere "fat joke."

According to Paul Flaherty, Joe's brother and a writer for *SCTV*, in the beginning Candy appeared to have few qualms about doing gags that exploited his body type. "*SCTV* did a parody of *The Great Gatsby* called 'The Great Fatsby,'" says Flaherty. "Or they would have John play a character named Hefty Neil in a parady of *Rocky*. Johnny, at that point, was quite willing to go along with that sort of thing. But I also remember Joe telling me that John had begged him, 'Promise me, promise me you will never ever see *The Clown Murders*.' And we held off for a really long time, but we finally watched it recently. Every mention of John in the movie was a fat reference or a fat joke. Every single one."

As large as he was, Candy could play miraculously against type, as he did in a *Dirty Harry* parody called "Harry Filth," in which he played a convincing Clint Eastwood–style tough cop, or when he transformed himself into a larger version of Jerry "the Beaver" Mathers for the *SCTV* spoof of the 1950s television sitcom *Leave It to Beaver.* That sketch, in particular, made a huge impression on a young actor named Tom Hanks, who was then an unknown on tour with the Great Lakes Shakespeare Festival. When he switched on the television in his motel room in Wooster, Ohio, Hanks discovered *SCTV*.

"Here was this huge guy in a ball cap, playing the Beaver," says Hanks. "The way he carried himself, and the way *SCTV* had nailed the odd cadence of this one-camera television show from the 1950s or '60s, wasn't laugh-out-loud, but I was laughing uproariously at how engagingly subtle it all was. In those days, comedy shows were bigger, and ingeniously small. It was so unique that I recognized some brand of bodacious genius right off the bat. This new brand of comedy was taking over ... a huge show-business tsunami and a whole different way of being funny."

In *SCTV*'s recurring talk show, "The Sammy Maudlin Show," Candy appeared as William B. Williams, the chuckling sidekick to Flaherty's Sammy Maudlin. Based loosely on Sammy Davis Jr.'s short-lived series *Sammy and Company*, Candy's Williams character was similar to Johnny LaRue, but with even lower self-esteem.

"This was a typical second-banana type who generally kissed Maudlin's ass," says Flaherty. "That chuckle thing that Williams did, with the shoulders moving, was something I had seen John do when he was laughing in real life, so I said, 'Give him a jolly laugh like that, John,' and he did!"

The unique chemistry between Flaherty and Candy generated a whole host of new characters for *SCTV*, among them Flaherty's Big Jim McBob and Candy's Billy Sol Hurok, the twangy rural host of their *Hee Haw*–like "Farm Report" sketches, in which two overall-clad farmers revealed themselves to be erudite cineastes, with their penchant for foreign films hilariously undercut by their equal admiration for action movies in which things "blowed up." Eventually, the premise evolved into "Celebrity Farm Film Blow-Up," a handy vehicle for the SCTV cast to impersonate famous real-life celebrities who "blowed up real good."

In her memoir *Lady Parts*, Andrea Martin reflected on the audaciousness of "Celebrity Farm Film Blow-Up," which managed to transcend its alarmingly violent premise largely on the strength of Candy and Flaherty's good nature.

"It sounds cruel now," Martin wrote, "but when you watch the sketch, you see innocence and glee and mischievousness in John's and Joe's eyes, not cruelty, and because of the fun they are having, the audience is having fun too."

By the end of *SCTV*'s first season, Candy was already emerging as the show's breakout star, but he was growing impatient and restless over the program's relative cult status in the US. In 1978, during an excruciatingly underattended press conference in Manhattan to promote *SCTV*, Candy's internalized frustrations came to the surface in a very public fashion.

"Nobody came to the press conference except for Marvin Kitman from *Newsday*," says Dave Thomas. "Andrew was really embarrassed, but nobody was more offended and hurt by that than John, and he took it on the chin for the whole cast. We all went back to the hotel, and then Catherine said, 'Let's all go to Studio 54!' So we went down to Studio 54, but they didn't recognize any of us at the door so they wouldn't let us come in; a double header of rejection for John."

Candy later recalled the incident with a touch of shame.

"I started barking out front [of Studio 54]," he told Robert Crane Jr. in 1982, "like a live sex show. That wasn't taken too kindly. I was hustled off for that one."

It was Thomas who "hustled" Candy off to a nearby Manhattan bar, where he drowned his sorrows and humiliation with copious shots of cognac.

"New York in the seventies was dangerous," says Thomas. "John got into something with some guy in this bar, and it took all my fucking diplomatic and comedy skills to walk him out of there and into a cab. Now, the reason I'm telling you these stories—and this is important, so I would like it if you would actually put this in the book—is because every one of these stories, there's a good reason why John was taking it on the chin for the press not showing up and not being allowed into Studio 54. John took all those things not just on behalf of the cast, but also all on himself. He wore it like a dark drape over his lovable, cheerful personality.

"So the reason I'm telling you these stories is that there's two sides to John. To just hear about the jovial side, where he made people laugh or showed his generosity by buying meals for the whole crew—those are things that you'll hear from lots of people. Yes, he did that kind of thing all the time. But what made him a really interesting human being, and what made him the essential John Candy with all the depth that audiences could relate to, is that he had this *other side*. He was conflicted. He was insecure and he had doubts about himself."

Right after *SCTV*'s 1978–79 season, as the show's production values—bigger sets, better hair and makeup—were growing ever more expensive, Global cut off their funding, forcing Alexander to put the show into hiatus. A saviour arrived in the form of Dr. Charles Allard, owner of the ITV Allarcom station in Edmonton, Alberta. *SCTV* was saved, and while nobody seemed particularly thrilled to move the production of *Second City Television* to Edmonton, their third season would now be seen across Canada on the CBC, while continuing in syndication south of the border. The isolation to Alberta's "second city" (after Calgary) would prove to be a creative shot in the arm. And Alexander's hands-off approach to the content side would also give Candy and his colleagues full creative control of *SCTV*.

"Andrew ran the business," says O'Hara, "and he never pretended to know more than we did about comedy, writing, or anything. He always laughed at what we were doing; John and Marty could always make him laugh."

But just as costumer Juul Haalmeyer was set to reunite with Candy in Edmonton, Candy was on his way out. During the hiatus, he had grown impatient with *SCTV*'s on-again, off-again status, and while he still loved working with his friends, he had begun to wonder if the series had run its course. With his star ascending, Candy, says Alexander, "got fed up and left."

"My feeling initially," Candy told Robert Crane Jr., "was that [*SCTV*] was a make-work project... to keep us going, because we had done other shows and pilots that were just fiascos. This one just seemed to work. Material was endless for that. It evolved very nicely."

But when "finances turned bad," Candy opted out of the Edmonton move for what he vaguely referred to as "a number of moral reasons. I didn't like the way the show was going. It was time for me to leave."

Seven

I Like Your Movie about the Fish

To understand why Candy bailed on *SCTV* just as it was gaining wider recognition, it's helpful to consider not only his grievances within the Second City organization at the time, but all that had happened outside of it. Concurrent with becoming the breakout star of *SCTV*, Candy had also been racking up an impressive resumé of extracurricular film and television work both at home and in Hollywood.

"He was getting a whole other level of recognition that some of the other cast members weren't," says Andrew Alexander, "although he wasn't one to lord that over everybody. John was still a team player who was always able to team up with the right person in the writing room."

On the other hand, Dave Thomas recalls Candy frequently expressing his desire to be rich and famous, if only to pay for his already expensive tastes in limousines, first-class flights, and fine dining.

"Sometimes he wouldn't have enough cash to pay for it," says Thomas, "so he'd borrow it from one of us. He was a young man with big ambitions. He used to say, 'One day I'm going to own this town.' I think John wanting to star in his own show was part of him becoming 'Johnny Toronto.'"

Despite Candy's Hollywood dreams, he got his first big break in an American movie filmed in Toronto, a mere three blocks from the Old Fire Hall.

Daryl Duke's 1978 film *The Silent Partner* was a heist thriller whose central action was set in a bank deep within the bowels of the newly opened Toronto Eaton Centre mall. Candy was a featured support player in a cast led by Elliott Gould, Christopher Plummer, and Susannah York. Featuring a jazz-based score composed by Montreal-born Oscar Peterson, *The Silent Partner* was likely the first Hollywood film in which Toronto didn't stand in for New York or some other American city. One of the earliest domestic films to take advantage of Canada's Capital Cost Allowance plan, which had been created to incentivize foreign investment in the Canadian film industry, it was a commercial success, earning praise from American critics such as Roger Ebert and Janet Maslin. *The Silent Partner* went on to win three Canadian Film Awards and was later described by *The Globe and Mail*'s Gayle Macdonald as "one of the few truly good films to come out of the tax-shelter heyday of the 1970s."

Significantly, *The Silent Partner* also gave Candy a soft launch into a film career playing an affable bank teller named Simonsen. Elliott Gould, who vaguely recalled hearing Candy's name through their mutual friend David Steinberg, says he was instantly charmed by Candy when he finally met him on location.

"It's lovely to me that *The Silent Partner* was where we introduced John Candy to the world," says Gould. "His smile, oh how it tickled me, I'll never forget that. It's almost like if I was on a polar ice cap before it started to melt, and that warmth would have been John Candy. He was just a regular guy; cherubic, bright, brilliant, talented, but not ostentatious. We all had this love for him, and he was so funny."

In one of their scenes together, Gould was supposed to refer to Candy's character by his last name. Gould felt that "Simonsen" sounded a little to "parochial" and "square," and suggested to Duke that everyone in the bank would probably know this man by his first name. Since the script hadn't indicated a first name for Simonsen, Gould simply improvised one.

"I looked at John," says Gould, "and just suggested he was Raoul. So in the take, when I said Raoul, I couldn't keep from smiling because it just felt so funny to name John Candy's character Raoul. So to me he's eternally 'Raoul from *The Silent Partner*' and I'm very pleased and privileged to have had the opportunity to give his character a first name. John just rolled with it; he was a natural screen actor who would have succeeded at anything he decided to do. Can you imagine him playing classical roles? He was talented and very intelligent. We make up so much in life, but life is the only thing we didn't invent, and John was a force of nature, and he did great; we didn't see enough of him."

Hollywood seemed to be coming to him, and in 1979, Candy appeared in another American production shot in Canada, Melvin Frank's comedy *Lost and Found*, with a cast that included George Segal and Glenda Jackson. Frank was initially concerned that a young and cherubic Candy couldn't play a convincing fifty-five-year-old used car salesman named Carpentier. The director instructed his hair and makeup department to camouflage Candy's baby face with a moustache and beard, and to dye his hair black, then give him a perm.

"I grew this real bad beard," Candy later told *City Lights* host Brian Linehan. "They said, 'Grow whatever you can and we'll fill in the rest.' And I had the worst beard in the world, it's gross-looking, gnarly. The permanent took for six months, and the dye came out in different colours. It went from a real bad raven black to a purple, then it started going into a pink—it was so embarrassing. God, I didn't realize how dumb I looked. Walking down the street and people are just looking at me. Oh, it was so embarrassing, and for what? I was not convincing as a fifty-five-year-old French used car salesman. I take full responsibility for *Lost and Found* not doing well. At least that's what Mel Frank said, he blamed me for that."

While these parts were a start, the seeds for Candy's true arrival in Hollywood film had been planted in Los Angeles during the summer of 1977, when Andrew Alexander sent the entire cast and writing team of *SCTV* down to a rented house in Bel-Air for a six-week Second City writing retreat with Harold Ramis, who had moved to Los Angeles to work on the screenplay for *National Lampoon's Animal House*.

"It was John, Dave, Joe, and me," says Catherine O'Hara. "Not everyone wanted to live together, so Andrea and Eugene had other places. I had a room with a pull-out couch, and John had the main bedroom. I think all of us Toronto young'uns would have died to go to LA in the winter, but no, Andrew sent us there in the summer. It was a change of pace, though, and I just remember waking up in the morning every day and John and everybody would improvise around the writing table and ease our way into the day. Harold, of course, would already have three sketches written by the time the rest of us started going."

Having become homesick after a few weeks, O'Hara opted to return to Toronto. She recalls Candy going out of his way to throw a bon voyage party in her honour. "It was so sweet," she says. "John got these garbage cans and lined them with plastic and ice and filled them with cans of beer and booze. Chevy Chase, Bill Murray, and Laraine Newman were there, and a bunch of other comedy writers, and some Chicago Second City people. We had a pool table. I still have my Polaroids from that night, and lots of pictures from that night of Chevy and John and people playing pool. It was really cool."

An estimated 350 people showed up at what was intended to be a private going-away party, and according to Flaherty, the gathering was a good indicator of how popular *SCTV* had become, at least within the LA entertainment community.

"It was kind of interesting who knew us by then," says Flaherty. "Steven Spielberg even showed up. It was amazing. It was one big blast. I'd talk to people and tell them we stayed at the house in Bel-Air, and they'd say, 'You guys didn't throw *that* party, did you?' Complete strangers knew about it."

Chase remembers that he really didn't know the *SCTV* crew very well at the time, but notes that comedy was such a small world in 1977 that it just seemed logical that the streams of *SNL* and *SCTV* would cross at a rented house in Bel-Air.

"I mean, how many people in the world are *really* funny?" says Chase. "Not that many. We all laughed at each other and appreciated each other's comedy. I just remember John and I really liked each other, and of course, we ended up working on a few things together later on."

Many of the people at the party that night recall Candy parading Chase around the house in a headlock. While Chase claims to have no memory of the incident, Candy mentioned it in a 1982 interview with *Oui* magazine. "Many parties where I went a little too nuts," Candy confessed with a tinge of regret. "I carried Chevy Chase in a headlock for a long time. I dragged him around a party for some reason. Or so I'm told. There are some things that are just too embarrassing to bring up."

The presence of Steven Spielberg at their little party was a surprise to many in the room, but it also proved to be significant. For it was here that a slightly overserved John Candy had his first fumbling close encounter with one of Hollywood's most successful and enduring legends. Years later, Candy elaborated on the exchange in a television interview on *City Lights* with Brian Linehan.

"Yeah, I had had a couple of drinks," Candy told Linehan, "and people were coming over to me saying, 'Steven Spielberg is here, he's here and he wants to see you!' And I'm like, 'Yeah, okay, right,' you know, 'Thank you. Excuse me, I've got a drink to get here.' And an hour later they say, 'He's waiting for you!' And thinking it was a joke, I went over there and there he was, just surrounded by a lot of people. And he [motions], 'John, John, I really like your work!' and I'm like, 'Ah, thanks very much.'"

Under the influence of too many rum-and-cokes, Candy was unable to recognize that Spielberg was seriously offering him a role in his next picture, reportedly telling the *Jaws* director, "I like your movie about the fish," before politely walking away.

"I think I said a few other things too," Candy told Linehan, "[but] it was all a blur after that."

Thirty minutes later, Candy felt a tap on his shoulder and was presented with the director's card and told that Spielberg was indeed serious. By the end of the week, Spielberg had offered him the role of Pvt. Foley in his next picture, the World War II farce *1941*.

Even in 1977, Spielberg was a massively successful and influential director. *Jaws* had terrorized a generation of beachgoers, while *Close Encounters of the Third Kind* had tapped into popular culture's interest in extraterrestrial contact. But *1941* was Spielberg's attempt to stage an all-star, blockbuster adventure comedy in the tradition of Stanley Kramer's 1963 ensemble caper, *It's a Mad, Mad, Mad, Mad World*.

A World War II–era comedy about a surprise attack on the city of Los Angeles by the Japanese Imperial Forces, *1941* seemed destined to become another Spielberg smash. He had tapped Candy and Joe Flaherty to join John Belushi and Dan Aykroyd, along with an impressive cast that included Michael McKean, Nancy Allen, and an authentic Japanese action hero, Toshirō Mifune. Excess was the order of the day, and Spielberg is rumoured to have used up over a million feet of film over 247 shooting days.

Spielberg's madcap blockbuster would be released on December 14, 1979, just seven days after the thirty-eighth anniversary of the Japanese surprise attack on the American naval base at Pearl Harbor on December 7, 1941. Despite being considered by many to be Spielberg's first flop, particularly after two back-to-back box office hits, *1941* did respectable business, earning back three times its $32 million budget.

But for John Candy, *1941* was one more tiny yet significant break on the road to stardom. And on his next project, he would reunite with both Aykroyd and Belushi, in the city where he had honed his comic chops, Sweet Home Chicago.

Eight

Something Borrowed, Something Blues

On April 28, 1979, John Candy and Rosemary Hobor were married at St. Basil's Roman Catholic Church in Toronto. Candy had met Rose, a ceramicist and abstract painter, ten years earlier on a blind date, but she had actually attended Notre Dame school, the all-girls counterpart to Neil McNeil. By all accounts they were a perfect match for each other. An independent woman with self-sufficient artistic passions, Rose cared little for the trappings of show business, and their union would afford Candy the kind of stable domesticity he would need to stay grounded as his career was taking off.

On their wedding day, Candy wore a funky, custom-made suit fashioned by an abstract artist and designer he had befriended in Chicago. Ordered over the phone from Toronto, the suit had arrived on the day of the service, and Candy had forgone the benefit of a final fitting. As he walked down the aisle at

St. Basil's in the boxy and ill-fitting outfit—one guest noted that it appeared to be fashioned out of "sackcloth"—Candy elicited a few unintended giggles from some of their guests, who included comedians from both the 1063 Avenue Road and Second City social circles. Sartorial missteps aside, it was a joyous occasion for the bride and groom, as was the rousing reception that lasted well into the early morning hours.

There was little time for a honeymoon, however, as director John Landis had offered Candy a small but memorable role in Dan Aykroyd and John Belushi's feature film *The Blues Brothers*. Filmed between May and October 1979, the film was based on characters Aykroyd and Belushi had created for *Saturday Night Live*, and their star-studded ensemble cast included musical greats like James Brown, Aretha Franklin, and Ray Charles, backed by celebrated musicians Steve Cropper, Donald "Duck" Dunn, Matt "Guitar" Murphy, and others from the SNL house band. Carrie Fisher, fresh from her star turn in *Star Wars*, displayed a previously untapped gift for comedy alongside high-profile cameos from Muppets mainstay Frank Oz, model/actor Twiggy, and Steven Spielberg as a county clerk.

Candy turned down a part in Robert Zemeckis's *Used Cars* to take on the role of parole officer Burton Mercer, which Aykroyd had written with him in mind.

"Landis loved Candy too," says Aykroyd, "and John was perfect for the part. He was a Chicago Second City alumnus, so it was perfect, and we all loved him."

Candy immediately identified with Aykroyd's vision for *The Blues Brothers*, having witnessed first-hand the origins of Aykroyd and Belushi's infatuation with blues music, back at Aykroyd's Toronto booze can, the 505, years earlier. But the screenplay that Aykroyd developed with Landis was also a tribute to the colourful, and richly musical, history of Chicago itself, set amid the juke joints and blues bars that Candy had originally been exposed to while bar-crawling with Bill Murray during his first eye-opening year away from Toronto.

Candy's most memorable moment in *The Blues Brothers* occurs during the film's concert finale, starring Cab Calloway. In a sequence filmed at the Palladium in Los Angeles (posing as a Chicago concert hall), Mercer orders three Orange Whips for himself and the two law enforcement officers accompanying him. While Aykroyd insists that Candy's choice of beverage was an improvisation, director Landis remembers it differently. Landis recalls that one of his assistants was related to a representative of the Orange Whip company, which was catering the refreshments for the location shoot, and thought it might be nice to include some subtle product placement in the scene.

"The camera was already rolling," says Landis, "so just before I said 'action,' I turned to John and said, 'Order some Orange Whips for your guys.' So it was kind of my suggestion, but the way John did it was just really funny. 'Who wants an Orange Whip? Orange Whip? Orange Whip? Three Orange Whips!' John gets a huge laugh in that scene every time it plays, because it was completely natural and funny, and totally *him*. I was always amazed and impressed with what a big laugh it got. That was just John, he was a lovely and naturally funny guy."

A pregnant Rosemary Candy visited the *Blues Brothers* set in Los Angeles in the summer of 1979. She later described her visit to journalist and family friend Rob Salem. "I was in the audience, up in the balcony," she told Salem. "As soon as the music started, I could feel [the baby] dancing away in there. It was a strange experience seeing John from that perspective, looking down on him in the middle of this huge room full of people. I was amazed at how magnetic he could be, at how much attention he could draw to himself by just standing there not doing anything. I was so proud."

Besides Candy's natural funniness and magnetism on the set, Landis says he couldn't help but notice Candy's weight gain, something his costumer (and Landis's wife) Deborah Nadoolman had also made note of while doing Candy's wardrobe fittings. Landis recalls being concerned for Candy's health, even then, and trying unsuccessfully to intervene.

"He was very Falstaffian," says Landis. "He always had bowls of candy bars in his trailer. He liked his food and his drink. I was like, 'John, don't eat like that,' but there was no talking to him. Still, he was unbelievably funny and wonderfully talented and just this sweet man who was our perfect parole officer, right?"

The extremely convoluted storyline for *The Blues Brothers* was almost as elaborate as the one for *1941*, but luckily for Candy this time, the chaos created a thoroughly entertaining musical comedy. Landis's seemingly off-the-rails production had raised eyebrows at Universal Pictures for its $27.5 million budget (high by 1979 standards), but in the end Aykroyd and Belushi delivered a genuine smash, taking in over $115.2 million at the box office. Today, *The Blues Brothers* is considered one of the best comedy films of its era.

In the wake of *The Blues Brothers*, Catherine McCartney introduced Candy to the LA star-maker Bernie Brillstein, at the time one of the most influential agents and managers in show business. Candy was impatient to capitalize on his increasing visibility and looking for the breakout role that would put his name above the title in Hollywood. To better field and procure Hollywood offers, he rented a house in Sherman Oaks as a kind of LA base of operations.

"Candy was like a man on a train that was clearly going somewhere," said Garry Blye, a fellow Canadian ex-pat whom Candy had met on the *Steinberg* show. Speaking later with author Martin Knelman, Blye recalled that "at the end of every project, [Candy] always had the sense that there was something better just around the corner, and he was in a rush to get it."

On February 3, 1980, John and Rose welcomed their first child, a daughter they named Jennifer, into the world. Later that year, the newly expanded Candy family finally moved to a place of their own, a farm in Queensville, forty miles north of Toronto, and quite near to his birthplace in Newmarket, Ontario. Candy had impulsively purchased the ten-acre spread, sight unseen, after reading a newspaper listing for a country estate with a pond and a barn. Lacking the counsel of a real estate agent, Candy had failed to notice there was running water going all through the house, and things got even worse when the family moved in that July.

"It turned out I got swamp property," Candy later explained on NBC's *Late Night with David Letterman*. "I learned about water tables; we're on a real high one. There's a lot of water running through our place. Now I've channelled it all around [the Candy home]. So now my lawn turns brown. So now my lawn is no good, so I have to put an irrigation system in. Lot of crushed stone and weeping tile that goes underneath it. Every movie I do kind of pays for another stone. We had to do the whole foundation of the house, had to dig that out. So it's been fun living there. There are about ten houses on the street and it's very pretty. It's like an Andrew Wyeth painting. I love it up there."

With a mortgage to pay off and a newborn baby to feed and clothe, Candy busied himself with constant work close to home, on Canadian-based projects such as the made-for-television film *The Courage of Kavik, the Wolf Dog* and the theatrical thriller *Double Negative*. Still fascinated by the idea of a satirical news program, Candy and Joe Flaherty kicked around an idea for an American series covering the US political conventions of 1980, but nothing came of it.

Having left SCTV, most of Candy's attention at the time was devoted to writing and starring in his own spin-off, called *Big City Comedy*. And to Andrew Alexander's further dismay, *Big City Comedy* would air head-to-head against SCTV in certain syndicated markets around North America.

But that wasn't Alexander's only problem with *Big City Comedy*, and as the rift between him and Candy that had initially begun over wage inequity widened, they became, for the foreseeable future, actual rivals.

Nine

Bright Lights, Big City

Andrew Alexander was not happy. Not only had his breakout star John Candy left *Second City Television*, but Candy had been lured away by his former partner and co-owner of the Second City brand, Bernard Sahlins, who had left the company to launch a rival sketch comedy program that he intended to call *The Second City Comedy Show*. This was problematic for Alexander in more ways than one. In the US syndication he had established a brand for *Second City Television*, but that would prove tricky if Sahlins kept his intended name. A compromise was reached when Alexander proposed that *Second City Television* simply rebrand as the initialized *SCTV*, and Sahlins would eventually rename his sketch program *Big City Comedy*.

Candy shot the pilot for *The Second City Comedy Show* in Provo, Utah, at a production facility owned by the Osmonds. After the pilot was picked up, *Big City Comedy* moved production back to Toronto's CFTO studios, the flagship facility of the CTV network, where Candy had begun his television career with *The David Steinberg Show*, even working with Steinberg's former director, Perry Rosemond. By the summer of 1980, production had begun in earnest on *Big City Comedy*, and both NBC and CTV committed to a fall debut, airing the thirty-minute program on "family hour," 7:30 p.m. on Fridays.

The supporting cast of *Big City Comedy* was mainly drawn from the Chicago Second City stage, and included Tino Insana, Tim Kazurinsky, Audrie Neenan, Don Lamont, Ann Ryerson, and Patti Oatman. According to Kazurinsky, Candy took responsibility for every aspect of the show, and his energetic leadership carried not only the cast but the entire production.

"He was not just the star of the show," Kazurinsky later admitted to writer Tracey J. Morgan, "he was head cheerleader as well as chief cook and bottle-washer. I was in awe of his magnetism."

Candy, Kazurinsky, and Insana were also part of the writers' room, along with Michael Short, Martin's brother, who came to *Big City Comedy* direct from finishing season two of *SCTV*. Short remembers Candy as an even-handed and equitable boss.

"John was a really smart guy who loved and appreciated everybody," says Short. "Usually nice guys aren't funny, but John was raised by his aunt and his mother, so if he was upset with you, he'd scold you gently, like a mom."

Juul Haalmeyer, the costume designer from *The David Steinberg Show*, was thrilled to be working with Candy again at CFTO.

"We had a great time working with all of John's friends from Chicago Second City," says Haalmeyer. "I loved Tino, Tim, and the wonderful Audrie Neenan, and they were always generous and approving of my designs. We never had a minute to talk about the [costuming] details, but with John, you just had to guess what his train of thought was, and he was always up for whatever I made for him. The more over the top, the more he loved it."

While Candy finally had total creative control of his very own sketch series, there were certain limitations placed upon him. Notably, Alexander insisted that characters Candy had created for *SCTV* were the intellectual property of Second City, which meant that Johnny LaRue was forbidden to appear on *Big City Comedy*.

As a workaround, Candy created a very LaRue-like character based on the nickname he had earned on the streets of Chicago, Johnny Toronto, and some brand-new characters such as the frilly-shirt-clad Mr. Mambo, who shook his maracas defiantly at all of life's challenges before breaking out into the Afro-Cuban dance he was named for. And, as famous as he had become, Candy was not yet a household name, so his network benefactors at CTV and NBC compelled him to invite a series of high-profile guest hosts, as *SNL* did. Candy complied, and was happy to invite the likes of Billy Crystal, Betty White, Jimmie "J. J." Walker, and other stars of the day, to bolster his repertory cast members in sketches.

Among the most surprising special guest hosts was Margaret Trudeau, the recently estranged wife of Canadian prime minister Pierre Trudeau, and mother of future prime minister Justin Trudeau. Having been embroiled in scandal and hounded by the paparazzi for her association with the Rolling Stones, "Maggie," as the press sometimes called her, had been pursuing acting roles in an attempt to establish an identity apart from her famous husband. In the September 27, 1980, issue of *TV Guide*,

Mrs. Trudeau confessed to writer John T. D. Keyes that she had only accepted the booking because she trusted and "respected John Candy," and that appearing on *Big City Comedy* was a bid to show the world that she could take a joke and even be in on it. This attitude was underlined by the cover of the magazine in which she appeared beside Candy, who was dressed in a Mountie costume.

UPON COMPLETION OF THIRTEEN EPISODES, Candy invited the cast and crew—nearly three hundred people—up to his new farm in Queensville for a wrap party.

"It was a great celebration," says Haalmeyer, "and everybody stayed overnight because they all got drunk, so they slept on the floor, some outside because the weather was nice, and we all had breakfast the next day."

To promote the series, Candy appeared with some of the cast to do a live show at the University of Toronto's Convocation Hall. In the audience was a young comedy enthusiast named Mike Myers, who recalls waiting at the stage door to meet Candy after the show.

"In all my life, there have only been two performers that I've ever waited at a stage door to meet," says Myers. "One was Lily Tomlin, and the other was John Candy after *Big City Comedy*. We waited in the cold, but when he actually came out and said hello he was very lovely. When I told him that I wanted to be on *Second City* someday, he suggested that I first take the Second City workshops, which I didn't even know about at the time. I went down to the Old Fire Hall and took workshops with Allan Guttman and eventually got hired at Second City, which started my whole career in comedy. So I'm forever indebted to John Candy for that advice."

Big City Comedy's early time slot meant the show naturally veered toward family-friendly material, and Candy missed the kind of risqué, mature subjects that he had become accustomed to on SCTV. And while Candy was personally earning more money than he had at SCTV, his expensive salary left little in the budget to pay for the kinds of production values he felt were necessary to compete with other network variety series. *Big City Comedy* was cancelled after only one season, a victim of low ratings and missed opportunities. While Candy had enjoyed making thirteen episodes of comedy, the overall experience of carrying the program on his back had been disappointing and dispiriting. Candy later vented to Robert Crane Jr. that he had been under the illusion that he had full creative control of the program, only to discover, to his chagrin, that he "didn't have it at all."

"As a result," he told Crane, "the show didn't do that well. I'm not saying that I could have saved it, but I would have liked to have been given a shot at it."

In 1984, Candy granted an interview to a precocious seventeen-year-old comedy fan and aspiring comic named Judd Apatow. Apatow, who was still decades away from his own future career as a wildly successful comedy director and producer, spent a great deal of his adolescence interviewing his comedy idols for his high school radio show. In the interview, later published in Apatow's anthology *Sicker in the Head*, Candy wrote off *Big City Comedy* as a painful learning experience.

"I learned what not to do in the business," Candy told Apatow, "and who not to work with a lot of the time. It was frightening.

I was naive in that I thought I was going to have some control and some say on who the cast members were going to be, who was going to be writing the show, who was going to direct, and this and that. But the cast was good; we were fortunate that way. It was a good group of people. It just was—again, they put us in the wrong time slot."

When Apatow pressed him about how seemingly uncomfortable Candy had been when he appeared as himself in the opening of the show, Candy admitted that he found it easier to hide behind characters.

"I'm not a stand-up comic," he told Apatow. "And there's a real frenzied energy when you're on a show like that, that I had never experienced before. So, it's frustrating. I've stood in front of audiences many times before, but when you've got that kind of pressure on—you feel that pressure from these comics who are really trying, who want to make it. And this is their shot."

Temporarily down, but by no means out, Candy was once again hustling for paying jobs so he could buy more stones to shore up the soggy foundations of his farm. Within a year, however, Candy would not only be reunited with some old friends, he would also be doing some of his best television work ever. On top of that, he was finally going to get his chance to go to military boot camp, if only in a movie.

According to the Chinese Zodiac, 1981 was to be the Year of the Rooster, but for John Candy, it would be the Year of the Ox.

Ten

The Year of the Ox

In November 1980, Candy was at his home in Queensville watching an episode of *Big City Comedy* with his family. While the grounds surrounding his newly acquired farm were muddy and damp, his living room was a cozy domestic scene, with baby Jennifer's toys on the carpet, Rose's ceramic works around the room, and Catherine O'Hara's framed drawing of Candy as Johnny LaRue on the wall. In a month he was to drive up to Kleinburg, Ontario, to appear in an episode of *Tales of the Klondike*, a dramatic television anthology series hosted by a man he had impersonated many times, Orson Welles. Also that month, NBC aired the pilot for an "improvisational journalism" series he had starred in called *Roadshow*. More significantly, however, he had recently been recruited to appear in Ivan Reitman's military comedy *Stripes*, as a plus-size grunt by the name of Dewey "Ox" Oxberger.

On the evening described above, Toronto journalist Rob Salem had just spent the day shadowing Candy, gathering material for a proposed magazine feature for *Toronto Life*, and he recalls sitting with the Candys as John awaited news from Reitman about when exactly he was needed to begin filming in Kentucky. In Salem's transcript for the article (which was ultimately never published), an unguarded Candy spoke openly about the "terrific rapport" he still enjoyed with his old SCTV castmates, at one point confessing, "I really miss it." Candy was also candid about his real estate woes, complaining that everything in and around the farm was "covered in mud" and joking that as soon as his soggy foundations dried out, he intended to "write a horror movie about it."

He was also enthused about yet another Reitman project in his future, a voice-acting role in the animated feature film *Heavy Metal*, based on the adult illustrated fantasy magazine of the same name. If everything went to plan, 1981 would be a good year. Late into the evening, Candy received the phone call he had been waiting for. It was Reitman informing him that Bill Murray had "closed his deal," and *Stripes* would roll out as soon as Candy could make it to Fort Knox, Kentucky.

Expectations were high for *Stripes*. Reitman's previous film, the 1979 summer camp romp *Meatballs*, had not only made a movie star of Murray, it had also grossed upwards of $70 million; not bad for a film that only cost about a million and a half. Those numbers announced to Hollywood that Reitman, who had already produced the 1978 smash *National Lampoon's Animal House*, could also be a bankable director. At the *Meatballs* premiere in Toronto, Reitman was already pitching his next feature film idea.

"I had this thought that there hadn't been an army comedy in quite some time," says Reitman. "I remember going up to the premiere and telling people, 'I think I got the next movie.'"

Stripes, which Candy later described as "*Animal House* goes to war," was initially sold to Columbia Pictures as a vehicle for the wildly popular stoner comedy team Cheech & Chong, but when negotiations fell through, Reitman quickly realized it would be better with Murray as the film's underachieving protagonist, the Louisville, Kentucky, cab driver John Winger. He cast Harold Ramis, who had punched up the screenplays for *Meatballs* and *Animal House*, as his unassuming comic foil, Russell Ziskey.

Early in *Stripes*, Candy's Ox admits to his fellow recruits that his primary motivation for joining the army is to lose weight and bolster his self-confidence. In real life, Candy understood the part implicitly, having once driven his White Knight to enlist at Parris Island. Reitman could sense that Ox's introductory monologue, in which the new recruit expresses his hopes that boot camp will transform him into a leaner and meaner Marine, resonated deeply with Candy, and he encouraged the actor to tap into his own frustrations when playing the scene.

"This aggressive character," says Reitman, "was the kind of character he had played on SCTV, so I just borrowed that as a focus for what I was hoping that he would do in the film. And he nailed it right out of the gate and improvised a lot of his lines, and there were a couple of scenes that he built from scratch, like where he plays cards in the bunk with the guys, or when Ox flirts with P. J. Soles and Sean Young. I was always shooting, so there was a lot of extra material."

Reitman noticed that as Candy's confidence grew, he became

a kind of group leader for the whole cast, as he and his platoon became friends both on and off the screen.

"That was a big help for me," says Reitman. "John was a very good actor, but he was also a good guy, so it's natural that he would befriend that big ensemble group. As the director, I needed supportive people who I had a history with, who I could count on to be helpful in terms of improv and comedy ideas. We all kind of knew each other from that Avenue Road scene with Eugene and Marty, and those Second City and *Godspell* people. John was like a good friend from the old country."

The forty-two-day shoot for *Stripes* took Reitman and his crew all over Kentucky, from Louisville to Elizabethtown, from the Jim Beam distillery in Clermont to the actual military facility at Fort Knox. While most of the cast stayed at the Ramada Inn in Elizabethtown, Candy stayed at a rented house with Rose and baby Jennifer. The Candys frequently invited members of the cast over to the house, and Rose would make spaghetti for anyone who wanted to come over.

In what would become a recurring pattern of hiring from within Second City, the supporting cast of *Stripes* featured Joe Flaherty and Dave Thomas in some well-placed cameos.

"They were this special and talented secret group coming out of Canada," says Reitman of the Second City players, "and it was wonderful working with any of them. It just so happened that when I was casting the movie, they all turned out to be the best people available."

One of Candy's most notorious scenes in the film was also the one that most humiliated him. In an elaborate set piece, Ox and his platoon attend a seedy nightclub called the Pom Pom Bar, where the popular attraction is an exploitative spectacle called "mud wrestling" in which scantily clad women wrestle in a mud pit for the amusement of the leering male clientele. At one point Winger convinces Ox to enter the ring and wrestle the women. If the scene wasn't already degrading enough to the women, it was equally distressing to Candy, who was self-conscious about his physicality. If he wanted to get mud all over himself, he could get plenty of it in privacy on the grounds of his Queensville home. While Reitman acknowledged some initial discomfort from Candy, and mild pushback from Thomas and Flaherty, who knew Candy better, the director felt at the time that there was comedy gold in the mud. Later in life, however, Reitman conceded that the sequence hadn't aged well.

"In hindsight," says Reitman, "it wasn't as good as many of the other scenes in the film. At the time, the mud wrestling thing was a gimmick that was used by a lot of nightclubs, so it seemed like a funny idea for the film. It took some time to convince him, and he finally agreed to do it slapstick, like Curly from the Three Stooges. Billy [Murray] cracked up during the very first take of it. Billy went hoarse from laughing so much in that scene, and I thought it was a lovely combination of the two of them. John seemed up for shooting the scene, and I didn't feel that he had any discomfort. I later heard from a few people that he did, so I felt bad about that."

Thomas, who played the mud fight announcer, remembers Candy telling him privately that he felt horrible about the scene. "John didn't like fat jokes, and besides, there were better ways to use John than a mud wrestling scene with a bunch of women."

Flaherty concurs, adding that Candy told him that he "despised" the day of mud wrestling on the set. "They got this actress who was a karate expert and she did not pull her punches.

She was giving John all these karate kicks, and meanwhile he was just drenched in mud. And after it was over, he said, 'I hated that... they just used me as a fat joke.' I think later, Ivan even apologized."

Candy largely kept his private shame out of the public eye, as he did while describing the muddy scene in a 1989 interview on NBC's *Later*. "That was just a lot of fun to do," Candy told host Bob Costas, "I had to do it for the team, for the uh, the Corps..." before hiding behind a comically lecherous boast that he had actually tried to extend his time with the mud-soaked women and mock-complaining about how he was forced to do the scene over and over again wrestling "six girls."

"That take didn't work, so you'd have to go take a shower with them," he added, sounding ever more like Johnny LaRue. "I mean, the first two times, I admit, it was fun, but then the sixth, seventh time, 'Scrub my back, okay, come on, let's go... let's hurry up and get this over with.' It was tough. And they paid me for that too."

Yet, his pain would occasionally slip out in interviews, as it did in a 1984 chat with the writer Cutler Durkee, where Candy went off about an unnamed reviewer who had referred to him as "the elephant" in *Stripes*. "Jerks like that are so obvious," Candy told the readers of *People* magazine. "They can't even be clever. Sure, I'm sensitive about my weight, I don't do fat jokes."

Toward the end of the shoot, Reitman recalls, Candy called him into his trailer with a modest proposal worthy of a film that had after all very nearly been a vehicle for Cheech & Chong.

"John says, 'We did good. We got this great movie,'" says Reitman. "But then he adds, 'Look, I know you've never smoked up, and you've been very good through the whole movie, but it's a scene where the main guys get stoned. Don't you think it's a good idea to get stoned for this?' He was like the devil on my shoulder in *Animal House*, trying to talk me into this idea."

Reitman relented and shared the joint with Candy in his trailer.

"It was the first time and last time that I ever got stoned when I directed a real scene," says Reitman. "While I was shooting in this state, I thought, 'Wow, this is the funniest stuff I've ever shot,' but when I looked at it later I realized I hadn't been in the right mind. I never did that again, but the whole thing just made me love John Candy more, because he had only done this as an act of love and friendship to me. He had thought it would make the scene funnier."

Stripes was released on June 26, taking in over $85 million in North America alone, to rank as the fifth-most attended film of 1981. The film would establish Reitman, Murray, and Candy as big names in comedy for the decade to come.

Back home, Toronto moviegoers were particularly proud of Candy's work in *Stripes*. Catherine McCartney recalled Candy sneaking into one screening and becoming overwhelmed by the audience's positive reaction to Ox on the screen.

"Everyone just burst into applause," McCartney told Tracey J. Morgan, "and John just had to leave, he was just so choked up. I think he realized that they accepted him."

Meanwhile, in the northern Virginia suburbs, a young comedian named Patton Oswalt, already a fan of *SCTV*, was blown away by Candy's performance in the picture. "I remember thinking what a force of nature he is," says Oswalt. "It's interesting when you watch *Stripes* today, you realize that Candy starts off as just another face amongst the chorus behind Ramis and

Murray. Then you could just feel [Reitman] realizing, 'Oh, this is the heart and soul of the movie right here.' As much as we love Bill and Harold, there's this whole other thing going on with this guy. At the end, when we see that *Tiger Beat* magazine cover, 'Win a Dream Date with Ox,' it still gets screams in the theatre. So for me, *SCTV* was when I first knew this guy existed in my lizard brain, but it wasn't until *Stripes* that I realized, 'Oh, that's a guy named John Candy and he rules!'"

THE ADULT SCI-FI FANTASY MAGAZINE *Heavy Metal*, owned by the publishers of the *National Lampoon*, had entrusted Reitman to produce an animated feature film based on themes and stories from their pages. The director was Gerald Potterton. *Heavy Metal*'s edgy screenplay, written by Dan Goldberg and Len Blum (who had written *Stripes* with Harold Ramis), was rooted in graphic depictions of nudity, sexual acts, and often violent imagery, and the film was set to a rocking soundtrack plus a lush symphonic score by Elmer Bernstein. To voice the animation, Reitman enlisted a wide variety of Canadian actors, plus Candy, who appears in three segments in the film. In "Harry Canyon," Candy is a desk sergeant in the dystopian noir fantasy, and in the cyber-political sex fantasy "So Beautiful & So Dangerous," he is a robot. But in "Den," Candy voices a shy and awkward teenager who finds a meteorite and is magically transported to a fantasyland where he has been transformed into the muscle-bound, naked, and frankly well-endowed title character.

"I smile when I remember hearing John's voice as Den," says Reitman. "It was kind of goofy and funny, and John uses his young boy voice, similar to the one he did to play Jerry Mathers in *SCTV*'s *Leave It to Beaver.* It's one of his funniest characters in the film and he's just great in the part."

In her review for *The New York Times*, Janet Maslin chided *Heavy Metal* for its low-level misogyny, yet singled out Candy for bringing his adorable heart to what was otherwise a testosterone-fuelled fever dream.

Unlike Den or Ox, the real John Candy hadn't quite transformed himself into a "lean, mean, fighting machine," and his ongoing struggles with body image, likely exacerbated by both show business and societal tendencies toward so-called fat shaming, meant that diet and health awareness were never far from his mind, and nor was the spectre of his father's early death from a heart attack. But if his body was a source of occasional shame, his career, at least, was in far better shape. 1981 was proving to be the year he finally made the big leap from television to feature films, getting big laughs and winning hearts in Hollywood.

All of which made it somewhat surprising when Candy chose this moment to return to *Second City Television. Big City Comedy* hadn't worked out, but the deep friendships he had formed in the Old Fire Hall days remained intact. To paraphrase Michael Corleone in *The Godfather Part II*, just when Candy thought he was out, *SCTV* was pulling him back in. And now, Andrew Alexander was making him an offer so good that he could not refuse.

Johnny Deluxe would finally be paid what he was worth, Johnny LaRue would finally get his crane shot, and John Candy was even willing to relocate to Edmonton, where he and his beloved *SCTV* castmates would go on to create some of their best television work ever.

Eleven

Johnny Gets His Crane Shot

Dave Thomas's voice-over in the opening of *SCTV*'s fourth season summed up precisely what had happened to the series in the time since Candy's departure:

"There once were seven people who started their own network. But every network has its day, and theirs was over. Or so they thought ... They were summoned ... by a force that none of them were able to resist ... New York City, the entertainment capital of the world, and showered with adulation and attention. They were given the red-carpet treatment and ushered into the highest executive offices. They were given contracts to put *SCTV* back in business. But abruptly, they were told to get the hell out of New York. The Big Apple just doesn't cut to hicks ... Yes, it was bye, bye, Big Apple, hello *SCTV*. Yes, *SCTV* is on the air!"

In Candy's absence, *SCTV* had added Tony Rosato and Robin Duke to the cast, along with Rick Moranis, who had teamed up with Thomas to create two popular characters, Bob and

Doug McKenzie, lovable "hoser" cable television hosts starring in a series of "Great White North" segments that parodied the Canadian content regulations mandated by the Canadian Radio-television and Telecommunications Commission (CRTC, the Canadian equivalent of the American Federal Communications Commission [FCC]). Such was their overnight popularity that they had managed to parlay their proverbial fifteen minutes of fame into a hit comedy album and the Billboard-charting single "Take Off," sung by Rush's Geddy Lee. But despite the characters' seeming ubiquity that year, *SCTV*'s perennial issues with financing had unexpectedly forced Andrew Alexander to put the series into indefinite hiatus at the end of its third season.

"We did some pretty good stuff in Edmonton," says Joe Flaherty, "and were getting a huge following on the CBC in Canada, but we were still in syndication in the US, playing mainly in a handful of markets like New York or Chicago. Some stations aired us after *Saturday Night Live*, which increased our visibility in the US market, but when we suddenly went into hiatus, nobody knew would happen to *SCTV*—which always seemed to be the case with us."

In a last-minute bid to save the show, Flaherty made a desperate phone call to NBC president Brandon Tartikoff, and to his great surprise, Tartikoff made a conditional offer to bring *SCTV* to NBC, providing that Alexander could persuade every member of the original cast to return. This was easier said than done, since some of the cast had recently struck up new deals elsewhere, believing *SCTV* was done. Catherine O'Hara had signed onto the cast of *Saturday Night Live*, who were also pursuing John Candy, while Thomas and Moranis had their own solo development deal over at CBS.

"It was like *The Magnificent Seven*," says Alexander, "with me trying to find all the people and round them up. And I had to really do a little bit of song and dance to try and inspire some of them to come back."

Flaherty frantically called up O'Hara, reminding her that she would never have the kind of creative freedom at *SNL* that they had all enjoyed on *SCTV*. Remarkably, she agreed and asked to be let out of her *SNL* contract. Moranis and Thomas were similarly willing to abandon their CBS deal and come home, but Candy had certain reservations. Given his history with Alexander, he wasn't sure if the money was right and held out for a better deal.

"Rick told Andrew, 'Just give John the money,'" says Flaherty, "and when Andrew agreed, John came back."

Candy did not mince words when he later explained how much financial stability, both in terms of his own fee and the budget of the show, had influenced his decision to return.

"I came back in when NBC stepped in," Candy told Robert Crane Jr. "There was a little more credibility there for the financing... They're putting all their money in now. It's a very expensive show to do."

The move to NBC would raise the profiles of everybody in the cast, perhaps no one more than Candy.

"Hollywood was beckoning," says Flaherty, "but for the most part Johnny was happy to be back."

SCTV Network 90, as the series came to be known, would air on NBC at 12:30 a.m. in a coveted slot following *The Tonight Show Starring Johnny Carson*. Creating the program in the relative isolation of Edmonton, empowered by the creative control that Alexander had granted them, Candy and his colleagues could be as inventive as they wanted to be without the distractions and restrictions that typically came in the form of network "notes."

"We got to run the show ourselves," says O'Hara. "When [Andrew] made the deal with NBC, they kept trying to send producers to work with us. It was like, 'You don't understand. That's not the way we're trained, thank you. We're spoiled. We run this show.' We were very focused on the work, and we all stayed in the same hotel, where we could meet to brainstorm."

Appearing on *Late Night with David Letterman* to promote the show, Flaherty and a chain-smoking Candy shared a few of the challenges of working remotely in the comparatively small town of Edmonton.

"It's a city of 800,000 people ... and it's growing every day," Candy joked. "It's a boom town! The city takes a bad rap, but it's a real nice city, and there's good people there. Everybody's working real hard on the show. Getting people [to come] there was a problem, we were begging a lot of people."

After Flaherty praised their new director John Blanchard, Candy noted that one of the pitfalls of their arrangement was sharing a local television crew who would leave on Wednesdays to go and cover the Edmonton Oilers hockey broadcasts.

"We would just kinda hang around," Candy told Letterman, "and wait 'til they got back and then we'd shoot some more."

Now promoted to head writer, Thomas assigned a team of expert writers with yellow legal pads to shadow Candy wherever he went, including when he stepped out of the office to run errands, and to take notes whenever and wherever inspiration struck.

"I just knew," says Thomas, "that when they were out riding around with John there would be sketch ideas coming up. And that's exactly what happened."

Away from family and the distractions of Toronto life, the cast were left with little else to do but hang out together, often watching television in each other's hotel rooms. Yet, even in their downtime, it was impossible for Candy and his funny and gifted friends to stop generating comedic ideas.

"Those three years in Edmonton," Eugene Levy later recalled, "were I think the best shows that we actually did. There was such a focus on the show."

Far from the prying eyes of network television executives, the hothouse conditions forced the troupe to bring out the best in all of them, and the isolation particularly helped solidify the chemistry between Candy and Levy, whose connection was immediately apparent in the push and pull between Candy's Dr. Tongue and Levy's Bruno (a.k.a. Woody Tobias Jr.) in *SCTV*'s *Monster Chiller Horror Theatre* sketches, often opposite Flaherty as Count Floyd.

"You lump those two [characters] together and wouldn't have enough intelligence to fill a thimble, I think," Levy explained to Jennifer Candy in a 2015 interview for her YouTube channel. "And yet they were just such great friends, you know, just bickering and fighting, but they loved each other, it was like an old married couple, kind of, you know? And it was great."

Dr. Tongue made for an unlikely Joe Buck in the *SCTV* parody *Midnight Cowboy II*, opposite Bruno as Ratso Rizzo. And O'Hara recognized what she refers to as the "underlying sweetness" Candy brought to Dr. Tongue, even when engaged in a bitter quarrel with Bruno in their parody of the 1970s disaster epic *The Towering Inferno*.

"Dr. Tongue says, 'I'm not going to speak to you, I'm not going to take your calls, I'm not going to answer the door... *for a whole week*!'" says O'Hara, underlining the point that "one week was about as long as he was willing to cut off his friend."

O'Hara also remembers Candy being a generous giver of gifts, but that his lavishness could sometimes be over the top, like Johnny LaRue, yet never as self-indulgent.

"In the most important ways," says O'Hara, "John was nothing like LaRue, who always had a lot of babes around him. John, on the other hand, would often have Rose with him or bring baby Jennifer to the set."

Candy's two-year-old daughter visited the set on a day when her father was dressed as the legendary drag performer Divine.

"I was doing this kind of a dirty lounge act," says O'Hara of her Dusty Towne character, "and when John came on dressed as Divine, Jennifer yelled out, 'Daddy!' It was so touching. But John looked great in drag, he just had a good face for it; beautiful lips and a cute little nose and big eyes, he looked really pretty. He was always up for whatever you wrote for him, and you knew he'd always add something great to it to make it funnier."

As Divine, or as *The French Chef*'s Julia Child, Candy was transformed by *SCTV*'s makeup artist Beverly Schechtman, Judi Cooper-Sealy's hair and wig designs, and costumer Juul Haalmeyer, who had followed Candy to Edmonton after *Big City Comedy* folded. One of Haalmeyer's favourite tasks for the show was to create a non-specific "ethnic look" for Candy and Levy's eccentric Shmenge Brothers.

As the hosts of *SCTV*'s popular polka-centric variety program *The Happy Wanderers Hour*, Candy and Levy's good-natured Shmenge Brothers were billed as the most famous polka duo to ever emerge from the fictional nation of Leutonia, described by Levy as "a country you've never heard of on the dark side of the Balkans."

The Shmenge Brothers were directly inspired by a televised polka music program, most likely one hosted by the Edmonton polka king Gaby Haas, that they had seen while channel surfing on Edmonton cable TV during one of their protracted hotel room hangs. Candy and Levy immediately realized the program's comic potential for *SCTV*, which was, after all, a send-up of local television as much as a celebration of characters.

"There wasn't a lot on TV that night," Candy later told NBC's Bob Costas. "So we watched these two guys on a local polka show. I said, 'Ah, look at those two shmenges!'"

Shmenge was a word derived from the Yiddish *schmegegge*, and a favourite utterance of a friend of Candy's, actor Stephen Young, who was fond of calling various people "a shmenge."

"I picked it up," Candy told Costas, "and I brought it into the group, and everybody was a shmenge. If you did this, you were a shmenge, you did that, you were a shmenge."

As Candy and Levy marvelled at the innocent charm of the polka broadcast, they hastily began to draft up a sketch in which Candy would become the clarinet-wielding Yosh Shmenge (he had played the instrument in high school), while Levy was transformed into his accordionist brother, Stan.

Beyond the fact that both actors knew their designated instruments well enough to fake them for the camera, they adorned their characters with certain signature details such as warts, a gold tooth, and radically altered hairstyles.

"Everybody just fell in love with 'em," Candy told Costas. "As soon as we came out we knew we had something... we did this salute to 'John Villy-ams,' it was the cheapest [laugh] with the shark's head over my head. 'Theme from *Jaws*!' It was a bad joke!"

Finally feeling respected, and happy to be among his

long-time friends, Candy brought a little "Johnny Deluxe" to their shared experience, often making sure they all flew together in first class. According to Andrea Martin, "no one was more fun to travel with than John Candy."

"Even though we were all treated equally on the plane," Martin wrote in her memoir, *Lady Parts*, "he demanded the most respect and was given it. Everyone loved John and felt elevated in his presence. No one was more generous than John to anyone, anywhere. Or more grateful. He was boisterous and lively and indulgent. Booze flowed; food was abundant. John made everything into an event...John would make the flight into his own personal party, and everyone on the plane would be invited."

Candy also found a duo chemistry with Flaherty, who had, after all, been the first at the Second City auditions to recognize his unformed brilliance. For his part, Candy was fascinated with Flaherty's ability to multitask while constantly generating fertile comic premises.

"Joe is always thinking," Candy later raved to Robert Crane Jr. "He's like the absent-minded professor. You could be talking to Joe for ten minutes and he won't be listening to you. He'll be talking about something else, [such as] how the [Pittsburgh] Pirates and the Steelers are doing."

Such was their trust and mutual respect that they were comfortable playing a number of characters who invariably antagonized each other, from Guy Caballero browbeating LaRue, to Count Floyd waving off Dr. Tongue, to Sammy Maudlin belittling William B. In real life, Candy was a keen student of human behaviour, but many of his SCTV characters possessed a limited self-awareness combined with a relentless stamina for abuse, something Candy elaborated on in his 1984 interview with teenage reporter Judd Apatow.

"We created lives for these people," Candy told Apatow. "We did it so many times that each [character] is special to me. Yosh and Stan Shmenge, they're brothers, and they have another life outside of that... Same with Doctor Tongue; Woody Tobias, Jr.; and Count Floyd. Their interactions with each other off-camera was just as interesting as what they're doing on-camera—even more so, actually. These two guys just bicker at each other all the time, but they still work with each other, they need each other... all these characters—it was just nice to be able to do all of those, and we could do whatever we wanted."

As extreme as Candy could be in many of his characters, he was just as comfortable playing low-key roles, such as Melonville mayor Tommy Shanks, or the amiable angler Gil Fisher, host of *SCTV*'s *Fishin' Musician*. The latter was created in response to a request from NBC to incorporate contemporary musical acts into the series, as the network had successfully done with *SNL* since day one. *The Fishin' Musician* was one of *SCTV*'s convenient ways to fold bands like Wendy O. Williams and the Plasmatics into the show's premise as a small-town television station.

The first musical act to appear with Gil Fisher was the Tubes, whose drummer and co-founder, Prairie Prince, remembers assembling with his bleary-eyed bandmates in the lobby of their Edmonton hotel at the unfriendly hour of 4 a.m. Piling into a van to take them out to film at a nearby lake, they were shocked to discover that their driver was none other than Candy himself, already made up as Gil Fisher.

"When the van pulls up," says Prince, "there's John Candy behind the wheel. He says, 'Welcome to Canada, boys. Now, are you ready to go fishing?' When our keyboard player, Vince [Welnick], shared that he had been unable to get any pot over the border, John handed him a bag of weed. They became best pals after that. Later we filmed our song over the lodge set at the studio, and it was really a special twenty-four hours for the Tubes."

When New Orleans legend Dr. John appeared on the show in the "SCTV Movie of the Week," *Polynesiantown*, the premise was that he was booked into Melonville's newest Polynesian restaurant, Johnny LaRue's Luau Room.

Candy and Flaherty's extended cinema noir sketch was loosely based on Roman Polanski's *Chinatown*. In *Polynesiantown*'s final "crane shot," a move borrowed directly from the Polanski film, Dr. John drawls, "Forget it, LaRue, dis is Polynesiantown," as he and Candy walk off down Melonville's main drag. SCTV finally had the budget to approximate the cinematic quality of the films they were lampooning, but this was the crane shot heard around the world, or at least around the NBC boardroom, where expensive production values were continually scrutinized. When Candy had insisted that the rental of the camera crane apparatus was entirely necessary, Alexander had reluctantly greenlit the cost and insulated his actors from the network bean counters.

"John always liked *big ideas*," says Dave Thomas, "like the throwing TVs out the window. You would get production people telling us that it would cost a lot of money ... and the hard part was always to convince them that it was actually going to be worth the expense."

After media critic Marvin Kitman wrote critically in *Newsday* about what he saw as the SCTV's extravagant budget, SCTV responded by incorporating the controversy into a plot arc that extended over several episodes. In one scene, Guy Caballero chastises LaRue for his indulgent budget while waving around a mock-up of a newspaper bearing the headline "Kitman Slams *Polynesiantown*." Caballero slashes the budgets for all future LaRue projects but gives him one last chance to produce an inexpensive man-in-the-street segment called "Street Beef." Armed only with a single camera and a boom microphone, LaRue sets out on the streets of Melonville to solicit citizens' opinions about *Polynesiantown* and its controversial crane shot. When opinions differ within the crowd, a huge street brawl breaks out, now filmed from above in an even costlier helicopter shot, not unlike one used in the film *Dog Day Afternoon*. After that, a series of subsequent sketches continue to dwell on the crane shot, until reaching a dramatic conclusion in which a deflated and inebriated LaRue sets out into the cold and deserted streets of Melonville for a very special "Christmas Eve Street Beef." Growing increasingly belligerent, LaRue becomes abusive to his crew, who finally abandon him. Hitting rock bottom, he seizes the camera and microphone and launches into a tirade for the ages before passing out in the snow. But then, in a Christmas miracle worthy of Charles Dickens, or at least Martin Scorsese, LaRue is awakened by the God-like voice of none other than Santa Claus, riding atop a camera crane adorned with festive string lights. Santa had given LaRue a crane shot for Christmas. God bless us one and all.

Candy won a Gemini Award for writing the scene with John McAndrew and Doug Steckler, and Flaherty remembers filming the scene on a cold December night in Edmonton.

"John was really cold when he shot that monologue," says Flaherty, "and he was really drinking in that scene, in fact, he got a little blitzed when we shot it."

Comedian, writer, and producer Ben Stiller watched the SCTV Christmas episode on television when it first aired. Having grown up around show business, he recognized, even as a child, the truth in Candy's portrayal of the desperation in socially climbing characters like Johnny LaRue and William B. Williams.

"His bare desire for success struck a chord," says Stiller, "maybe from growing up in a house full of actors. I still watch the SCTV Christmas special every year, and when LaRue drunkenly breaks down and gets his crane shot, that moment just distilled every drunken actor's trajectory before or since. He wasn't very old when he did that, so I don't know how he understood that level of show business cynicism at that age. I mean, I was young too, but for some reason, I connected with it. I also loved William B., who was such an unctuous sideman, but Candy just brought so much humanity to him. You really felt his pain at being dissed by Sammy. Candy was a brilliant actor because he allowed us to empathize with his characters. He was vulnerable and real within some very unreal situations. He had that thing that all brilliant improvisors have, which is an understanding of what the funny choice is, but never making that choice just to be funny. He was *real* first, which made it all funnier."

While Candy was proud of all that he and his SCTV team were accomplishing in Edmonton, he steadfastly refused to accept any idea of competition with his friends at *Saturday Night Live*, whom he considered the "real" trailblazers.

"We're riding the crest of a wave that SNL started," Candy told Robert Crane Jr., adding that being part of the NBC family had only been positive for both shows. "We're in more markets, and we're on kind of a regular schedule. This is an expensive show to do, and there's not much money generated at that time—12:30 at night until 2 in the morning. It's hard for them to justify our being there. What gets them is we keep getting such good press. They can't just drop us."

After appearing on NBC's short-lived *Billy Crystal Comedy Hour*, Candy, who had declined *SNL* producer Dick Ebersol's offer to join the cast during its sixth season (1980–81), agreed to do a cameo on the program during an episode hosted by actor George Kennedy, with musical guest Miles Davis. Andrew Alexander says that he refused to let Candy fly to New York during what he refers to as *SCTV*'s "ridiculous production schedule," which left little time for side projects. Candy, however, ignored the boss, and on October 17, 1981, Alexander was shocked to spy Candy in the background on *SNL*, "dressed up in some sort of Mexican sombrero for some sketch."

Candy was once again becoming restless, impatient for the big Hollywood break that always seemed just around the corner. When *SCTV* returned to Toronto to produce the next season at Magder Studios, *Creem* magazine's Susan Whitall was dispatched to the city to write a feature story about what she at the time called "the best comedy on American network TV right now."

While in Toronto, Whitall was able to obtain interviews with most of the cast, but Candy declined to be interviewed. It later transpired that he was under the impression that the review that had hurt his feelings by referring to him as an "elephant" had been written for the pages of *Creem*. There's an old saying that "an elephant never forgets," and in this case, neither did Candy.

"I'd been there since 1975," says Whitall, "so I told them that this writer had never written for us, and certainly never wrote about John for us. But John didn't budge. I was told by the others that once John got an idea like that, you're just not going to convince him. Everybody remarked to me about how sensitive John was about that sort of thing."

SCTV's return to Toronto also meant enlisting help from Second City mainstage actors such as Mary Charlotte Wilcox, Ron James, and John Hemphill, to bolster the cast. Original cast members were coming and going, and Harold Ramis, whose career as a director was just taking off, even made an appearance. This would be the last season for Catherine O'Hara, Rick Moranis, and Dave Thomas. John Candy was still around, but his eyes looked increasingly south to Hollywood.

That's not to say there was no more fun to be had, and Candy and Flaherty were brilliant together in an episode where *SCTV* ruthlessly, yet lovingly, sent up Canadian film and television. This gave them an opportunity to parody *Goin' Down the Road*. Jayne Eastwood, who had starred in the Canadian indie film in the 1970s, gladly accepted a chance to appear in *SCTV*'s version, *Garth and Gord and Fiona and Alice*.

Canadian-born comedy historian Kliph Nesteroff considers the *SCTV* parody "tone perfect, and even if you don't know the original movie, Candy and Flaherty's performances transcend the references and make it still funny." He also marvelled at Candy's ability to capture the "essence of a naive Cape Bretoner heading to Toronto."

Working in Toronto put Candy closer to home, but now the question was how and when he would make it back to Hollywood. The answer would soon come in the form of a standout cameo in a Chevy Chase comedy penned by a former magazine writer for the *National Lampoon* named John Hughes.

Twelve

"The Moose Out Front Shoulda Told Ya"

On March 5, 1982, Candy received horrible news from Hollywood: John Belushi, the seemingly indestructible man that he had nicknamed "the Bear," had been found dead at his bungalow at LA's Chateau Marmont, at the tragic age of thirty-three. Candy had first met Belushi at the Second City in Chicago, and he considered him as much a mentor as a friend. Later, when Belushi rolled through Toronto with the *National Lampoon* road show, Candy had volunteered to chauffeur the Bear around the town, proudly showing off his hometown.

Candy had always been haunted by sudden loss, having lost his own father at a tender age, but losing Belushi not only sent him into an existential funk; significantly, the nature of Belushi's death by misadventure shocked Candy into finally taking stock of his own recreational drinking and drug use. If the seemingly invincible Belushi could fall, Candy thought, it was surely an omen that things needed to change.

"When you lose someone, it causes you to reflect on your own life, to look inside," Candy confessed to writer Robert Crane Jr. "John's death [was] very tragic and very untimely. I think all death is untimely. I'm not a big fan of it. It made me look around a little more—how I was living, what can happen to you, how things like that can happen ... This is a very hard subject for me. John meant a lot to a lot of people. He was a very giving man. I just hope people remember the good things about him and what he brought, instead of the bad, what people assume is bad. After a while, it takes something like this to jolt you and say it's not worth it. I don't drink rum and Coca-Cola much, you know. I did learn that because of that incident. I don't drink a lot of that anymore, and I did before."

Yet, in a different interview with Crane, Candy confessed to being a Jekyll and Hyde character. Most of the time he favoured a quiet life in the country with his family, but every so often, when left to his own devices, his demons got the better of him.

"When I'm living the other side," Candy told Crane, "[I'm] more like Johnny LaRue ... there is a tendency to go overboard. I try to keep a close rein on that."

It was distasteful enough that some in the press had tried to paint him as "the new Belushi," and now, with the clear spectre of mortality added into the equation, Candy knew it was time to put his head down and take stock of his bad habits.

"I can only keep doing my work," he told Crane. "I'm not really giving people any ammunition for the comparison between us, so the less said about it the better."

Candy had gotten to know Belushi's brother James, commonly known as Jim, in 1977, when the two of them worked on a comedy pilot called *Gangway for Comedy*, and after the events of March 1982, Candy and Dan Aykroyd rallied around the younger Belushi like a brother.

"They were the first ones who approached me," says Belushi, "and told me 'I'm really sorry that you lost your brother.' They put their arms around me, physically and metaphorically, and cared for me during that traumatic time."

Having vowed to curb his indulgences, Candy even hired a personal trainer. Keenly aware of his reputation as the "fat guy," he began to wonder if he could somehow transcend his body type.

"I think I could [still] be as funny if I were 100 pounds lighter," Candy told Crane. "I could be more versatile if I lost the weight. When your face is slimmer, there are more ways you can change it with makeup. Psychologically, I would feel better if I was lighter … People identify me and know me as being big, and I don't think there's going to be any radical change coming up. I don't think I'm going to do *Rocky XII*. I'd like to keep my weight down for health reasons. I really don't think about my weight, I think about my character. I mean, my brain isn't that fat, I'm six-three and I stand out in a crowd. In terms of my abilities, I'd like to think that I could do anything. I'd probably be able to do more if I were thinner. I've always had a running battle with it."

Candy told his close friends that he hoped to lose forty pounds by the time he shot his next film, *Drums over Malta*, co-starring Joe Flaherty and Eugene Levy, for Universal. He had been pleased with the original screenplay, written by SCTV writers Paul Flaherty and Dick Blasucci, but the studio executives at Universal had "notes." After months of "development hell," comedian and director David Steinberg, one of Candy's earliest champions, was hired to help steer *Drums over Malta* into something the studio could get behind. Steinberg invited Candy and his family to stay at his guest house in Los Angeles, where they could "punch up" the shooting script. But according to Steinberg, Candy found it hard to focus.

"It was like kicking a boulder up a hill for him," says Steinberg. "John was writing little ideas on napkins, but he wasn't writing a 'script' script. This personal trainer kept coming to see him, supposedly to get in shape for the movie, but John didn't seem like he was being worked out. The script just wasn't coming together fast enough, so that's when we brought in another writer, Dana Olsen."

Candy is funny enough in what became known as *Going Berserk*, playing a good-natured chauffeur named John Bourgignon, but Steinberg readily admits that the film leaned a little too heavily on improv, and the result was a resounding flop upon its release.

A review of *Going Berserk* by the *New York Times* film critic Janet Maslin foretold a trend with film critics who would torpedo Candy's less successful films while leaving Candy unscathed. Maslin singled out Candy as "easily the funniest thing" in an otherwise "affably stupid comedy that's saddled with too much plot that hasn't nearly enough energy to go with it."

While Candy appreciated the good review, he later admitted that he sometimes felt guilty about the preferential treatment.

"You don't take [the roles] just to [think] 'I'll get paid for it, that's great, I don't care about the rest of it, you know, as long as I look good in it,'" Candy told NBC's Bob Costas. "That's ridiculous. Not me, anyway, there's a lot of people like that, I'm sure, but if you're not involved with the assembly of putting the picture together and even beyond that, the marketing of the picture, which these days ... that's as important as the script."

While Steinberg and Candy would have better luck improvising their way through a Canadian cult film called *My Dinner with Duddy*, in which Candy plays what Steinberg describes as "a blowhard raconteur," the year would end with Candy finally getting to experience what it was like to shine in a well-written and well-marketed American box office hit.

Candy had taken on a memorable cameo role in *National Lampoon's Vacation*, directed by Harold Ramis. The film benefited from the post–*Animal House* box office clout of the *National Lampoon* brand, plus the popularity of its lead actor, *SNL*'s breakout star Chevy Chase. *Vacation* had begun as a 1979 *National Lampoon* magazine story called "Vacation '58," written by John Hughes, which was an extrapolation of real-life events from Hughes's childhood. *Vacation* hilariously chronicles an ill-fated road trip by the Griswolds, a suburban Detroit family who drive out to California to visit Walley World, a more legally feasible appellation for Disneyland.

Hughes, who had started out in the advertising business, had progressed to writing short stories for magazines such as *National Lampoon*, and in the aftermath of *Animal House*, Hollywood came calling on anyone who had written for them. Hughes was ready, having already amassed boxes and boxes of treatment ideas. His subsequent screenplays for 1983 films like *Mr. Mom* and *Vacation* would translate into a burgeoning career in Hollywood and, fatefully, an introduction to John Candy. Their meeting, however, would come about only after a failed test screening of the original cut of *Vacation*.

In Hughes's original storyline for *Vacation*, Chase's character, Clark Griswold, was sent to prison for brutally kidnapping Walley World owner Roy Walley at gunpoint. Test audiences reacted in horror to the brutality of the finale, so Hughes was asked to write a gentler ending that toned down the violence. In the revised ending, Griswold simply forced an affable park security guard named Russ Lasky to give his family an exclusive guided tour of Walley World.

"The rewrite gave me an introduction to John Candy," Hughes later wrote, "with whom I would eventually match the coherence of cruelty, sorrow, disappointment, and farce that underpinned 'Vacation '58.'"

After Bill Murray passed on the role, Candy was happy to do it, for a price. According to Matty Simmons, the publisher of *National Lampoon*, Warner Bros. paid Candy $1 million, an unheard-of fee in the 1980s. Yet, while Simmons teased Candy about his fee on the set, he later conceded to journalist Nick de Semlyen that Candy's late cameo in *Vacation* proved to be worth twice that amount; Simmons recalled telling the actor, "I'd pay you $2 million if I could."

To Hughes, Candy was worth even more. An avid fan of *SCTV*, Hughes was not only honoured to hear Candy deliver the security guard's most memorable line—"Sorry folks, park's closed. Moose out front shoulda told ya"—their meeting also marked the beginning of a significant and long-lasting alliance between the two men. And over the ensuing years, the Hughes and Candy families would also become close.

According to John Hughes's son James Hughes, who along with his brother John Hughes III came to know Candy as an honorary uncle, "having created a character that John Candy embodied was, for him, the single most positive experience that came out of the whole movie."

Shooting the Walley World sequence at Six Flags Magic Mountain in Valencia, California, Chevy Chase, apparently having gotten over the headlock incident from their first meeting, was impressed with Candy's dedication to the role of Lasky.

"John was funny," says Chase, "but he wasn't a clown, you know? He really *became* that security guard when he took me around on the rides and stuff, and he was just the nicest guy ever to work with and spend time with, and he always had a funny story about other shows he'd worked on. I adored him."

Candy was still moonlighting on *SCTV*, but in the words of Joe Flaherty, "he had one foot in and one foot out." He was not alone; Catherine O'Hara and Eugene Levy were also coming and going, and in the summer of 1983, Rick Moranis and Dave Thomas were striking out on their own, after their Bob and Doug feature film, *Strange Brew*, earned back double its $4 million budget.

While appearing on NBC's *Late Night with David Letterman* in late December 1982, Candy addressed the comings and goings of the cast, and confessed that it was "getting kind of lonely" over at *SCTV*'s set at Magder Studios. What had kept Candy and his castmates loyally returning to *SCTV* was a mutual respect for their unique chemistry, yet while they would continue to break new ground on the series, the end was near.

Martin Short joined the *SCTV* cast during what he called the "ramp-up to the exodus." After a decade of friendship, he was excited that he and Candy could finally collaborate. In one of Short's favourite scenes, he played a time-travelling Ed Grimley opposite Candy, as Jackie Gleason's character, in a parody of *The Honeymooners*.

"John was Ralph Kramden," says Short, "and the two of us just looked funny together. It was a great scene, and he was brilliant in it."

When *SCTV* moved to Cinemax the following year, Candy officially exited the cast, later telling Letterman that *SCTV* had been "excommunicated from NBC." While Candy was still open to making the odd cameo appearance on the series and wouldn't rule out joining them in a rumoured Second City feature film, he made it clear to Letterman that *SCTV* was no longer where his creative energies lay. It was time, he said, to enjoy the country life up on his Queensville spread.

"I'm farmin' now," he told Letterman. "I gotta spend some time up there... You reach a point where there wasn't much more that I could offer [*SCTV*], but it was a great show to do."

After Candy made it official, Cinemax offered to continue the series with only Flaherty, Martin, Levy, and Short, but according to Flaherty, "it just wasn't in the cards."

Still, Short says he was grateful to have worked with Candy at all on a show that he remembers as "a celebration of characters and observation, even more than jokes. And John himself was the greatest character of all of us. I remember one time on set I looked out and saw John and Andrea laughing and joking with each other, and thinking, 'My god, *they* have worked together for ten years.' When you're thirty, that seems like a lifetime. But maybe that's why everyone was so good with each other, we had such a long history together and so much trust in each other."

In all, John Candy appeared in over 160 episodes of *SCTV* over a seven-year run, during which time the show won two of its fifteen Emmy nominations plus an ACTRA Award.

Looking back in 2021, Flaherty was adamant that, despite equal billing, Candy was always the star of the show.

"We all thought that John was the most photogenic," says Flaherty. "He had the greatest quality onscreen and people just liked looking at him. We sort of made John the star because we felt, even as far back as the stage years, he *was* the star. I still remember saying to Dave [Thomas], 'You know who I think a big star is going to be from our show, who's going to have a career? John Candy!' And you know what? I was right."

Despite being considered the breakout star of *SCTV*, Candy remained humble about his achievements, sharing credit equally with his castmates.

"There were seven strong characters," Candy told Robert Crane Jr., "and it was one of those rare cases in television that if you looked at it from different angles you could see all the players' special influence. Everybody shone on that show. We [were all] supporting players and we each got a chance to star. It was a unique show. Everyone worked equally as hard."

On October 22, 1983, Candy finally got to host *Saturday Night Live*, with musical guests Men at Work. The occasion also marked the debut of Jim Belushi as an *SNL* cast member, and the two appeared in a number of memorable sketches including one where Belushi interacted with Candy as a Catholic priest operating out of a phone booth "confessional."

"There was a lot riding on my first episode on *SNL*," says Jim Belushi. "If I was ever going to get beat up by media [for not being my legendary brother], it would be on that first episode, so I was nervous. But then who walks in as the guest host of my first episode? Johnny LaRue, himself."

Candy did his best to bring the spirit of the Bear back to *SNL* that night, to guide and protect the younger Belushi and himself.

"Candy said, 'Jimmy, this is *your* first show on *Saturday Night Live*,'" recalls Belushi. "So John and I sat in the little writers' room for hours with Michael Short and Paul Flaherty, who he'd brought along, and ordered up these big corned beef sandwiches and steak fries from the Carnegie Deli and came up with sketches. I never laughed so hard."

Candy had hoped to return to cohost SNL with Eugene Levy the following year, but a writers' strike put an end to that plan. While he did make one more appearance on the program, on March 2, 1985, Candy never hosted the show again, and in the words of former SNL writer Bob Odenkirk, Candy holds the dubious designation as the long-running series' "most-burned potential host."

When *National Lampoon's Vacation* was finally released on July 29, 1983, it became an instant hit, raking in over $60 million at the box office. *Vacation* brought Candy to a whole new audience of filmgoers, including director Ron Howard, who was about to cast Candy opposite Tom Hanks in a downtown fish-out-of-water story that would make him a star in his own right.

Thirteen

A Fish Out of Water

"I think *Stripes* started it," John Candy explained to his old friend Peter Gzowski in a 1991 appearance on CBC Radio's *Morningside*, "but *Splash* solidified it... after that, things started rolling."

Empire magazine's Ian Freer playfully, yet accurately, described the plot of Ron Howard's comedy *Splash* as: "Boy meets mermaid. Boy leaves mermaid in sea. Mermaid tracks down boy in New York. Boy and mermaid fall in love. Boy and mermaid's happiness jeopardized by insane mermaid hunter."

Since *Splash* contained mature themes and partial nudity, Howard and his producing partner Brian Grazer had secured a release through Disney's newly created imprint for grown-up content, Touchstone Pictures, and set about casting the picture. They had earmarked Tom Hanks, at the time a relatively unknown sitcom actor, for the role of the loud and loutish brother Freddie Bauer, but after searching in vain for an A-list movie star to play the romantic lead, Allen Bauer, they gave it to Hanks and continued looking for a suitable co-star.

Howard had been impressed with Candy's work in Ivan Reitman's 1981 military comedy *Stripes* and had already briefly considered casting him in his film *Night Shift*. After securing tapes of his work on SCTV, Howard "became aware that John Candy was hilarious" and offered him the role of Freddie. At first, Candy told Howard that he would prefer to play the role of the evil scientist Dr. Walter Kornbluth, and Howard very nearly agreed with him based on the fact that he and Hanks looked nothing alike.

"I kept thinking, 'Tom and John can't be brothers,'" says Howard. "But Brian insisted that since John was hilarious and Tom's great, the audience would be entertained and want to believe they're brothers. And of course, he was one hundred percent right."

Candy had new representation in John Gaines and Marty Klein at the Agency for the Performing Arts (APA), and according to Grazer, he was "paid meaningfully more [on *Splash*] than everybody else." The two lead actors met for the first time, along with Eugene Levy, whom Candy had suggested for the role of Kornbluth, at a table read at Ron Howard's home in Encino, an affluent Los Angeles suburb in the San Fernando Valley. For Hanks, already a big fan of SCTV, the prospect of playing opposite both Candy and Levy was intimidating, and he recalls feeling anxious at their first readthrough in Howard's living room.

"Man, suddenly this was like jamming with Lennon and McCartney. It just froze me so much. I was just trying to hold my own comedically with these two kings."

But by the time Hanks shot his first scenes with Candy, on location at a New York vegetable market at the beginning of

March 1983, his confidence had been "greatly improved by John's magnanimous charm."

"You know," says Hanks, "in some ways, John was bigger than life, but he was also just a good hang. We'd have a Diet Coke in his trailer and just goof around."

Daryl Hannah, fresh from her breakout role in *Blade Runner*, was cast as Madison the mermaid. While Hannah spent a great amount of time sewn into her thirty-five-pound prosthetic tail, even during lunch breaks, she later recalled Candy and Hanks keeping her spirits up and feeding her french fries from the side of the tank. She told *Empire*'s Phil de Semlyen that she "absolutely adored" Candy.

"Tears-coming-out-of-your-eyes, pee-your-pants hilarious," Hannah said of Candy's antics on the set. "I used to sit on his lap all the time and he would talk for me while I mimed what he was saying. I would just be his ventriloquist doll."

While Howard recalls that Candy "could be very disciplined" as far as sticking to the script, he encouraged both of his leads to improvise whenever they felt it was appropriate. He says that many of Candy's ad libs did so well in early test screenings of the film that they remained in the final cut. "I think John saw this role as an opportunity to really act," says Howard, "and he had a couple of scenes where he had to play these earnest and straightforward brotherly emotions. John has this scene where Tom says, 'Jeez, I fell in love, finally found the perfect girl. And it turns out she's a fish.' And John's line, 'Love ain't perfect,' just perfectly described the theme of the whole movie. I wanted John to play it as big brotherly advice coming from this playboy philanderer who yearns for what his younger brother was feeling. He had moments in the picture where he played it really grounded and connected, which I think we began to see more and more of in his later movies."

Howard's lean $11 million budget required a tight shooting schedule, which inspired a speedy working environment as they completed *Splash* in Los Angeles that June (additional underwater scenes were filmed in the Bahamas). According to Howard, the breakneck pace directly influenced one of Candy's most memorable scenes in *Splash*, filmed at an actual racquetball facility in Los Angeles.

"It's the scene where Freddie is smoking cigarettes in the racquetball court," says Howard, "when John winds up hitting himself in the head with a racquetball, then hitting the floor. This place was only available to us for about eight hours, so on the morning of the big day, I went down there early, with my shot list. I was already anxious when I realized that John wasn't there yet, so I was becoming a little worried about his health. After we called around, we finally got word he was finally on his way in."

When Candy eventually arrived, well after his call time, he rambled apologetically about having run into Jack Nicholson at the bar of his Hollywood hotel the night before. Nicholson had recognized him and insisted they have a drink or two. Flattered and amazed that Nicholson even knew who he was, the now-fast friends ended up closing the bar at 2 a.m. Nicholson then insisted they go back to his home to continue the party, and Candy never made it back to his hotel. And now, still drunk from the night before, Candy was pleading with his director to be sent home. Howard, with time running out on his rented location, made it clear to Candy that time was money, and he was precariously short on both.

"John's eyes were welling up with tears," says Howard. "He

was a wreck, whimpering, 'I stayed up all night, Ron. I can't possibly work. I'm still drunk. I'm so sorry. Jack wouldn't let me go, Ron, Jack Nicholson wouldn't let me go!'"

Howard had no choice but to implore Candy to sober up, quick, and get on with it. Candy, to his credit, complied.

"He never complained after that," says Howard. "He just nodded, got ready, and shot that entire racquetball scene giving it one thousand percent. It was a 'two-shot' with Hanks, so John does the jokes, then serves the ball. It comes screaming back and hits him right on the head, and he falls straight down. He hit his head for real, on the second try. I didn't have to do any cutaways. Hanks didn't break, and the whole scene was comedically perfect. I think that since John felt like a screw-up, he mustered up all his energy and got it right on the second take."

After thunderous applause from the cast and crew, Howard wrapped for the day, satisfied with one of his favourite scenes in the can. Candy later described the incident as an "inspired day" when promoting *Splash* on NBC's *Later with Bob Costas*.

"I didn't realize just how fast those balls move," Candy told Costas, "and it hurt, too! I have this great smile on my face, which you can never see but then it hit, I was so excited, but then in a split second I realized that I had to fall, otherwise we're gonna have to do this again. So I took the hit, I smiled, and then I dove down. That was the hardest part, the diving down, because there was no stopping—it hurt, it was a good one. Moments like that, they're worth it."

WHILE CANDY AND LEVY share very few onscreen moments in *Splash*, they were close on the set, enjoying what Grazer describes as "this amazing chemistry together," befitting their decade-long history at Second City.

"They loved laughing with each other," says Grazer, "and could often finish each other's sentences."

A month into the *Splash* shoot, Candy invited Hanks and Levy to join him at an after-hours recording session, along with Joe Flaherty, Martin Short, and Howard Hesseman, at Dick Orkin's Radio Ranch. Candy was putting together some recorded comedy sketches to be played back at a benefit event in Toronto for his old high school, Neil McNeil. According to Hanks, the session turned into another "all-nighter."

"John kind of lived Elvis Presley hours," says Hanks. "I don't know when he ever went to bed."

Candy had agreed to fly to Toronto to host Neil McNeil's Silver Jubilee Dinner-Dance at the Sheraton Centre, on May 21, 1983. As excited as Candy was to be there, Jonathan O'Mara, his childhood friend from McNeil, remembers him becoming "physically ill" from nervous anxiety before taking the stage.

"He didn't want to bomb in front of his old schoolmates," says O'Mara. "So he had also invited Catherine O'Hara and Joe Flaherty along for moral support. But when he took the stage, you'd never know he was nervous, and the show was hilarious. Still, he told me afterwards, 'Oh Christ, O'Mara, I never want to do that again.'"

Immediately after the benefit, Candy flew back to California to complete *Splash*, his luggage stuffed with enough Toronto Blue Jays merchandise for the entire cast and crew. Hanks recalls that, for the second time on the shoot, Candy came straight to work having indulged too heavily, this time from enjoying the in-flight beverage service.

"Luckily drunk John was just as hilarious as sober John," says Hanks. "At one point, this guy holding the sound boom was shaking and couldn't keep a straight face. My son Colin was there, running around, and he was also laughing. This scene should have been done in seven setups, but we must have taken thirty, thirty-seven, forty-five takes of this scene because we couldn't stop laughing. Even Ron started laughing during some of the takes. I remember John couldn't keep his shoes on, he said, 'I gotta sit down. I gotta get these shoes off my feet. You got any rum?' He was just trying to stay drunk. It was just the greatest thing. It just made us all love him so much, when you see this scene in the final movie, it's pretty damned funny. It was, hands down, the best day of the shoot. I actually thought that if all movies are made like this, this is the greatest job on the planet Earth. Because all we did was laugh."

Ron Howard regrets that he never had the chance to direct Candy again after *Splash*. "I didn't know John all that well, in terms of his life," says Howard, "but during the period we were working on *Splash*, I absolutely adored him."

GIVEN CANDY'S SUCCESS WORKING with Ivan Reitman on *Heavy Metal* and *Stripes*, and his long personal history with Dan Aykroyd, it may be surprising to learn that Candy ultimately passed on an offer to reunite with both of them, plus his *Stripes* castmates Bill Murray and Harold Ramis.

Aykroyd had originally imagined *Ghostbusters* as a vehicle for himself, John Belushi, and hot new *SNL* star Eddie Murphy. After Belushi passed away and Murphy passed on the project, Bill Murray was brought in to complete what became a fearless foursome of Ghostbusters, alongside Aykroyd, Ramis, and Ernie Hudson. Reitman, who had cast Sigourney Weaver to play Dana Barrett, reached out to Candy to play her neighbour, Louis Tully. To Reitman's surprise, Candy didn't jump at the offer.

"We had been quite close on *Stripes*," says Reitman, "but when he didn't call me right back, I called him and asked, 'Hey man, what do you think?' John just said, 'I don't know.'"

Aykroyd remembers Candy telling him that he would agree to the Tully role if he could play it "full-on Tyrolean German, with these two massive dogs. But Ivan told him that we already had the terror dogs."

While certain published accounts have speculated that the fee Reitman was offering was far less than what agent John Gaines was demanding, the truth is that Candy simply didn't feel right about the movie, later telling Bob Costas that he and Reitman "just didn't see eye-to-eye on certain things."

Candy did, however, suggest that Reitman offer the role of Tully to his SCTV co-star Rick Moranis, who parlayed the supporting role into a tour de force that kickstarted his own film career.

IN JANUARY OF 1984, as *Splash* was being prepared for release, Candy rejoiced in the news that Rose was pregnant again. While waiting for his second child, he worked with his writers on an original screenplay called *Con Job*, and agreed to guest-star on an SNL spin-off program that Lorne Michaels was developing for NBC called *The New Show*. Between January and March, Candy made three appearances on the sixty-minute sketch comedy series whose cast drew equally from SNL and SCTV talent, joining fellow guests Laraine Newman, Gilda Radner, Steve Martin, Catherine O'Hara, and Carrie Fisher, and series regulars Dave Thomas, Valri Bromfield, and Buck Henry. While Candy played in a variety of scenes, reprising his popular impression of Orson Welles in one, playing the title role in "Roy's Food Repair," and indulging in physical comedy with Thomas and Radner in the slapstick "Good Mailman, Bad Mailman," he was perhaps most memorable in a black-and-white film parody of the 1961 poolhall drama *The Hustler*, as Jackie Gleason in the role of Minnesota Fats, opposite actor Kevin Kline.

Thomas was happy to find their old Second City chemistry still intact in a *New Show* sketch about Mikhail Gorbachev receiving a hospital visit from Yuri Andropov. "By this time in our careers," says Thomas, "we were both comfortable enough with each other, and with the camera, that if we became bored with the script, we'd just start ad libbing. John and I just got into a rhythm, like we had done onstage at Second City. It was fun to get to *play* again."

When *Splash* finally surfaced in the cinemas on March 9, 1984, it instantly created ripples that changed the careers of everyone involved. Touchstone's first cinema release took in an estimated $70 million over its initial run and made movie stars of both John Candy and Tom Hanks. Candy's performance was universally acclaimed by film critics, including his champion at *The New York Times*, Janet Maslin, and *The New Yorker*'s Pauline Kael, who wrote that Candy was "perfectly named" and "a mountainous lollipop of a man. Preposterously lovable. He doesn't add weight, he adds bounce and imagination."

Candy, who was offered a lucrative three-picture deal with Touchstone Pictures, later told film interviewer Brian Linehan that getting a rave review from one of America's most influential film critics transformed the film industry's perception of him as a box office star.

"I think it was very influential for *me*," Candy said. "I received a lot of phone calls [the] week that came out. As people started taking me a little more seriously ... people were actually offering me more work on a regular basis."

Steady work meant more than just a consistent revenue stream to feed his family; commanding a star's wages would become necessary to feed his own indulgences for the finer things. Even when he had been a struggling actor before joining the Second City, Candy had always lived like a rich man.

"Fame," the poet Emily Dickinson observed, "is a fickle food upon a shifting plate."

And now, as the Hollywood machine kicked into high gear, Candy had a lot on his plate in more ways than one. If fame and fortune did not exactly fill him up, they did afford him the luxury of introspection. He was becoming increasingly aware that he needed to take better care of himself if he was going to take on all the work that was coming his way.

Fourteen

Candy's Millions

Having noted that *Splash*'s Freddie Bauer was an avid *Penthouse* reader, the magazine dispatched a writer to shadow Candy for a profile. Journalist Robert Crane Jr. flew to Toronto with Candy, then on the cusp of major stardom, as he waxed candidly about the moral ambiguity and outright depravity seething underneath the desperate streets of Hollywood.

"People smell blood very quickly in Los Angeles," Candy told Crane. "If you're hurting and not working... people stay clear of you. There is a tendency [in LA] to live only in show business. How boring. It's a one-factory town. People you think you know, you don't know. People you trust, you shouldn't trust. You don't know if you're trusting yourself, or if you're doubting yourself all the time. Am I telling the truth now?"

The antidote to the shallowness of LA, Candy suggested, was his double life in Queensville as a gentleman farmer with a newly expanding family. The irony, Candy lamented, was that he often felt compelled to take on certain degrading jobs—including television commercials—to provide for them.

"Sometimes you do have to sell those refrigerators," Candy joked, "or you can be a 'true artiste' and starve. There are those who do that, and I have great respect for them ... I know that if my career just drops off, I can always go out there and sell a refrigerator, or gum, or dandruff shampoo better than a lot of guys on television."

Not only did Candy have more mouths to feed, his Queensville property was still in constant need of maintenance. In her memoir, *Lady Parts*, Andrea Martin noted that at one point her husband, *SCTV* writer Bob Dolman, visited the farm and observed workers installing a radar dish, "gardeners building a river," and "a barn that housed every car he'd ever owned."

While the success of *Splash* and his new multi-picture deal had surely eased Candy's financial burden, the increased visibility meant that his cherubic face and plus-size body were plastered on billboards and bus wraps all over North America. Candy found the new scrutiny unsettling; not only was he getting bigger in the show business sense, but his six-foot-three frame now weighed in at three hundred pounds or higher. While he had made no secret of his struggles with body image, his late-night eating and drinking habits did little to help the matter. Still, at the end of the day, as Candy told *People* magazine in 1981, he was "the one who has to look in the mirror, and after a while it begins to eat at you."

His rapid weight gain had also caught the attention of one of his comedy heroes, Carl Reiner. Reiner was a big fan of Candy's brilliant comedic mind, but he privately worried that his indulgences might lead him, like John Belushi, to an early grave. Reiner reached out to Candy about nutritionist Nathan Pritikin's Pritikin Diet Plan, which advocated a diet of fruits, vegetables, whole grains, and no red meat, in tandem with a regimen of regular physical exercise. Candy couldn't believe that he was getting health advice from the creator and co-star of *The Dick Van Dyke Show.* Candy held Reiner in such esteem that something about his pitch compelled Candy to check into the Pritikin Longevity Center in Santa Monica in March 1984 for a supervised twenty-six-day program. During this time Candy agreed to undergo intensive medical study, nutrition education, mandatory exercise, and a strict diet. While at Pritikin, he drank no alcohol, smoked no cigarettes, and rediscovered exercise in a more meaningful way than he had at any time since the days before a knee injury had ended his dream of playing football. He cycled five miles a day and found some peace of mind away from the demands of life in show business.

That said, when director Walter Hill phoned him at the Pritikin Center, Candy took the call. Hill had recently coaxed magic from Eddie Murphy in *48 Hrs.*, and now he wanted to know if Candy might be available by the end of the month to co-star with Richard Pryor in *Brewster's Millions*. Candy agreed, and on April 30, stepped out of the facility pounds lighter, relaxed, and ready to report to Hill in Los Angeles, just before the 1984 Summer Olympics were set to begin that August. After July 28, when traffic became unbearable, Hill completed the production in New York.

Hill's *Brewster*, the latest in a long line of screen adaptations of George Barr McCutcheon's 1902 comedic novel, cast Pryor as Monty Brewster, a former pitcher for the Chicago Cubs, now relegated to the minor-league Hackensack Bulls. The central comedy engine of the film is a morally questionable challenge: In order to inherit $300 million, Brewster must successfully squander a $30 million bankroll within one calendar month. "Money," boomed the voice-over on the theatrical trailer for *Brewster's Millions*, "everybody wants it."

Getting paid was a prime motivator for many of the key players involved in the project, including Hill, Pryor, and Candy, who played the hard-partying baseball catcher Spike Nolan, the wingman to Pryor's Brewster. While Candy and Pryor worked well together, they lacked the exquisite chemistry that Candy had come to expect in previous screen pairings. Offscreen, their relationship was chilly, despite Candy's best efforts to charm him.

"John would walk through the stage doors and start entertaining the grips or electricians, getting lots of laughs with low jokes," Hill later told writer Nick de Semlyen. "Richard would come through the stage doors and find the most obscure seat over in the darkest corner and sit there. He was friendly with John, but wary—John could see that there was some bridge he wasn't going to get across there. And one time Richard got mad at me, saying he wished I'd treat him with the same respect that I treated John. It was bullshit. I probably laughed too much at John's jokes."

At one point Candy tried to appeal to Pryor by inviting Eddie Murphy to visit him on the set. While Pryor was indeed happy to see Murphy, he used the meeting as an opportunity to further freeze out Candy. In his memoir, *Black Is the New White*, Pryor's close friend, the writer Paul Mooney, described the meeting from an entirely different perspective. "Richard and Eddie huddle up right away," Mooney wrote. "John Candy looks over to them and frets. He's jealous of their instant friendship. 'Richard hates me,' Candy says. 'Richard doesn't hate you,' I say to him, even though I know for a fact Richard can't stand the man."

Before Candy had wrapped on *Brewster's Millions* in New York, Ivan Reitman visited the set bearing a boombox and a cassette tape of Ray Parker Jr.'s catchy title song for *Ghostbusters*. Candy consented to appear in a music video as a part of a collage of celebrities that included Chevy Chase, Teri Garr, and Carly Simon. While Candy was genuinely happy to see Rick Moranis enjoy massive success in the *Ghostbusters* role he had waved off, his own experience on *Brewster's Millions* gave him pause about the projects that he was committing to, as he balanced his desire to do good work with the need to pay off the mortgage on the farm. He had been working non-stop for the past decade, and his brief respite at the Pritikin Center had only served to remind him that he hadn't had a proper family vacation in years. On the other hand, he knew that it was better to make hay while the sun was shining, painfully aware that fame's fickle spotlight would only be trained on him for so long.

"Once your career starts going," Candy told Robert Crane Jr., "you're always afraid to take some time off because, if you do, people will think the worst of you and they'll forget about you real fast, and you'll be gone. Things are going real nice for me now. I don't intend to blow it by burning myself out. It ain't worth it. Nothing's worth that—no career, all the notoriety, it means nothing. It's wonderful and it's hard to give up, but I think I could. Busting your tail no matter how much you love the business, love what you're doing, you ain't gonna love it if you're in a box under the ground or if you're in some hospital, shaking in the corner and doing Big Bird imitations."

The Big Bird reference would become mildly ironic when Candy accepted a small but memorable role in *Sesame Street Presents: Follow That Bird*. Jim Henson and director Ken Kwapis had brought the production to Toronto's International Studios, now Cinespace Film Studios, where Henson also produced the television series *Fraggle Rock*. With Rose expecting their second child, Candy was glad to spend the remainder of the summer filming closer to home with Muppet mainstays Jim Henson, Frank Oz, and Big Bird himself, Caroll Spinney, along with his good friends Joe Flaherty and Dave Thomas, and a non-Muppet cast that also included Sandra Bernhard and country music legend Waylon Jennings.

In *Follow That Bird*, Big Bird journeys far from his nest in search of birds of a feather, only to discover that his real family is right back home on Sesame Street. Something similar could be said of Candy, who had left Toronto to explore the world and was now shuttling between his family life in Queensville and his movie life in Los Angeles.

Back in LA, Candy had been eagerly developing his screenplay for *Con Job*, with writers Michael Short, Doug Steckler and John McAndrew, which he hoped would be the first film in his three-picture deal with Touchstone. Concurrently, he and Levy were preparing to write and star in a Shmenge Brothers mockumentary for HBO called *The Last Polka*. *Con Job*, loosely inspired by the 1960 British comedy *Two-Way Stretch*, was a political satire of the "prison industrial complex," in which a crafty politician hastily drafts a plan to reconfigure a financially insolvent college into a privately owned, maximum security, for-profit prison.

Assuming that he now had some clout in Hollywood after the success of *Splash*, Candy was shocked when Touchstone refused to greenlight *Con Job*. He was still shaking his head in disbelief when he recounted the sad tale on Brian Linehan's *City Lights* in 1986. "I don't know what happened," Candy told Linehan. "I started out with Tom Wilhite, who was an executive at Disney right after *Splash* ... he was the only one in town here who had expressed interest in me producing and writing."

By the time the *Con Job* screenplay reached Jeffrey Katzenberg, by then the new boss at Touchstone, the project, and Candy's deal, had died on the vine.

Still, it wasn't all bad news, and Candy gladly accepted an invitation to be a guest of honour of *The Harvard Lampoon*, the prestigious and influential college humour publication and comedy think tank whose alumni had founded the *National Lampoon*. *The Harvard Lampoon*'s president at the time was a young college student named Conan O'Brien, who later recalled that when Candy arrived on campus, his first stop was a bakery to buy a box of chocolate eclairs. When a shy and nervous O'Brien politely asked if Candy was still on his much-publicized diet, Candy joked, "Don't worry, kid, they're Pritikin eclairs!"

In October 2022, O'Brien revisited the story on his podcast, *Conan O'Brien Needs a Friend*. "I grew up watching SCTV," said O'Brien, "and was just enchanted with this guy. He was everything I wanted John Candy to be in person; and you know sometimes that's not the case ... [but] he was the John Candy that I was hoping he would be times ten. I remember talking to him pretty late at night, having a chat with him, and he asked me what I was thinking of doing and I said, 'I might like to try comedy.' And he looked, like, through me, into my eyes, and like Johnny LaRue, he said, 'Kid, you don't *try* comedy, you do it because you have to.' And I walked away from that thinking, 'He's right.' I mean, if I'm in, I'm all in."

Disappointments aside, 1984 was still one of the better years in Candy's life. While there could be no doubt that the critical acclaim and box office success for *Splash*, and Candy's arrival as a star, were the biggest headlines in his professional career, such milestones were eclipsed by a joyous occasion in the Candy household. On September 23, 1984, Rose and John Candy celebrated the arrival of their second child, Christopher, a brother for Jennifer. Candy would have preferred to spend the final months of the year at home with his newborn baby, but by November, he was off again. This time, he was flying to Mexico to reunite with Tom Hanks as a pair of Peace Corps volunteers bungling in the jungle. While it was hard to leave home, Candy was eager to find out if the chemistry he and Hanks had shared on *Splash* was a fluke.

Fifteen

Jungle Hotels and Summer Rentals

In November 1984, as the Christmas decorations were going up around his Queensville home, Candy's career was heating up and his family had grown. With a newborn son at home, he had passed on an invitation from Lorne Michaels to co-star in *¡Three Amigos!*—a role that ultimately went to his friend Martin Short—ostensibly because he didn't want to travel to Spain to film it. But despite his misgivings about leaving home so close to Christmas, Candy was in great spirits as he arrived in the sleepy Mexican town of San Juan Bautista Tuxtepec, Oaxaca, to begin a month-long location shoot for Nicholas Meyer's Peace Corps comedy *Volunteers*, which would reunite him with his *Splash* co-star Tom Hanks.

Set in 1962, *Volunteers* follows a crew of idealistic Peace Corps volunteers tasked with building a bridge in a remote village in Thailand. On paper, the film featured many of the same elements that had made *Splash* a hit, notably Hanks, back this time as an entitled Yale graduate named Lawrence Bourne III, an opportunistic playboy who sneaks onto a Thailand-bound Peace Corps jet to flee his serious gambling debts. Once on the plane, he winds up sitting next to Candy's Tom Tuttle from Tacoma, a true believer in the ideals of the Peace Corps who has one tragic flaw. Under duress, Tuttle proves himself to be highly susceptible to brainwashing and propaganda. Of course, this was the perfect comedy engine for Candy's strengths, and Tuttle is a naive and vulnerable man-child who is transformed into an oafish and brainwashed automaton with hilarious results, after being kidnapped by local communist insurgents. Candy sank his teeth into the role; at one point Tuttle belts out the Washington State fight song for his rebel captors as though it is his national anthem.

Rita Wilson, in her first feature film, co-starred as fellow volunteer Beth Wexler, and her onscreen romance with Hanks in *Volunteers* blossomed into a real-life union that continues to this day. According to both Wilson and Hanks, their courtship was greatly enhanced by the laughs they shared while watching Candy work.

"Tim [Thomerson] was doing his Charles Bronson imitation for John while they were pretending to fly a helicopter in one scene," says Hanks, "and John was riffing right along with him, making us both laugh in the back seat of this chopper."

"John was just cracking these filthy, filthy jokes," adds Wilson. "And it was one of the most fun days of shooting. Tom and I were laughing so hard."

Candy had gratefully taken up Wilson's offer to trade him her spacious suite for the tiny room that he had initially been assigned, and she remembers Candy beaming as his driver and personal assistant, Frankie Hernandez, stocked the shelves of the hotel's presidential suite room with "boxes and boxes of Pritikin snacks."

"John just seemed so happy when I gave him the bigger room," says Wilson, "because he was the kind of person who liked to entertain friends and guests, and he was always a generous host."

The isolated Mexican town of Tuxtepec was a seven-hour drive southeast from Mexico City, and while it did a serviceable job standing in for the jungles of Thailand, the remote location made it difficult for the cast and crew and catering to bring in equipment, food—and rented elephants. Meyer later joked that making a film there was "like having a picnic on Mars." With no direct flights out of Tuxtepec to Toronto, Candy went to work with his team to arrange flights home to check in on his young family whenever he had a free weekend or mandatory holiday.

"We were filming over Christmas," says Wilson, "so we had a little bit of a hiatus, and I remember John being very adamant that he would get home for Christmas. He chartered a private plane to get him all the way to Toronto, which I just thought was fantastic, and it showed me just how much he valued the time that he had with his family."

In part to assuage his homesickness, Candy bonded with Hanks, Wilson, and the rest of the crew at nightly group dinners in the hotel's dining room. Hanks remembers Candy at these gatherings as the proverbial life of the after-party.

"It was a high point of the day," says Hanks. "After we were done filming, we'd all gather and all we did was eat and laugh. John was the ringleader. He was still a big guy, but he'd lost a bit of weight and seemed to be eating incredibly healthily at the time. I think for those Second City people, it was as much about the hang afterwards as the work."

While Hanks and Candy enjoyed a blossoming personal rapport off camera, their onscreen chemistry failed to ignite this time, and *Volunteers* would never be the *Splash II* that moviegoers and studio executives might have hoped for.

"In *Splash* we were playing brothers," says Hanks, "but we were protagonists in this, and I didn't get to play in as many scenes with John, because his character gets kidnapped by the communists so early in the film and he disappears for a lot of the movie. So to be honest, I feel that what happened between takes on that film was funnier than what went in the movie; the entertaining, the kidding around. My only regret is that I just didn't get to hang out with John enough."

Candy did, however, get to hang out with a few of his Second City friends—Eugene Levy, Robin Duke, and Catherine O'Hara—at Toronto's Manta Sound studio on February 10, 1985, as they lent their voices to the charity single "Tears Are Not Enough," as part of an impressive list of Canadian pop stars—including Joni Mitchell, Geddy Lee, Neil Young, and Bryan Adams—under the group banner Northern Lights, to raise money and awareness for Ethiopian famine relief. For Candy, spending time with his Second City friends again was one of the highlights of the day at Manta Sound.

And throughout that year, Candy teamed up with other Second Citizens on diversions such as Robert Boyd's comic documentary *The Canadian Conspiracy*, and *Martin Short's Concert for the North Americas*, directed by *SCTV*'s John Blanchard, a concert film interspersed with taped in-studio sketches that would run on the US Showtime network that November. Short observed that, during the ten-day shoot for the special, Candy was still pulling all-nighters after work.

"The last day was a night shoot," says Short, "and we probably wrapped around 3 a.m. Then John, Eugene [Levy], and I went to one of our trailers and started drinking. Eugene, I think, left before us, but John and I stayed there until about 6:30 a.m. I remember that quite vividly."

Candy was struggling to maintain the basic tenets of the Pritikin plan. His relationship with food, in particular, dated back to the comforts of his earliest memories, when his Polish grandmother regularly fed him rich ethnic comfort foods such as cabbage rolls, boiled potatoes, and pot roasts. Nobody walked into the Candy house without getting fed. In the wake of his Pritikin counselling, many of his friends and family, and even his mother, Evangeline, did their best to accommodate his new menu requirements. But there were still plenty of cabbage rolls and coffee on hand when Candy and Levy collaborated on the Shmenge Brothers concert documentary, *The Last Polka*, which aired on HBO and CBC in March. They had written the special as a stylistic parody of the 1978 Martin Scorsese concert documentary *The Last Waltz*, but where Scorsese's film chronicled the farewell concert by the Band, *The Last Polka* told the story of the Leutonian brothers' long and storied career as the Happy Wanderers, using interviews, archival footage, and a staged farewell concert filmed in Toronto. It was a labour of love for Candy and Levy, and yet another chance to drag along their talented compatriots from *SCTV*, including director Blanchard, and many of the same hair, makeup, and costume aces who had worked on the series. Catherine O'Hara, along with her sister, Mary Margaret O'Hara, and Robin Duke appeared in the film as the Lemon Twins.

"It was really fun playing the twins, all *three* of us," says O'Hara. "I actually watched *The Last Polka* again just a few months ago, and it's so well done. All the 'archival' footage looks so real, all that 'paparazzi' footage of us on the beach where they're revealing that the Shmenges were having affairs with the Lemon Twins. It's beautifully shot."

The film's titular concert was staged at Toronto's Danforth Music Hall with a real audience made up of around 1,500 enthusiastic SCTV fans who had answered a newspaper ad and had lined up around the block to get a ticket. While Candy and Levy had a basic understanding of their instruments, their musical contributions were pre-recorded by session musicians.

"You watch it now," says O'Hara, "and you can't tell they're faking it; they're both so believable. And they were so sweet together, and had such love for each other that came through in all of their characters. When they say goodbye at the end, with John, that makes me cry so much."

They faked it again on a February 26, 1985, appearance in full costume on NBC's *Late Night with David Letterman*, miming along with Paul Shaffer and the band, on "The Cabbage Rolls and Coffee Polka."

"[Eugene] and John were very particular that the sync be perfect," says Shaffer, "even sending us the score to read along on our respective instruments. I think, in that little exchange, we all saw a little bit of the perfectionism that we'd loved on SCTV."

DURING THE *VOLUNTEERS* SHOOT in Mexico, Candy had taken a phone call from Ned Tanen, then president of Paramount Pictures. Tanen told Candy that his hero Carl Reiner had agreed to direct a film for Paramount on one condition: John Candy must be the star. Candy didn't hesitate to sign on, and for the first time in his career, his would be the sole name above the title on the poster. In March 1985, Candy flew, with his whole family in tow, to Saint Petersburg, Florida, to begin nine weeks' work on Reiner's *Summer Rental*.

Candy starred as Jack Chester, an overworked Atlanta-based air traffic controller who is sent on a mandatory five-week vacation after mistaking a blip on his radar screen for another plane, narrowly avoiding a mid-air collision. When Chester's family arrives in the fictional coastal resort town of Citrus Cove, Florida, hilarity ensues.

In an interview with Tracey J. Morgan just before his passing in 2020, Reiner referred to Candy as "a major comedy mind" who was "just a joy" to direct. Having worked with some of the greatest comedy minds of his generation, from Mel Brooks to Dick Van Dyke, Sid Caesar, and Imogene Coca, Reiner valued Candy's gift for spontaneous comedy.

"Every day on the set we had so much fun," Reiner told Morgan. "He didn't just give you what you had rehearsed, he would give you extra stuff [and] find these moments in the movie that could only be his ... I was very careful to make sure I didn't lose any of his ad-libs, going in that hot sand he was hysterical, I will always remember [Candy's scene] on the beach. It is one of those things you don't forget."

Candy was moved by Reiner's confidence in him and his generosity with the process of filmmaking itself. He later raved to interviewer Brian Linehan that the experience had inspired him to want to direct a feature film of his own one day.

"Carl walked me through it," Candy told Linehan. "That was

the first time that anybody had really said, 'Well, what do you think? What do you like, do you like your take here, or do you like this take over there?' I was like, 'My god, I love this man! This is what making movies is, yes!'"

But once again, Candy's self-consciousness about his body type nagged at him during the making of *Summer Rental*. Minutes from a February 12, 1985, production meeting at Paramount, attended by Reiner, Candy, and the film's writers, reveal that negotiations had transpired over every detail of how Jack Chester could be portrayed, and there appears to have been much debate over a scene involving a seafood restaurant that was "used to illustrate the volume of food that the children are accustomed to seeing the father eat."

In a *Playboy* interview from this time, Candy confessed that with his slow metabolism, a solid regimen of cardiovascular workouts and lifting weights was the only way he could burn fat. "I can eat a normal fifteen-hundred-to-two-thousand-calorie-a-day diet," Candy told Robert Crane Jr., "and [still] put on lots of weight. I try to use the treadmill twice a day—at least an hour in the morning and an hour in the evening. My goal is to learn to discipline myself. I've never liked exercise."

As the man who had told Candy about the Pritikin plan, Reiner was sensitive to Candy's struggle and catered the *Summer Rental* shoot with a Pritikin menu. At first, Candy was grateful and happy to comply with the diet, but over the course of the production, Reiner began to notice empty pizza boxes in Candy's trailer, along with discarded candy wrappers and other signs of snacking. Sadly, Candy would continue to suffer this cycle of keeping and breaking diet plans for the rest of his life.

On August 9, *Follow That Bird* opened to a box office gross so disappointing that it temporarily put Jim Henson's dream of a Muppet Cinematic Universe on hold. The following week, *Summer Rental* fared slightly better, taking in $25 million in domestic box office receipts, by no means an embarrassing showing. But Candy's crowd-pleasing vacation romp wasn't the kind of box office home run that he and his agents might have hoped for if they wanted to prove that his name alone could, in Hollywood parlance, "open a picture" as a leading man.

"We shot it too fast," Candy later groused to the *Chicago Tribune*'s Gene Siskel, adding that both a threadbare script and a tight release schedule had left Reiner to rely on improvisation and charm to make it all work. "Carl and I tried to resolve the problems and make each moment as funny as possible, but it didn't work, despite some wonderful performances by Rip Torn and Richard Crenna."

Finally, on August 16, *Volunteers* arrived at the cinemas to mixed reviews, earning back twice its $10 million budget, to rack up nearly $20 million at the box office.

Candy's face was on millions of screens that year, but none of the films would do for him what *Splash*, *Stripes*, or even *National Lampoon's Vacation* had done. While he had held his own against Pryor in *Brewster's Millions*, released in May and earning back three times its $15 million budget, the critical reaction had been mixed at best. Work offers continued to roll in and his fees were getting higher, but privately, Candy lamented the inconsistent quality of the scripts he was receiving. He was frustrated with the studio system, where good ideas either died in development or suffered the indignity of death by committee. In a soul-baring interview with Patrick Goldstein for the *Los Angeles Times*, Candy shared the wisdom he had received from his agent, John

Gaines, who told him: "It's not called show *art*, it's show *business*."

"Until the money comes out of your pockets," Candy told Goldstein, "you can rant and rave all you want, but they hold the purse strings. I'm always hearing about these great scripts, but then they say, 'Oh, it needs a rewrite.' And then before you know it, there's another rewrite, and then it needs a little polish, and by the time it's done, it's almost unrecognizable ... And of course, if the movie bombs, then everyone dumps on those guys! You try not to make it a situation of 'them versus us' ... but I've always had a little rebel in me, and I've always battled with authority. That was the great part of Second City—we were all rebels, so we were in it together."

It was true, Candy loved Second City so much that he had even chosen his next picture, *Armed and Dangerous*, as an opportunity to co-star with Dan Aykroyd in a rare comedy from action director John Carpenter. But by the time the cameras rolled, Aykroyd and Carpenter were out, and very little remained from the project that Candy was contractually committed to film. If he was ever to gain control of his runaway career, *Armed and Dangerous* would not be the picture to help him do it.

Sixteen

"I'm My Own Best Friend"

As Candy's struggle to find the perfect script continued, he nonetheless closed out 1985 as one of the most famous, and best-paid, Canadian actors in Hollywood. In the fall, he had been included on the list of *Playgirl* magazine's Ten Sexiest Men alongside *Miami Vice* star Don Johnson and music producer Quincy Jones. Explaining why the magazine considered Candy a "turn-on for today's woman," *Playgirl* wrote that "male sex appeal in the 1980s involves much more than simply being a 'hunk,'" and singled out Candy as someone who "turns us on with good humour." Candy, they concluded, was "an actor who trusts his wit, doesn't cop out with mere slapstick, and has dynamite dimples."

While his friends teased him relentlessly about the dubious, if flattering, honour, John and Rosemary Candy were far more concerned with feathering the spacious nest that was their new two-million-dollar family home in Mandeville Canyon, in the

Brentwood district of Los Angeles. The new place was just a few streets away from Sunset Boulevard, where Candy liked to drive his shiny new black Mercedes. Having a second home in Hollywood made practical sense for Candy at the time. LA was where the work was, so why not move the whole family down there too? In a catch-up interview with Brian Linehan, the *City Lights* host reminded Candy that his daughter, Jennifer, had once confessed to him that she had already become tired of Canadian winters by the age of four. Nonetheless, Candy insisted that he would "never get rid of" their spread in Queensville.

Candy hadn't so much left home as home had followed him to Brentwood, and he was pleased that Joe Flaherty, Andrea Martin, and Martin Short were among their new neighbours. "That community is all together again," Candy explained to Linehan, adding that if he could just convince Eugene Levy and Catherine O'Hara to join them, "we'll have everybody down there."

Among his other neighbours were Jim Belushi and Beatrice Arthur, the star of television's *Maude* and later one of *The Golden Girls*, who offered to throw the Candys a welcome-to-LA party. But another new neighbour would arguably have the most significant impact on his future in Hollywood. John Hughes had moved his family to Brentwood the previous year, and now, he and Candy lived less than a mile away from each other. According to John's son, James, the Hughes and Candy families shared many a group dinner and backyard barbecue at each other's homes.

"The ages of the kids really lined up," says James Hughes. "Jen Candy and I are a year apart; Chris is a few years younger. My brother John [Hughes III] is a few years older than me. We all got along really well. And I think for my dad, a big part of the equation was finding a collaborator that he could work with and to also have this kind of family union."

Meanwhile, Candy desperately wanted to get out of the two-million-dollar contract he had hastily signed a year earlier to appear in *Armed and Dangerous*. At the time of his signing, a Columbia Pictures press release had described the film as an action comedy from director John Carpenter that would co-star Candy and his good friend Dan Aykroyd. As Candy was wrapping on *Volunteers*, he received word that the film was now a very different prospect. Carpenter had left the project, citing artistic differences with Aykroyd. Then Aykroyd, who had been Candy's main reason for wanting to do the picture, left the cast. In light of these developments, Candy assumed that *Armed and Dangerous* would be shelved indefinitely, but when accountants at Columbia Pictures calculated that they stood to lose less money if the film went ahead, they brought in director Mark L. Lester and told Candy that he was contractually obligated to appear in what was now a vastly different project that still required a suitable co-star. At the time, Candy had been collaborating with Eugene Levy on a script for a buddy picture. He went to Levy and told him that, since their screenplay was still in progress and *Armed and Dangerous* was already greenlit and ready to shoot, perhaps he would like to join the cast. At Candy's urging, Levy read the script and liked it. To demonstrate their onscreen chemistry, Candy and Levy couriered over a tape of *The Last Polka* along with a selection of highlights from their SCTV work. Columbia consented and Levy was in, rounding out a cast that also included relative newcomer Meg Ryan (last seen in *Top Gun*).

"It's very easy to work with Eugene," Candy later told Brian Linehan. "Writing the scenes that we have for the show or scenes in the picture, they seem to flow, the dialogue comes out."

Candy and Levy had plenty of fun shooting the film in and around Los Angeles, but when it was finally released, on August 15, 1986, *Armed and Dangerous* was widely considered another misstep for Candy, both critically and commercially. In many of the interviews Candy granted that summer, he seemed deflated and apologetic, even admitting to the *Los Angeles Times* writer Patrick Goldstein that he was finding it harder and harder to promote his own work, adding that he was desperate to have more input and control over the projects he took on.

"I need to write and develop my own work," Candy told Goldstein. "For a long time, I was on a good roll, going from picture to picture, and I just couldn't carve out the time. Now I'm pushing myself harder to take control. I don't know if I can do it or not, but I'd like the opportunity to try."

Assisting Candy on the two-week media junket for *Armed and Dangerous* was Robert Crane Jr. The two had hit it off six years earlier, when Crane was a journalist. Eventually, Candy invited Crane onto his team to help manage his press schedule, which afforded Crane a front-row seat during Candy's ascent to the top of the Hollywood food chain. He compared Candy's dramatic rise to the Beatles' arrival in America in 1964. "Only, John Candy was like all four Beatles wrapped up into one person," says Crane, "and I was like the Beatles' road manager Mal Evans, getting him from cars to hotels and on and off airplanes. Going through an airport terminal with him was unbelievable. His physical size made him easy to spot, so fans always approached him for an autograph. He would stop, talk to them, pose for photos, and sign things. It just wasn't in his nature to refuse them. All of the attention he was getting was just jaw-dropping to me."

After the whirlwind press junket, Crane accompanied Candy to Vancouver to fulfill a commitment he had made to his friend the broadcaster Terry David Mulligan to guest-star on the pilot for a celebrity fishing program called *Terry and the Tiger*, in which Mulligan and the NHL hockey player Dave "Tiger" Williams would take notable guests out for a day of fishing in Campbell River, British Columbia. The premise was not unlike *SCTV*'s *Fishin' Musician*, but after the exhausting press junket, Candy approached his seventy-two hours on Vancouver Island as a chance to relax and have a few beers, then a few more, with Williams, and according to Mulligan, the two closed every bar in Campbell River that night.

When Candy finally arrived back in Mandeville Canyon, he appeared hopeful about a number of prospects that had come to him, including a screenplay that Hughes had written expressly for him, plus another one from Mel Brooks. There was also an offer from CBS television to reunite the *SCTV* cast for a one-time network special.

All of these projects were in various stages of readiness when Candy boarded a plane to England in the spring of 1986, to film his memorable turn in the big-screen adaptation of Alan Menken and Howard Ashman's 1982 off-Broadway musical comedy *Little Shop of Horrors* at London's historic Pinewood Studios. The multi-million-dollar extravaganza was directed by Frank Oz, whom Candy had met on the Muppets' *Follow That Bird*, with a cast that included *SCTV*'s Rick Moranis and Broadway star Ellen Greene, plus a cast of top-flight comedy actors, including Bill Murray, Christopher Guest, Jim Belushi, and Steve Martin.

Oz's set was fun and playful, and like many of Candy's directors, he encouraged his cast to improvise wherever they felt it was appropriate.

"You have somebody like John Candy," Oz later told *Filmhounds'* Jordan King, "you don't say 'Do the words.' These are brilliant people. So, all that stuff that John did, he just made up."

In *Little Shop*, Candy was playing a fast-talking disc jockey named Wink Wilkinson whose *Weird World* program plays host to the film's carnivorous talking plant, Audrey II. In real life, he was about to launch a syndicated radio comedy program with producer Doug Thompson, whom he had met while doing commercials in Toronto ten years earlier. After Thompson hired Candy to voice *Rock 30*, a thirteen-episode radio series celebrating the thirtieth anniversary of rock and roll, they vowed to do more radio in the future. They had committed to begin recording *That Radio Show with John Candy* in the fall of 1986 but had yet to write anything for it, so Candy asked Thompson to join him in London to conceptualize with him at his Chelsea hotel. It seemed like a good idea at the time, but in practice, Thompson found Candy increasingly distracted, as much by the excitement at Pinewood as by the nightlife in London. In lieu of writing, Thompson helped Candy burn through what he recalls as a "handsome per diem." And Candy also took full advantage of his twenty-four-hour access to a chauffeur-driven limousine to shuttle them both to exclusive nightclubs such as Stringfellows, in Covent Garden.

Thompson recalls one night when Candy's agent, John Gaines, had flown over from LA to visit. Candy took Gaines out for a night on the town, including a stop at London's Hard Rock Cafe on Old Park Lane. According to Thompson, Gaines was alarmed at Candy's stamina and tolerance, and begged his client, unsuccessfully, to go back to his hotel and get a good night's sleep before filming in the morning. Nonetheless, Candy appeared bright-eyed and attentive when he arrived at Pinewood at six o'clock sharp the following morning. To celebrate what Thompson remembers as "a brilliant performance," he and Candy joined several members of the cast at a large group dinner at the posh St. James's Club in Mayfair.

"Around this one big table," says Thompson, "were Oz, Moranis, Billy Murray, Steve Martin and his [then] wife Victoria Tennant, plus John Gaines, and [Candy's] other agent Marty Klein."

Gaines represented both Candy and Martin, and the conversation turned to a John Hughes screenplay that Candy was excited about.

"At the time," says Martin, "I was really judgmental of comedy and of who I worked with, so I watched [John Hughes's] *Sixteen Candles*, and I thought, oh, this is really funny, and his timing is impeccable. I thought, yeah, I'd really like to work with him."

While Martin and Candy exchanged small talk that night, Candy had other business to attend to with Mel Brooks and Moranis when he returned to LA.

Before leaving London, however, Candy squeezed in a meeting with one of his heroes, Monty Python's Graham Chapman. Three years prior, Chapman had attempted to cast Candy in *Yellowbeard* and had approached him about a subsequent project. The following evening, Thompson and Candy set out for Chapman's home in Highgate to discuss potential collaborations. Thompson, however, recalls the evening devolving into yet another episode of "feasting and drinking" well into the wee hours of the morning, by which time Chapman insisted on having his guests cram into his tiny MG for what Thompson recalls as "a harrowing drive" back to Chelsea. And while these two comic minds would later discuss a variety of projects, including *Ditto*, about a man who creates multiple Xerox copies of himself, and a television series called *The Dangerous Film Club*, none of these would come to fruition before Chapman succumbed to complications from cancer in October 1989.

Candy's ninety-minute syndicated program, *That Radio Show with John Candy*, debuted in the fall of 1986 on thirty radio stations across Canada. Thompson says that Candy "had a ball" creating vivid comedic characters without elaborate makeup, costumes, or sets, "and bringing back old characters John didn't get to do in his movies."

In October 1986, as *Little Shop of Horrors* approached its Christmas release, Candy was back in Los Angeles, reporting for duty on MGM's Soundstage 39 (the same stage on which *The Wizard of Oz* had been filmed in 1938) to begin shooting *Spaceballs* with Mel Brooks.

"I love laughter on a set," Brooks proclaimed in the 2003 behind-the-scenes documentary about the making of his *Star Wars* parody, and by all accounts his was a fun, if demanding, work environment. Since the 1970s, Brooks had directed a series of high-concept comedies that parodied the tropes and conventions of various cinematic genres. *Blazing Saddles* shot up the western, *Young Frankenstein* drove a stake through the heart of horror, and now, *Spaceballs* took the space opera of *Star Wars*, and to paraphrase Billy Sol Hurok, "blowed it up real good."

"Space is the new frontier," Brooks later joked, "why don't I wreck it?"

The idea for *Spaceballs* had formed after Brooks told a Hollywood executive that he needed to go back to "planet moron." After making sure George Lucas wouldn't sue him, Brooks hired Lucas's Industrial Light & Magic company to do all of the post-production work on what would become one of the costliest films of 1986.

"I'm a mawg: half man, half dog," Candy announced as the adorable Chewbacca-inspired Barf. "I'm my own best friend!"

Besides Joan Rivers, who voiced the robot Dot Matrix in post-production, Candy and Rick Moranis, who played the Darth Vader–esque Dark Helmet, were the most experienced film actors in a cast that included Bill Pullman, in his first screen role, and *Beverly Hills 90210* star Daphne Zuniga, a relative newcomer who found it hard to concentrate on her lines as Candy did his best to crack her up on set by waggling his ears and tail before the cameras rolled.

In his 2021 memoir, *All About Me!*, Brooks recalled how he and his effects team transformed "big, warm, lovable John Candy" into Barf the mawg by outfitting him "with doggy ears and a swishing tail that sometimes had a mind of its own." Candy's makeup designer, Ben Nye Jr., worked with *Spaceballs'* costume designer Donald Lee Feld, known professionally as Donfeld, and prosthetic designer Ken Diaz, while Rick Lazzarini operated Barf's animatronic ears and tail. In *The Making of Spaceballs*, Nye revealed that Candy had asked him to model his look on his own yellow Labrador, Keema. Brooks, however, insisted that the prosthetics didn't cover Candy's bankable face.

"Mel said, 'We're paying all this money to see this guy who's really funny,'" Nye recalled, "and he's got this really funny face, and no, we don't really want to cover it up."

Candy found it challenging to act with the animatronic tail and ears, and at times became frustrated with Brooks about who controlled his performance. He found it hard to be spontaneously funny with a team of technicians operating his costume and prosthetics, but according to Pullman, Candy kept his cool despite it all.

"It was a real testimony to his character," Pullman told *The Hollywood Reporter*'s Ryan Parker. "He never got angry. He would sit down; say he needed a break, and everyone would just back off. Then he would get up and say 'OK, let's try it again.'"

Candy later remarked that he had been impressed and flattered that Brooks would take his suggestions, then calmly incorporate the ones that worked and a few "crazy thoughts" of his own. "That's what makes him Mel Brooks," Candy declared in a 1987 promotional video. "We had to find the dog qualities. Obviously we had the ears, but it was the hair we were very concerned about because ... dogs' ears are up here, so mine are blocked off down here. I gave myself big sideburns ... and a DA [a men's hairstyle popular in the 1950s, characterized by sides slicked back and a pointed, tapered end at the nape of the neck] in the back to the ponytail so I tried to be a very cool dog, with the soul patch."

In Brooks's memoir, he celebrated one particular Candy improvisation, during a scene in which their Winnebago-like starship crash-lands in the desert. "As he undoes his seatbelt after the crash," Brooks wrote, "he quips: 'Well, that's going to leave a mark.'"

While Candy apologized to Brooks for going "off book," Brooks thought it was one of the biggest laughs in the movie and left it in the final cut, later writing that "it was beautiful. Nobody else could be that funny and quick."

In a 2017 essay for *The New York Times* entitled "The First Time a Fellow Actor Had My Back," Pullman wrote that Candy, for reasons he would never know, had kept watch over him. In his essay, Pullman remembered that, as an inexperienced film actor, he had been struggling to find a way to hold his own in scenes with Candy and Moranis. Candy asked his driver, Frankie Hernandez, to invite Pullman back to his spacious trailer for lunch. After a heart-to-heart talk, they were called back to the set, but on the way out of Candy's trailer, Hernandez produced a box of doughnuts.

"John didn't miss a beat," Pullman recalled, "he grabbed one and pushed the box my way: 'For your blood sugar, Pullman. I see you yawning.'"

It was both a gift to the young actor and an implicit bribe to buy his silence about the doughnuts.

"I was being introduced to a ritual with endless variations," Pullman wrote. "John would chuckle and rib Frankie, Frankie would roll his eyes. John would find one way after another to curse the [Pritikin] diet."

Brooks and his wife Anne Bancroft had taken an instant liking to John and Rose Candy and invited them to a concert at the Hollywood Bowl by an opera singer whom Candy had parodied many times, Luciano Pavarotti.

"We did a picnic basket," Brooks told Tracey J. Morgan, "and John was so funny. Pavarotti had a big white handkerchief, and after he sang, he mopped his brow with it, and he took a bow and waved this white handkerchief in the wind. Candy turned to me and said 'Oh look! He's surrendering.' His quick wit was always there and always ready."

But, like his best friend, Carl Reiner, Brooks was also

concerned for Candy's health. He recalled making surprise visits to Candy's trailer, trying in vain to keep him on the Pritikin plan.

"He would be eating a turkey leg," Brooks told Morgan. "I was kind of the *food police* for a while. I would go through his trailer, I would search it for candy and stuff like that, sometimes I would find a great big Hershey bar, or ham, and I would get it out of there and he'd cry (joking). I made him vow, pledge, that he would not eat French fries or drink beer or do anything that would put on extra weight."

Spaceballs was released on June 24, 1987, and was a reasonable summertime hit for Brooks. But while Candy was funny and adorable in his floppy ears, Barf did not turn out to be Candy's best friend. *The Hollywood Reporter*'s Duane Byrge dismissed the film and chastised Brooks for reducing the "ever entertaining and talented" Candy to "loping around in an outlandishly inflated jumpsuit and doggy ears."

By now, Candy was seemingly critic-proof, his charm so irresistible that the general public continued to root for him even in his worst films. Audiences came out to see John Candy being John Candy. But even in his sneering review of *Spaceballs* for *The Washington Post*, Hal Hinson lamented that "the great John Candy performance we keep hoping for [is] still out there somewhere, waiting for takeoff."

While savaging *Spaceballs* for arriving a decade too late to parody *Star Wars*, *Chicago Sun-Times* critic Roger Ebert suggested that a more topical subject for Brooks to satirize might have been the recent spate of "John Hughes' teenage films." The irony was that Candy's new Brentwood neighbour had offered him the role of a lifetime, which would at last showcase the vulnerable dignity that audiences already loved about him. Candy had "cried with laughter" when he read Hughes's screenplay for *Planes, Trains and Automobiles*, and could barely conceal his excitement about it when he spoke with Patrick Goldstein for the *Los Angeles Times*. "It's really what I've been waiting for," Candy said. "It's like it was written for me, which makes a big difference. You could just see the movie in your mind."

Seventeen

Getting There Is Half the Fun

"It's a hysterically funny story," Candy raved to Brian Linehan in 1986, while discussing John Hughes's bespoke screenplay for *Planes, Trains and Automobiles*. "I laughed a lot when I read this and I'm looking forward to working on that in January and February of 1987."

Hughes had come a long way since writing *National Lampoon's Vacation* and was now directing his screenplays, and a succession of his well-received youth-oriented comedy films had earned him a reputation as "the Steven Spielberg of teen films." Despite being in his mid-thirties, Hughes had a keen ear for realistic teen language in films that didn't pander or talk down to them. Between 1984 and 1986, Hughes had directed *Sixteen Candles*, *The Breakfast Club*, and *Ferris Bueller's Day Off*, and had written the screenplays for *Pretty in Pink* and *Some Kind of Wonderful*.

"Life moves pretty fast," Hughes had famously written for *Ferris Bueller.* "If you don't stop and look around once in a while, you could miss it."

Not wanting want to miss any of it, Hughes wrote it all down, as fast he could, filling boxes and boxes with stories, outlines, and movie scripts to draw from whenever he needed one. Having moved from Chicago to quietly upscale Brentwood in 1984, with his wife Nancy and their two young boys, James and John III, Hughes, in his later films, began to deal with the more grown-up themes of parenthood and suburban life. The man whom Roger Ebert considered "the creator of the modern American teenager film" was growing up, just like his newest friend and neighbour, John Candy.

Besides being born just months apart in 1950, the two men had a lot more in common. They laughed at the same things, had a keen interest in popular music, and shared an abiding nostalgia for holiday gatherings and family feasts. Even their journeys had been similar: they had both endured the harsh winters of the Great Lakes region while launching their respective careers in windy Chicago, Hughes in advertising and Candy at the Second City. Success had brought both of them to Hollywood, mostly out of expedience, but their hockey-loving hearts had remained firmly around the forty-ninth parallel.

"Dad always loved that he grew up close to the Canadian border," says James Hughes. "He talked about that a lot. He was a Detroit Red Wings fan, and their rivalry with the Toronto Maple Leafs was a big part of his hockey culture."

In 1986, Hughes had been all set to deliver his latest film, *She's Having a Baby*, to Paramount Pictures in time for its release in the summer of 1987. But during a meeting with Paramount's

Ned Tanen, Hughes told him about a treatment he had written based on a torturous road trip he had taken during his advertising days. He had been trying to make it home to Chicago from New York in time for the US Thanksgiving holiday, but on this occasion his typical three-hour commute had devolved into a harrowing five-day misadventure with detours in the American Midwest, exposing him to an entirely different class of American traveller than he had been accustomed to when flying business-class. One of them was a loud and guileless travelling salesman whose many years on the road had made him unflappable amid the chaos.

"He knew *everything* about this kind of situation," Hughes told the *Rocky Mountain News*. "I kind of hung out with him. I was so impressed by this guy's understanding of the situation."

This salesman inspired Hughes to create the role of Del Griffith, and Hughes knew instantly that Candy was perfect for the role. Tanen was also impressed, so much so that he wanted to greenlight *Planes, Trains and Automobiles* immediately on one condition: it had to be ready to open during the November 1987 Thanksgiving weekend. That release date presented a conflict for Hughes; he was already bogged down with post-production on *She's Having a Baby* and it seemed impossible to shoot and edit a whole other film concurrently. After reluctantly delegating *Planes, Trains and Automobiles* to one of his protégés, director Howard Deutch, Hughes told Candy the good news.

When Candy first read Hughes's screenplay, he laughed, he cried, and laughed again, and he surely must have noted that his own career in comedy had begun with a man named Del: the comedy guru Del Close, who had first invited him to join Second City in Chicago. Now, Hughes had created a character

Candy could fully inhabit, in a film where he would share top billing with one of the reigning kings of comedy, Steve Martin.

Deutch was well into pre-production when Tanen called Hughes to tell him that Steve Martin had officially signed on to play Neal. After apologizing profusely to Deutch, Hughes pulled him off *Planes, Trains and Automobiles*, explaining that he just couldn't resist the chance to direct both Martin and Candy, and offered him another of his scripts, *Big Country*, to direct as a consolation prize. Paramount agreed to hold back *She's Having a Baby* until 1988, and formally announced to the trade papers that Hughes would begin shooting *Planes, Trains and Automobiles* with Martin and Candy in February 1987. The looming spectre of a labour action by the Directors Guild of America at the end of June meant that Hughes, already facing a tight turnaround, would only have just over three months to complete principal photography on this $15 million, flagship release for Paramount.

To get better acquainted before they set out on their real-life road trip, Steve Martin paid a visit to the Candy home in Mandeville Canyon. "I had thought he was fantastic on *SCTV*, of course," says Martin, "so I already had great respect for him and thought he was really funny. It was a little awkward at first because you're getting to know someone, but eventually we just really made each other laugh. Well, at first, we weren't trying to make each other laugh. We were just being nice and saying hello."

During the eighty-five-day shoot, Martin and Candy would be spending most of their time together, much of it on location in many of the northeastern US locations depicted in the film. Hughes's race to make the Thanksgiving deadline became as chaotic as the tale he was shooting.

"Everything that happened onscreen also happened in the production of the movie," says Martin, "missing planes, not having the right weather, landing somewhere in Rochester then realizing no, the snow is in Buffalo now, so we had to move the entire production to follow the weather patterns."

Filming commenced near Buffalo, New York, on March 2, 1987, on an unopened stretch of Route 219. To alleviate some of the stress during shooting delays, long days, and cold weather, Martin and Candy developed a running comedic banter between them on the set.

"John could always make me laugh," says Martin. "He had this bit he would do where he would pretend that he was in one of those old Italian gladiator movies that had been dubbed badly into English. He'd say something like, 'Kneel before your queen, Centurion,' but he would move his mouth after he'd finished the line. It just made me laugh every time. It's hard to explain this, but it was something to do when the shoot was getting long and difficult, because we were actually in those freezing circumstances. We had this thing, we'd come in in the morning and we'd fake frustration by faking a punch-out to each other. I'd pretend-hit him in the face and then he'd pretend-hit me back, and we would both just laugh and laugh at that. And it's hard to explain why that was funny. It was just, everything was so difficult that you were just taking it out on each other."

Martin and Candy were both as excited about working with each other as they were about the ways in which the Hughes script would allow them to stretch as actors. For Candy, getting to play the unsophisticated travelling salesman, a big man like himself, gave him an opportunity to showcase both his flair for broad comedy and, for the first time onscreen, his innate vulnerability. Likewise, the relative straightness of Neal Page allowed Martin, the erstwhile "Wild and Crazy Guy," to stretch his dramatic muscles.

"It wasn't 'sketch comedy,' where John had started," says Martin, "and it wasn't standup, as I had done. Something you face on every movie, is 'How big do you get?' or 'How small do you stay?' *Planes, Trains* walked that line between the characters feeling very real, but then there are these jokes where you get punched in the face and almost get run over by a car or washing my face with John's underwear."

Hughes's sprawling 150-page script was considered long for a broad comedy with commercial aspirations. "A typical script is around 110, 120 pages," says Martin. "So I asked Hughes, 'What are you going to cut?' He looked at me and said, 'Cut?' Meaning nothing."

Besides a hefty word count on the page, Hughes was equally fond of letting certain of his actors ad lib if he trusted their improvisation skills. Candy and Martin, two of the sharpest comic minds of their generation, quickly found a natural groove together. Martin remembers plenty of this riffing during a scene in which actor Michael McKean played a state trooper.

"It's, like, ten degrees outside on this stretch of road," says Martin, "and while we were cross-talking this dialogue, I would ad lib something, then the crew would have to turn the camera around to shoot the other side to get my coverage. Then John would ad lib something, so Hughes would say, 'Well, we got to get that on film.' So they turned the camera back around, which is a big deal. Turning the camera around is what takes all the time."

McKean recalls that after a full day of improvising against a background of sunny skies and green grass, the three actors went to dinner immensely satisfied with what they had come up with. But when they returned to their location the next morning to shoot the reverse angle "pickups," they discovered that intense overnight snow squalls had blanketed their little stretch of Route 219 under a coat of white, forcing Hughes to shoot the entire sequence again, from the beginning. For McKean, there was at least one upside—more time to get to know Candy.

"I became quite fond of him," says McKean. "I was already a big fan of *SCTV*, and while that whole cast was just phenomenal, I always thought there was this kind of sweetness about John."

As the shoot dragged on, both Candy and Martin realized that, while Hughes the screenwriter had written brilliant dialogue, Hughes the director was more than willing to burn through multiple takes of the same scene, allowing endless improvisation in pursuit of capturing "lightning in a bottle."

"We both had a good insight into our comic timing," says Martin, "and we liked the scenes [as written]. These characters were so well defined that swapping lines would not be logical, but we came up with stuff on the set and Hughes was all for it."

And so was Candy, at least at first.

"We'd still be in character," Candy later recalled, "and we wouldn't hear 'cut!' Our eyes kind of flashed just a little. You realize he's not going to cut... so then you stay in character, and you go, 'Well, what about this?'"

Fearing that the best parts of the script might be lost amid the hours of freestyle riffing, Candy and Martin made a kind of pact to rein things in.

"We said, 'No more ad libbing,'" says Martin, "'because this is going to go on forever,' and we mostly obeyed that rule. John and I really liked each other, so we never thought about *chemistry*, we just did what we were supposed to do and there was never any hint of competition. I think it's like the old cliché about the tennis match, that you play better if you're playing against someone really good."

Among the most talked-about sequences in *Planes, Trains and Automobiles*, when the reluctant travelling companions are forced to share a tiny, single bed in a rundown motel, was born out of improvisation.

"John ad libbed that line when I say, 'Those aren't pillows,' which was made up on the set," says Martin, "and Candy gets up and awkwardly starts talking about 'manly' things like sports teams, 'How about those Bears?' And it's just funny."

Candy thought so too, later recalling that the only hard part of filming the scene was doing it over and over again for Hughes and his punch-drunk crew.

"They had the camera rigged up over our heads," Candy explained. "You'd see the cameras start, you know, they'd look at us and we'd see that, we'd start laughing and then everybody started. 'Now kiss his ear, nibble it, just nibble it, just—lower, lower.'"

Hughes was also known for pre-selecting his preferred music cues for a given scene, and in this case, he had asked that Emmylou Harris's cover of Patsy Cline's "Back in Baby's Arms" be played back, loudly, on the set while Martin and Candy squirmed on their comically cramped mattress.

"Every time we got in that position, we'd hear the music," Candy later remarked, "and we'd start laughing. Then we'd settle down and we'd see the cameras start shaking ... everybody lost it."

When they weren't filming, Candy made sure there was always plenty of time for socializing, and James Hughes recalls the whole Hughes family paying a visit to St. Louis, where Candy took everyone to a hockey game between his beloved Toronto Maple Leafs and the St. Louis Blues.

"I was, like, an eight-year-old kid watching Doug Gilmour get his forehead stitched," says James Hughes. "It was incredible, and John just had this immediate rapport with all the hockey players."

At the end of March, Candy invited all of his friends from the film crew to watch the television broadcast of the Academy Awards up in his hotel room, ordering upwards of a thousand dollars' worth of room-service beverages and picking up the tab for an estimated twenty pizzas. Even as far back as the Colgate TV commercial, Candy had always enjoyed an easy rapport with a film crew, and Robert Crane Jr. observed a similar mutual respect when he paid a visit to the Sony Pictures soundstage in Culver City on the day when Candy and Martin were filming the "Mess Around" driving sequence.

"I'll never forget seeing John," says Crane, "standing outside the soundstage having a cigarette, dressed in full bright-red devil garb with the horns, the red face, the cape, the whole thing. While we talked, he introduced me to each member of the crew as they walked by, and he seemed to know everybody's name, shaking hands with all of them. Teamsters were driving by saying, 'Hey, John, you're looking good.'"

In the original screenplay, Del was described as a slovenly, grotesque slob, but after a few miserable test screenings, Hughes and his team came to the unanimous decision to dial back a lot of his obnoxiousness in post-production.

"Their original encounter at the airport was a much more extended sequence," says James Hughes, "with a lot of sight gags of him eating a chili dog or smoking. Del was more 'the passenger from hell' than Dad was going for. Dad's editor, Paul Hirsch, noticed that people were not connecting with him in these test screenings."

In 2022, Hirsch revealed to *Vanity Fair*'s Jason Bailey that audiences had even walked out during some of the film's four test screenings.

"The audience started to perceive John Candy as *using* Steve Martin," Hirsch told Bailey. "Steve was paying for everything. In our hurry to shorten the picture, we had taken out part of a scene at a train station where they're parting—not for long, but we don't know that yet—and Candy says to Steve, 'Give me your address, I'll send you some money.' And Steve wants no part of this guy, never wants to hear from him again. He says, 'No, no, that's okay.' So, we restored that. And that was it. That one exchange changed everyone's attitude about the character, that he'd offered to pay."

Yet it was the act of removing a key page of dialogue from Del's big reveal at the end of the film, where he finally confesses that he is a homeless, nomadic widower, that gave the film added pathos and emotional heft.

"I think that sequence is cut with such economy," says James Hughes. "Just a few lines that tell his whole story. Originally, that was a much longer sequence, with a lot more expositional dialogue of Del really laying out his whole life, his wife's illness, and how he couldn't live in an empty house once she had passed away. How he'd made the decision to sell the house and live on the road."

Martin says that it was while Candy was filming Del's big reveal, in footage largely trimmed from the theatrical release, that he became convinced of his dramatic ability.

"I took from that what a great actor he was," says Martin. "In these final scenes where I go back to find him after I've abandoned him and say, 'Well, thanks. Bye.' Well, the script had at least a page of Candy talking, and I didn't say much. It was a lengthy scene. I remember we were sitting on two wooden benches in the railway station, and it was cut down to almost nothing. This scene was performed so beautifully by John, and he made me cry every time. And there is a coffee shop scene, the first time I say goodbye to him. It's in the last five minutes of the movie. I remember the line that killed me was when he said, 'Every year I travel on my own. And every year around the holiday, I latch onto somebody. But this time I couldn't let go.' It still makes me cry. It really surprised me, because when I was watching the film I thought, 'Oh boy, here it comes.'"

While the full Griffith speech packed an emotional punch, the scene drew unintentional laughter in test screenings, forcing Hughes to reimagine his edits.

"It was almost *too* emotional," says James Hughes, "and slowed down the pace of the movie. Paul Hirsch said the film came screeching to a halt in order for everybody to hear his story. John showed some real range in those moments, and in his delivery of those lines and the telling of this story."

Hughes's breakneck odyssey had begun in the shadow of a Directors Guild of America strike that was to begin on June 30, an on one final marathon filming day that stretched into the early morning hours of July 1, Hughes completed principal photography. Ironically, that directors' strike lasted roughly three hours, the same length as Hughes's gargantuan first assembly cut of *Planes, Trains and Automobiles*. But after Hughes and Hirsch emerged from the cutting room, a ninety-two-minute print was ready just in time for the American Thanksgiving holiday season. Mission accomplished.

As he had on all of his recent movies, Candy had been mindful of his health as he went into *Planes, Trains and Automobiles*, promising himself that he would stay on the Pritikin plan, and Martin recalls being impressed with how Candy "was eating popcorn with no butter out of his little bowl." Candy brought his personal trainer to the shoot and even had exercise machines installed in his hotel room. But Martin also remembers that while Candy would often joke about his struggles with his weight, "the only time he would get upset is if *someone else* made a joke about his weight. He could do it, but nobody else could get away with it."

A tactless exchange with a journalist asking about Candy's weight cast an ugly pall over the official press conference for *Planes, Trains and Automobiles*. Prior to the film's November 25 release, Paramount had assembled roughly three hundred reporters from around the world to come to Los Angeles and ask questions to a panel of Hughes, Martin, and Candy. When Candy arrived an hour late to the conference (he was already shooting his next film, three hundred miles away) one insensitive reporter from Japan jokingly compared Candy's body type to that of a sumo wrestler, adding that the Japanese "admire big people because we are a nation of small people," and finally asking, "Do you plan to diet?"

At first, Candy seemed taken aback by the weight question, but he tried to stay calm and upbeat with the tactless journalist, earnestly replying, "I do eat a lot of junk food, and I think about [dieting] for health reasons."

But Martin, his improvisation skills sharpened from the shoot, rushed to both save Candy and restore the otherwise good vibes they had been having at the press conference.

"At one point during filming," Martin quipped, "John went down to 110 pounds, which I thought was a little excessive."

Laughter ensued, but the moment had already touched on one of Candy's deepest insecurities. While he was a big man, his dignity was never in doubt, and Candy was gratified that Hughes had appeared to understand this when writing him a role that represented the full range of his humanity.

Candy's friend Dave Thomas also praised Hughes for affording Del Griffith the kind of dignity that Candy himself had not been granted.

"John was touched that somebody thought enough of him to write him some dignified roles," says Thomas, "and the world could suddenly see he was able to do a really convincing dramatic scene. Well, of course. Brilliant comedy actors typically make great dramatic actors. Drama is easy. Comedy is much harder."

This was a sentiment shared by practically every one of Candy's Second City colleagues.

"I believe people believe they're seeing John when they see him in any role," says Catherine O'Hara. "That big love comes across in everything. He was completely open. When he says, 'I like me,' you want to kill Steve Martin's character for having the nerve to hurt John Candy. You just want to protect him because you love him so much."

Martin Short found his performance "heartbreaking" and relatable, while Eugene Levy raved to *Forbes* magazine's Scott King that Candy "just destroyed you emotionally and made you laugh out loud."

Comedy actors of later generations, such as Ben Stiller,

Patton Oswalt, and Brendan Fraser, also found inspiration in Candy's work in *Planes, Trains and Automobiles*.

"I don't think there is a better comedic duo performance in movies," says Stiller. "It was both extremely heightened and incredibly real. Any person who aspires to be a comedic actor can learn all you need to know from the acting in that movie."

Oswalt observes that the vulnerability Candy brought to Del had always been there, even as Ox in *Stripes*.

"Like Jackie Gleason before him," says Oswalt, "Candy had this incredible sense of balance and gracefulness and almost wispiness in how he moved through the world. It's because it's the *soul* piloting this tank, and when you see that, you just have to root for him."

In a 2023 episode of the *Fly on the Wall* podcast, actor Brendan Fraser, who won an Oscar for his portrayal of an obese man in *The Whale*, said that he had been floored by Candy's projection of dignity as Del.

"It was a beautiful piece of acting," Fraser remarked, "and... I don't think we've seen that kind of sensitivity attached to owning who you are when you live in a larger body like that."

Planes, Trains and Automobiles is widely regarded today as both a holiday staple and Hughes and Candy's best work in film, despite coming in third at the box office on its big holiday opening weekend, behind *Three Men and a Baby* and Disney's reissued *Cinderella*. In 2022, a 4K Blu-ray reissue was eagerly received by fans of all ages, many of whom came ready to drool over the added seventy minutes of previously unseen footage. Up until then, the only way to see anything from the original long cut of *Planes, Trains and Automobiles* was in one of Hughes's impromptu household screenings for friends and family.

"If you were hanging out in his office," says James Hughes, "Dad would disappear for a moment and he would come back with the original cut of *Planes, Trains*. He was so proud of all the work that he did with John Candy. Some great moments of John's acting were lost due to the way the ending was restructured and the paring down of that revelation."

The 1987 promotional season for the film coincided with Candy's launch of another syndicated radio series, *Radio Kandy*, and he convinced Hughes to let him and producer Doug Thompson record three official radio spots for *Planes, Trains and Automobiles*, including one where Candy, as Dr. Tongue, spars with Joe Flaherty as Count Floyd, reviewing the movie in the style of Siskel and Ebert.

The *real* Ebert wrote that *Planes, Trains and Automobiles* transcended the conventional buddy comedy because it was grounded in "the essential natures of its actors," who "don't play characters" as much as they "embody themselves. That's why the comedy is able to reveal so much heart and truth."

But Ebert also recalled a moment when he had chanced upon Candy in the bar of a New York hotel smoking and drinking alone. Remembering their brief conversation, Ebert made an almost psychoanalytical speculation that Candy seemed depressed.

"People loved him," Ebert wrote, "but he didn't seem to know that, or it wasn't enough. He was a sweet guy, and nobody had a word to say against him, but he was down on himself. All he wanted to do was make people laugh, but sometimes he tried too hard, and he hated himself for doing that in some of his movies. I thought of Del. There is so much truth in the role that it transforms the whole movie. Hughes knew it ... Steve Martin knew it and played straight to it."

Martin concludes that while Candy was "a complicated person," he never took it out on anyone, except perhaps himself.

"I think he had this little broken heart inside of him," says Martin. "I'm not a shrink, but there was something in his soul that was melancholy. I didn't live with him, so I don't know, but he always seemed happy doing the work, and any sense of his private pain, you had to infer. And when you're around somebody, there's a difference between constantly jovial and a jovial angst. Some people are just born with a little melancholy."

For Hughes, *Planes, Trains and Automobiles* was a giant step toward successfully writing about grown-ups, and while the features he wrote expressly for Candy would both strike gold at the cinemas, a Candy cameo in *She's Having a Baby* did little to save the film from box office and critical disappointment when it was finally released in 1988.

Candy spent the fall and early winter of 1987 in and around Bass Lake, California, transforming Hughes's *Big Country* into director Howard Deutch's feature comedy *The Great Outdoors*. After his chaotic road trip with Martin, it was poetic that his new wingman was a fellow Second City alum with whom he had shared many memorable cross-country drives, Dan Aykroyd. There was something vaguely Canadian about an Aykroyd/Candy comedy set at a cabin on a lake among the pines. In many ways, it felt like going home.

Eighteen

"Big Bear Chase Me"

According to James Hughes, son of John Hughes, his father's decision to write for men his own age coincided neatly with the arrival of John Candy as a kind of muse. "It's kind of telling that *Planes, Trains*... was among Dad's first adult projects, along with his script for *The Great Outdoors*, and they were both designed around John Candy. That was something that Dad wanted to build on."

In Candy, Hughes had found more than a collaborator; as their two families blended, their bond strengthened into a kind of brotherhood. Similarly, while the competitiveness of two brothers-in-law provided the comedy engine for *Big Country*, the screenplay that Hughes had delegated to director Howard Deutch to be filmed as *The Great Outdoors*, Candy and his co-star Dan Aykroyd also shared a brotherhood of their own. Having come of age together on the Second City stage, they had both appeared on CBC's *Coming Up Rosie*, and in Steven Spielberg's ill-fated World War II comedy, *1941*. While Candy had stayed with *SCTV*, Aykroyd had gone to *Saturday Night Live*, yet he had nonetheless written a part for Candy in *The Blues Brothers*. Even after Candy had declined Aykroyd's offer to appear in *Ghostbusters*, they remained fans of each other's work, with no signs of sibling rivalry between them.

When Deutch came to the project, after being pulled off *Planes, Trains and Automobiles*, it was still called *Big Country*, with only Candy attached to it.

"When John heard that Danny was interested," says Deutch, "he said, 'We've got to do this with Danny.' So that was that. He loved Aykroyd and so did I."

In *The Great Outdoors*, Candy plays a well-meaning Chicago-based family man named Chet Ripley who books a summer getaway with his wife at a lakeside cabin in northern Wisconsin. Aykroyd plays his avaricious yuppie brother-in-law Roman Craig, who shows up unannounced and uninvited with his wife, Kate, played by Annette Bening, making her screen debut. Excited about working with Candy again, Aykroyd helped tinker with the screenplay to showcase Candy's delicate balance of physical comedy and vulnerable charm. "I've still got a copy of the original *Big Country* screenplay here," says Deutch, "with Aykroyd's notes all over it."

"We had an absolute wonderful time working on the script with Howie Deutch and Hughes," says Aykroyd. "Candy was absolutely perfect—his boiling, restrained anger in that movie is so funny, and he's being pushed to the brink by my character, who is almost a straight-up sociopath. It was so great to see these characters as foils. He got to do some nice acting in that film."

While the film was shot entirely in and around Bass Lake,

California, the freshwater and evergreens of the film's fictional Pechoggin, Wisconsin, may as well have been in Ontario's Muskoka Lakes district or any of the pine-scented playgrounds frequented by both Candy and Aykroyd in their youth.

"We were totally in an element that we both knew," says Aykroyd. "All of us Canadians knew the cottage experience and the joy of being on a lake in the summer and resort communities. I think we ended up making the definitive 'cottage country' film of all time, which meant so much to us. We understood the way to play that, the leisurely vacation attitudes that the women played and that family rivalry that you get in some of Hughes's other great movies like *National Lampoon's Vacation*. We were able to tap into that vein a bit. All in a milieu, of course, that we totally understood."

According to Tarquin Gotch, who worked closely with Hughes at the time, Candy's Chet Ripley was his latest in a long line of proxy characters.

"I think all Hughes's movies were really parallels to the various times in his real life," says Gotch. "*She's Having a Baby* was about him and Nancy having a family, and from there we're into *The Great Outdoors*, *Uncle Buck*, and *Home Alone*, where it's about the world of family life in white, middle-class Chicago. He was always evolving, always moving, and he was brilliant at documenting all of it."

Howard Deutch recalls working on projects with Hughes in his Brentwood office in all-night sessions that lasted well into the morning.

"I'd usually fall asleep maybe around one or two," says Deutch, "but Hughes never slept. Then he'd get a phone call from Candy, and both of them could talk sometimes for four hours. Hughes loved Candy more than any other person he worked with that I'm aware of. I mean, he loved the cast of *The Breakfast Club*, and he loved a lot of the people that he worked with. But if I had to pick one person that John Hughes would want to go away on vacation with, it was John Candy; he adored him."

Universal Pictures saw *The Great Outdoors* as a potential summer blockbuster and sent a crew of around three hundred skilled workers to Bass Lake to make sure that every cent of their estimated $24 million budget was on the screen. Deutch, accustomed to directing smaller movies such as *Pretty in Pink* or *Some Kind of Wonderful*, was under enormous pressure but happy that Hughes had put him to work with Candy and Aykroyd. Observing Candy during their time at Bass Lake, Deutch was impressed with his passion for filmmaking and for people.

"While he was signing autographs," Deutch recalls, "he'd say, 'You know how lucky I am to get to do what I do, dance and sing and tell jokes and act?' I mean, he was seriously in love with what he did and the people around him. That affected me ... he was such a good person and that made you want to be a better person."

Deutch admits that he was "not a happy camper" when Candy first arrived at Bass Lake with a big beard covering most of his big, bankable face. Candy insisted that the facial hair made Chet look more "outdoorsy." Universal Pictures, on the other hand, had other ideas, and asked Deutch to ask Hughes to ask Candy to shave. Hughes refused, which put it back on Deutch to be the bad guy.

"Candy told me, 'If you make me shave this off, this movie will always be a black spot on my soul,'" says Deutch. "It broke my heart because there was nothing that I could do about it. It wasn't like I was in a position of great power. It was what the studio demanded to make the movie."

Having won the battle of the beard, Deutch was soon beset by a host of logistical problems, ranging from mosquito bites and unpredictable weather to frigid lake temperatures. One morning, Deutch was set to film a key water-skiing sequence in which Chet is trying on water skis for the first time and Roman, towing him in a motorboat, sadistically hits the gas with his hapless brother-in-law in tow, dragging him around the Lake.

"On the morning that we were to shoot this scene, which was supposed to be taking place in the summer," says Deutch, "it snowed. But you know, every moment of every day had some kind of nightmare like that."

Despite partying late into the night before, Candy showed up on time and braved the cold water, even managing to stay on his skis. Tarquin Gotch from the Hughes Company paid a visit to the set shortly after the water-skiing sequence, and found Candy mostly on his best behaviour, save for a slight cold after spending a day in the freezing lake.

"No matter how much he liked to party, he always turned up on set on time and prepared," says Gotch. "When I visited him up there, he was sick from what looked to me like pneumonia, but you could rely on John Candy, and there was no shirking what had to be done."

But according to Deutch, the vacation atmosphere on the set did little to help with Candy's health regimen, and to Deutch's dismay, he would often eat and drink late into the evening.

"He was always on time and always did what we asked him to do," says Deutch, "and he was so sweet to my children. But I remember one time we were in his trailer, and I looked in the refrigerator. It was loaded with so much food. I thought, 'This is not good.' I just worried because sometimes in the morning, he was very red and ruddy, so [the makeup artists] had to cover it because he'd stayed out late, maybe he didn't go to sleep, that kind of thing, or drank too much. But this was not an ongoing problem. I'm not exaggerating; it happened maybe once or twice. But enough that it worried me because I adored him."

Arguably, Candy's most challenging task in the film involved his interactions with Bart, the large grizzly bear that appeared in the film as Jody the Bald-Headed Bear. Bart was already a seasoned animal performer in film and television, having played the title role one year earlier in *The Clan of the Cave Bear*, alongside Candy's *Splash* co-star Daryl Hannah. Bart may have been a big star, but to Candy, this four-hundred-pound Kodiak was the inspiration for one of his most memorable lines in the film: "Big bear, big bear, chase me!"

In order to sell the believability of the chase between the bald-headed bear and Chet, Deutch needed Candy to be in the frame with Bart. While today, such a scene could be faked with computer graphics or even AI, such technology was unavailable in 1987, and Candy nervously agreed to the dangerous sequence, provided the appropriate safety measures were taken.

"Of course, I didn't want John to be in any real danger," says Deutch. "But I had asked everybody to do stuff that was a little bit on the edge of being dangerous, so John trusted me and made the scene work, even if he wasn't happy about it. When he breathlessly says, 'Big bear, big bear, chase me!' you really believe he was being chased by a bear, and that whole scene works thanks to John Candy."

In another memorable sequence, someone dares Chet to eat a ninety-six-ounce steak nicknamed "The Old 96er" in order to win a free dinner for his entire party at a local steakhouse. Despite the scene's implicit message that it was "funny" when a larger man eats too much, Deutch recalls no complaints from Candy as cameras rolled at Ducey's Bar & Grill.

"I just remember the difficult logistics of shooting the scene on location at this real steakhouse," says Deutch, "but John never told me he was unhappy with that scene, in fact he never complained to me about anything in the movie other than not wanting to be so close to the bear. He was always just so collaborative."

Today, despite the perennial praise Deutch receives for the other "teen movies" he did for Hughes, interviewers still want to talk to him about *The Great Outdoors*. He credits the onscreen chemistry between Candy and Aykroyd for making the experience just about worth the hardship.

"The scene where Danny unloads emotionally on Candy and he's about to cry," says Deutch, "I don't think they were used to doing so many takes, and we did about fifty. Honestly, I thought he'd never talk to me again. But it is thirty years later, Danny just called me and we're talking about a project based on his Roman character. He obviously liked his performance, and thankfully so did Hughes, so it was all worth it. Almost."

Released the following summer, *The Great Outdoors* went on to gross over $41 million worldwide. The general fan consensus was that it was a dependable Candy vehicle but nowhere near as universally loved as *Planes, Trains and Automobiles*. The critics, on the other hand, were less impressed, and this time even Candy wasn't spared. *The Washington Post*'s Hal Hinson complained that the usually buoyant Candy couldn't keep the film afloat, noting that "perhaps for the first time in his career he looks genuinely unhappy."

Some of Candy's closest colleagues had begun to feel that, either out of loyalty to his friends or the temptation to sign on to lucrative agreements, he had been too quick to say yes to projects that they felt were beneath him. Their hope was that, with John Hughes now on his side, Candy might finally be on the path to higher-quality work. But while *The Great Outdoors* had mostly kept Candy's career above water, he was not out of the woods yet. And while Candy waited for the next Hughes project to throw him a life vest, he was forced to wade through a succession of lesser projects that floated his way.

Nineteen

Frostbacks and Greenbacks

In the year after *The Great Outdoors*, Candy appeared to be taking jobs based on whether they offered either money or fun—or both. One that ticked both boxes was "Cursed with Charisma," an episode of HBO's *Really Weird Tales* described by its producer and host Joe Flaherty as "a sort of *Twilight Zone*-y thing, but comedy," in which Candy played an extraterrestrial visiting a small town on Earth. Like Hughes, Flaherty was one of Candy's Brentwood neighbours, a good friend, and a frequent dinner guest. While both men enjoyed the shoot, Flaherty couldn't help noticing Candy struggling to keep to his strict diet regimen.

"Those Pritikin meals were just godawful," says Flaherty. "But for a time, John really was losing weight. Then he fell off the wagon and kind of blew up."

Candy's career was also blowing up. But while his agent, John Gaines, was now commanding upwards of $3 million a picture for him, such fees invariably tempted him to do things like lend his voice to Don the horse in the lamentable Warner Bros. comedy *Hot to Trot*. Released to an almost non-existent marketing campaign on August 26, 1988, *Hot to Trot* was a commercial and critical disaster that mercifully attracted very little attention apart from its Razzie nominations.

According to Bobcat Goldthwait, who starred in the picture, Candy's involvement in *Hot to Trot* is the only fond memory he has of it. Having long been a fan of *SCTV*, Goldthwait had found himself a little star-struck when Candy invited him to lunch at a nearby Hollywood diner. "I could barely speak," says Goldthwait. "I remember being a kid back in Syracuse watching Candy as Divine in *Peter Pan*, and thinking 'Oh, if he can do it, boy it would be awesome if I could do it too.'"

Career worries aside, Candy was enjoying his domestic life and settling into his Mandeville Canyon home. In an interview with Brian Linehan back in Toronto, Candy shared a few glimpses of his new life in California, remarking that Jennifer, having at one point grown tired of Canadian winter, was now homesick, whereas LA-born Christopher only knew of their Queensville property as a fun place to go in the summer. Candy said that when stories of local crime dominated the LA news, he sometimes considered fleeing back to the Great White North.

"But then," he told Linehan, "Rose is like, 'Well, it's no different there, you know, the crime rate is going up there too, you know, if it's gonna happen, it's gonna happen."

Relative newcomers to Hollywood themselves, Rita Wilson and Tom Hanks were frequent dinner guests at the Candys' Mandeville home, which seemed to Wilson to be "bigger than life. Jen and Chris had a huge backyard to play in, with a big trampoline out there. John and Rose were completely generous hosts, and nobody went home hungry."

One Canadian tradition that had followed Candy to Hollywood was hockey, and he was a frequent attendee of the Los Angeles Kings games at the Great Western Forum (now the Kia Forum), often as a guest of the team's owner, Bruce McNall, who introduced him to the Kings' newest acquisition, Wayne Gretzky, recently imported from the Edmonton Oilers. While Gretzky and McNall would later become business partners with Candy, for now Candy's main item of business was launching his own company, Frostbacks Productions, to commission, acquire, and produce bespoke projects for him. The sole mission of the enterprise was to free Candy from being at the mercy of whatever scripts came to his doorstep through his agents at APA. After first hanging a shingle outside a tiny apartment in Hollywood, Candy moved the company to a two-storey building on San Vicente Boulevard. Frostbacks was a safe space for Candy to plot his next career moves, record radio shows, or do voice-overs. Over time, however, with a fully stocked bar, it became a kind of clubhouse for Candy and his rapidly growing cast of friends and professional acquaintances, Dan Aykroyd among them.

"We would come over to talk about ideas," says Aykroyd, who around this time pitched Candy about a project he had in mind, known at the time as *Valkenvania*, "and we'd have these long three- to four- to five-hour lunches catered in."

Robert Crane Jr., now working full-time for Candy, recalls that in the cozy backroom of what he jokingly refers to as the "Frostbacks Bar & Grill," it was easy to forget about time.

"John never ever drove himself home if he'd had too much to imbibe," says Crane. "We'd work it out that one of us co-workers that night would be designated to drive him home."

Second City's Andrew Alexander visited Candy at Frostbacks and found him comfortably holding court in a seemingly endless conversation that touched on both the old days and the challenges of the moment. Alexander recalls that, within the safety of his inner sanctum, Candy could vulnerably share his doubts and anxieties about the future.

"I got the sense," Alexander says, "that once he had lived past the age of father's death, he felt that he'd been given a bonus. He really did try to go the healthy route, but it was a challenge. I remember recommending that he go see a certain heart specialist the next time he came back to Toronto, but he was reluctant to do it. I think he knew that the doctors were going to tell him he had to change his lifestyle, so John resisted that on some level."

One of Frostbacks' first co-productions was a film called *Who's Harry Crumb?* in which Candy played a bumbling detective and master of disguise. In some ways, Crumb was not unlike the Inspector Clouseau character created by his hero Peter Sellers, and Candy dared to dream of a Crumb franchise of his own in the tradition of *The Pink Panther.* The stakes were always high when Candy took on a film project, but now, as an executive producer, he had something extra to prove.

The tagline on the poster for *Who's Harry Crumb?* promised a new private eye with "Nerves of steel. Body of iron. Brains of stone." But as Candy flew into a cold, wet Vancouver to begin principal photography with director Paul Flaherty in the spring of 1988, his nerves were anything but steely. To make things easier on himself, Candy surrounded himself with a number of familiar faces, including Joe Flaherty, Valri Bromfield, Tino Insana, Jim Belushi, and Stephen Young, plus Annie Potts from *Ghostbusters*, and Jeffry Jones from *Ferris Bueller's Day Off.* In a syndicated interview for the Associated Press, Candy said he felt "very good about this one," adding that the comedy was "very reminiscent of some of our work on *SCTV*." Elsewhere in the same interview, however, Candy shared his frustration with certain Hollywood executives, who, he said, "know nothing about comedy," but he felt certain that he was in good hands this time with producer Arnon Milchan, who had a proven track record that included hits like Martin Scorsese's *The King of Comedy* and Terry Gilliam's *Brazil*.

"My associations in the future will be with people I feel I can depend on and trust," Candy told the AP. "I'm looking at my pictures a little more carefully now. If the odd cameo comes up, you've got to look out for money, we all have to make a living. But... I want to make sure they're done right."

Chris Candy later recalled visiting the *Harry Crumb* set at the age of six, accompanied by his mother and sister, and being amused by his father's unique profession. "He was dressed up in this incredible blue leather outfit with a bald wig and self-tanner," Chris told the CBC's Carol Off. "He looked like this Eastern European hairdresser. And I just remember looking at this massive man—my father—as this character, going, 'OK, this is not normal.' It absolutely makes me smile just thinking of him. At that point, I knew there was something unique and interesting happening."

In the middle of the Vancouver shoot, Candy flew to Montreal to host HBO's special live broadcast from the 1988 Just for Laughs international comedy festival at the Théâtre St-Denis, on July 23. Candy was honoured to be hosting a lineup that included stand-ups like Richard Belzer and Steven Wright, plus his friend Graham Chapman, but backstage, a nervous panic was getting the best of him. With his thirty-eighth birthday months away, he had already lived three years longer than his father, Sidney, had, and the confidence that seemed so unshakeable to his fans began to falter. Writer and producer Peter Kaminsky witnessed his friend's discomfort, and later revealed to *People* magazine's Karen Schneider that before he went on, Candy would stand alone "with his eyes shut, breathing in and out. Eating, ingesting, smoking. For John, it was a way of swallowing that anxiety."

The anxiety had yet to abate by the time he returned to Vancouver to finish *Crumb*, by which time his initial good feelings about Arnon Milchan had all but deteriorated over a disagreement about the tone of the film.

"Arnon had felt that John was playing Crumb a little too angry," says Paul Flaherty. "To be honest, I kind of agreed with him, but Johnny didn't want to change it. I couldn't talk him out of it even if I wanted to."

Matters got even worse after certain test screenings for *Who's Harry Crumb?*, when a number of audience members wrote insulting remarks about Candy's weight on their comment cards, which wounded him greatly.

"Of course, the majority of audiences loved John," says Paul Flaherty, "but some of the cards were so brutal they even hurt *my* feelings. I can't imagine writing 'BIG FAT FUCKING SLOB' in big letters on a card. It was just some of the most inappropriate, vulgar, and vicious fat-shaming stuff. It really shocked me."

By the time *Who's Harry Crumb?* opened on February 3, 1989, the reviews were mostly negative, and after a disappointing first weekend at the box office, it left the cinemas with little fanfare. Candy took the rejection personally, putting the lion's share of the blame for the film's poor performance on what he felt was a minimal marketing campaign from the studio, TriStar Pictures.

"These guys," Candy complained to Brian Linehan, "they sank the picture. And they all got promotions for it. 'Hey, a bomb, alright! Give that guy a raise! Give him a better office.' What happened?"

While Candy was still in Vancouver shooting *Crumb*, he had found time to record the pilot episode of *Radio Kandy*, which was syndicated to over three hundred individual radio stations in the US. On one episode of the program he publicly chastised TriStar for its lack of promotion for *Who's Harry Crumb?* In general, the whole experience had confirmed his distrust of studio executives.

"I question a lot more than I did before," Candy told Linehan. "I'm not afraid, you know? What are they gonna say to me? Just be straight... that's all I ask with them... I'll be straight with you."

Back at Frostbacks, with Del's trunk from *Planes, Trains and Automobiles* holding a place of pride at the foot of his desk, Candy and Crane sorted through a stack of scripts, passing on most of them. One of these was *The Telephone*, whose only attraction was its screenplay by *Dr. Strangelove* screenwriter Terry Southern and songwriter Harry Nilsson. Among the other rejects were two biopics of controversial plus-size comedians. One was about the scandalized Roscoe "Fatty" Arbuckle. While Candy had enjoyed the history lesson in the film, playing a character named Fatty felt unwise at the time. Another hard pass was an offer to play his friend John Belushi in *Wired*, an adaptation of the Bob Woodward book that Candy had dismissed as a "sensationalized" exploitation of events that had traumatized his social circle.

Candy flew Paul Flaherty out to Hollywood to develop new projects for Frostbacks to produce. While in the office, Flaherty noted that Candy, the executive, had become far more cost-conscious than the Johnny Deluxe he had known in the days of *SCTV*.

"I flew out first-class and put myself into a good hotel," says Flaherty. "A couple of days later, I get a phone call from John's lawyer screaming at me for the expenses. It was different now that John was the producer, and he was shovelling out all of this money for this big suite of offices and a full staff. There were lots of meetings for things that never got off the ground."

Since Frostbacks was funded by "greenbacks," it was time to get back to work. To make a quick three million dollars, Candy returned to Montreal to appear in *Speed Zone*, a madcap road race comedy meant to be the next installment in the lucrative *Cannonball Run* franchise. But after Burt Reynolds left the series, Orion Pictures, with a large infusion of cash from the Canadian Film Development Corporation, needed to recast the project with a Canadian to star. John Candy was just such an actor. When the cameras finally rolled on *Speed Zone*, on October 18, 1988, Candy and Brooke Shields were its co-stars. Even while doing it for the money, Candy wanted the comedy to be top-notch, so he brought along *SCTV* writer Michael Short and director Jim Drake, and asked Joe Flaherty and Eugene Levy to join him in the cast.

Appearing on Jennifer Candy's *Couch Candy* program in 2015, Levy admitted that while he had been underwhelmed by the script, he had agreed to come out to Montreal for the promise of a fun hang with Candy, who had assured him that "Nobody's gonna see it, and we'll have a ball doing this movie."

Levy and Candy did have some laughs in Montreal, but as the production quickly went over budget, a circular firing squad of blame plagued the enterprise. In the end, *Speed Zone* was yet another flop for Candy with the critics, but his prophecy had held: nobody went to see it.

In January 1989, however, Candy's losing streak appeared to be coming to an end. At last he was returning to Chicago to reunite with Hughes on a film that, for the first time, combined Hughes's expertise in teen comedy with his current interest in writing for men his own age. By this time, Candy had grown wary of predicting box office success, but he was certain about two things: the script for *Uncle Buck* was hilarious, and the role of the avuncular Buck Russell would allow him to finally play to the full range of his strengths as an actor.

And besides, there would be pancakes.

Twenty

Everybody's Favourite Uncle

When suburban Chicago parents of three Bob and Cindy Russell are urgently called away to Indianapolis, they desperately need a babysitter for their fifteen-year-old Tia, eight-year-old Miles, and six-year-old Maizy. After exhausting a short list of more suitable guardians, they settle on Bob's brother Buck, a chain-smoking heavy drinker who lives alone in a small Chicago apartment. While Buck dutifully, if reluctantly, takes on the family obligation, he makes it clear that he would much rather be down at the track betting on horses and enjoying the life of an uncommitted and unmarried man. For their part, the Russell kids aren't too thrilled about being left with their slovenly Uncle Buck either. Predictably, since this is after all a John Hughes film, the two reluctant factions come to understand each other and bond, recognizing the power of family. Promoting *Uncle Buck* after its release, Candy explained that he was thrilled to be working for Hughes again in a simple family film where "no one flies" and there were "no major car chases."

"It's just a good movie," Candy declared, while describing his undomesticated title character as "a neat guy to have as your uncle, because he can say and do things your father can't do ... It's quite an adventure for Buck, being in the suburbs ... I think he lived on takeout food most of his life ... He's a bit of a rounder, a gambler" and "a well-meaning guy" whose schemes don't always pan out.

Hughes told the press that Candy, with two young children of his own, was perfectly suited to the role, and singled out the subtlety his star had brought to one particular scene where Buck experiences unexpected pangs of guilt while taking the young children to the racetrack. "He knows it's wrong," said Hughes. "He's in the car and he looks in the rear-view mirror and he sees these two sweet little kids that he's gonna take to the track when he meets his gangster buddies and they bet, and he can't do it. And I know that when he was doing that scene, that when he looked in the mirror, he wasn't looking at two little actors, he was looking at two real kids. That was him, that was him, the father."

In a 1989 interview with Brian Linehan, Candy confirmed that he had dealt with his film kids exactly the same way he did at home. "Buck doesn't talk down to these kids," Candy told Linehan. "I think that's why they like him ... he treats them as an equal. They're given that respect and that self-esteem and that comes across."

According to Candy, Hughes later confessed to having been so focused on directing the big picture, that he hadn't fully appreciated how realistic his interactions had been with Tia

(Jean Louisa Kelly), Miles (Macaulay Culkin), and Maizy (Gaby Hoffmann). He added that the separation of duties was one of the great things about his collaboration with Hughes. "He covers one side," Candy explained, "and I'll cover the other side and put them all together. And I don't know what he does over there, half the time. When I look at it, I go, 'Gee, how'd he *do* that? I didn't know they were shooting like that.'"

James Hughes recalls that he and his brother visited the *Uncle Buck* set more than any other, not just to see their dad but to hang out with their de facto Uncle John, and on a few occasions, Jen and Chris Candy. "The set was at an empty high school in Northfield, Illinois," says James, "about twenty minutes away from our home. I especially liked it when the Candy kids were visiting. I remember John Candy giving me a Toronto Maple Leafs jersey, and a little later, for my ninth birthday, he gave me a Los Angeles Kings jersey with my name on it and the number nine. I still have it. These incredible gestures that fostered a lifelong love of hockey in me. Once we formed this alliance with the Candy family, hockey became the dominant sport in my family and carried on for decades beyond that."

Jennifer Candy later told *Vanity Fair*'s David Kamp that, by this time, the two families had "basically merged," adding that Hughes had been so impressed with the Candy farm in Queensville that he purchased his own hundred-acre parcel of land in western Illinois that he called Redwing Farms. James Hughes confirms that the Candy farm "really had an impact" on his father. "Seeing that it was even possible to have a rural getaway like that, and a place of refuge. Pardon the pun, but it planted the seed."

Early in the production of *Uncle Buck*, John Hughes took a camera crew to Chicago in hopes of shooting a few additional scenes at a Chicago Blackhawks game, to illustrate a story that Buck tells his friends about one of the greatest days in his life, when he scored a goal during a promotional shoot-the-puck contest in between periods. In the stands at Chicago Stadium were the combined Candy and Hughes families. In the concrete expanse underneath the stadium seats, Candy practised hard for his moment on the ice and got some slapshot advice from Blackhawks legend Stan Mikita. When he finally skidded out onto the ice, replete in his *Uncle Buck* wardrobe, Candy took three shots but failed to get even one into the net. The footage was never used, and the moment is lost to time.

While the Candy and Hughes families were strengthening their bond, Candy's entourage, affectionately self-identified as "the Chongos" for no apparent reason, were becoming a kind of family too. In addition to Robert Crane Jr., Candy's crew included his stand-in, Bob Elmore, and Frankie Hernandez, whose job title was driver, despite the fact that he rarely, if ever, actually drove a car anymore.

"In Candy world," recalls Crane, "you may be titled as one thing, but you did something else, or you did five other things in addition to what your little title was. And since John liked to entertain, Frankie's actual job was to take care of John's dressing room and to keep it well stocked with food and drink. Frankie knew where John's copy of the script was at all times, and he was also trusted with counting John's per diem. John was getting, I think, about $2,500 a week in his per diem, and I remember seeing Frankie in the trailer making these neat stacks of cash. Whenever John had cash, it was always rolled up into a ball in his pocket. If you ever needed cash from John, he would just throw this ball of cash on a table and then you'd have to go through it and find out what was in there."

Candy had met Hernandez when he was a crew member on *Going Berserk*. When Hernandez had noticed that Candy had a tiny trailer, he'd offered to help.

"Frankie asked him if he was the star of the film," says Crane. "John, being humble, says, 'Well, yeah. I guess.' Frankie pulls out the call sheet, sees that John Candy is at the top of the call list, and says, 'Look, you're number one on this sheet, and *this* is your dressing room?' As a Teamster, Frankie knew who was supposed to get what, which really helped John in the early days of adjusting to Hollywood. He became a major player in John's life, and John never forgot about that. He always had him by his side, and they were working together until the very end."

While Bob Elmore (infamous for his portrayal of Leatherface in Tobe Hooper's *The Texas Chainsaw Massacre 2*) was Candy's official stand-in, the big man also appeared to some to be Candy's bodyguard. Candy's other regulars included makeup artist Ben Nye Jr., hairstylist Dione Taylor, and clothing designer Silvio Scarano.

Hughes shot well over a million feet of film on *Uncle Buck*, breaking the previous record he had set on *Planes, Trains and Automobiles*, as Candy and his writer/director bounced ideas off each other as the cameras rolled.

"Hughes might whisper an idea to Candy," says Crane, "lean in and say, 'What if we did this?' And he'd let Candy throw in ideas on the set too. It was the same with Laurie Metcalf, playing this, kind of, the nosy neighbour, Marcie. Hughes loved Laurie, and she worked so well with Candy. Hughes gave both of them lots of latitude. They even worked up a little dance number together. Laurie, who came from the Chicago stage, was exactly the right person for that role."

In an interview for the Chicago NBC affiliate, Metcalf later spoke with great affection about working with Candy on what was one of her first screen roles. "I was really green during that," Metcalf recalled, "but John Candy is about the nicest person you'd ever wanna work with. I was petrified to do the dance. We'd sort of choreographed it, so I wanted to rehearse it over and over and over again. And I knew he didn't want to ... but he did it with me, over and over and over again before we [filmed] it, so he was a great guy. I think it's commitment. You have to commit!"

Co-star Amy Madigan, at the time enjoying a career boost from the hit film *Field of Dreams*, witnessed an almost telepathic level of communication between Candy and Hughes on the set, and was similarly struck not only by Candy's generosity with his castmates, but by his innate ability to keep things fun.

"He would really work with you to figure out what you needed and wanted as an actor," Madigan later told *Vanity Fair*'s Julie Miller. "[It's] what you hope that actors do, but oftentimes they don't. You would be doing a closeup ... and he would just throw this stuff at you to crack you up. He'd be like, 'Do you need a ride?' or 'I'm going to go out to dinner with some people. You want to come along?' He was very inclusive in that type of thing, which was really nice."

The youngest cast members, Jean Louisa Kelly, Gaby Hoffmann, and Macaulay Culkin, were all mandated to keep up their schoolwork in a makeshift classroom within the abandoned New Trier West High School that Hughes had taken over for *Uncle Buck*. As Tia, Kelly had particularly fond memories of a shoot at bowling alley that took on a party-like atmosphere after Candy and Hughes both invited their kids. According to Kelly, much of the dialogue for her scene with Candy in "The Beast," a dilapidated 1977 Mercury Marquis Brougham, was workshopped to include on-set improvisations.

"We're sitting there talking to each other," Kelly later told *Vanity Fair*, "and [Candy] was sort of throwing stuff at me, and I was just responding to it like the unpleasant person that I was. I don't really know that you can write that stuff and get the same kind of organic authenticity that you would get when you're just responding with [unscripted] lines."

While Gaby Hoffmann, who later went on to a critically acclaimed role in the Hulu series *Transparent*, was suitably precocious as youngest niece Maizy, Candy had an undeniable chemistry with a young newcomer named Macaulay Culkin. Culkin later recalled that while the role of young Miles was his fourth time on film, *Uncle Buck* was the proof-of-concept for his imminent career as the best-known child star of his generation, when Hughes cast him in his production of *Home Alone*. In one of the most celebrated sequences in *Uncle Buck*, Miles interrogates his mysterious uncle, quizzing him on such personal details as where he lives, whether he owns or rents his apartment, what he does for a living, and his marital status and why.

"Mac came in and there was a number of pages of dialogue," Hughes later explained to the CBC, "and it was supposed to be fast, [but] Mac couldn't get through 'em. He was a little boy, so I thought, 'Oh god, how're we gonna do this?' John [Candy] said, 'Put the camera on my back, I'll say the lines to Mac, and he'll repeat them back to me."

Candy became Culkin's de facto uncle on the set, mentoring

the young actor and running dialogue with him as much as he needed. "There's a video somewhere," says Robert Crane Jr., "and you can clearly see John guiding him, even on the audition tapes. I got the sense that Macaulay loved him and looked up to him. I mean, here's this eight-year-old kid with this established actor, but they had great timing. Macaulay was fearless."

In a December 2024 interview with journalist Amy Kuperinsky, Culkin was still praising Candy's kindness toward him on the set of *Uncle Buck*.

"He'd always ask me how am I doing? You'd be surprised how often people don't ask you 'how are you doing?'"

MUCH LIKE HIS CHARACTER, Candy's heart of gold was tinged with a tendency to be a bad boy, and Hughes had at least one time on the shoot when he felt the need to rein in his star's social life. One morning as he prepared to go to the set, Hughes heard on the radio that Candy had been seen out on the streets of Chicago on an all-night pub crawl the night before. According to Tarquin Gotch, who had accompanied Candy that night and was with him at work that morning, Hughes was not amused. While his star had shown up for work on time and ready to work, Candy was visibly hungover as he flopped into the makeup chair. Hughes not only felt that Candy's behaviour was disrespectful to himself and his crew, he was also concerned for the health of a man he now considered a close friend. Candy had been chain-smoking, and his weight had reportedly shot up to 330 pounds. According to Gotch, Hughes took Candy aside and "read him the riot act," admonishing him for his recklessness. Candy, for his part, heeded his friend's words and apologized profusely before turning in what Gotch remembers as a "perfect performance."

Over the course of the filming, Hughes had also realized that, as with Del Griffith, the ne'er-do-well Buck Russell needed to be more likeable if audiences were going to feel for his predicament. "There was a harder edge to him initially," Candy later revealed. "We shaved a lot of that off and gave him more of a vulnerability."

What emerged was a title character that Dave Kehr of the *Chicago Tribune* later described as "a great, happy mass of urban, ethnic funk." Candy had successfully dialed in the likeability factor, and on August 16, 1989, *Uncle Buck* opened as the hit Candy had been waiting for. After slogging through twelve-hour workdays, and after exposing nearly one million feet of film, John Hughes's $15 million film became the first John Candy solo starring vehicle to open at number one in North America, where it remained for four straight weeks, grossing nearly $80 million worldwide at the box office. *Uncle Buck* was not, however, universally loved by the film critics. Roger Ebert complained that the film's violent implications, such as Buck taking a power drill to a teenaged boy, made for "an uncomfortable undercurrent in the material" that was too dark for its own good.

That said, *Uncle Buck* is mostly remembered today as one of Candy's most beloved characters and everybody's favourite uncle. Audiences are charmed by *Uncle Buck*'s chaotic breakfast scene, with giant pancakes and flying sausages, a spatula-wielding duel, and a symphony of clanging pots. Despite Ebert's concerns about violent implications, filmgoers root for Buck as he interrogates a pizza delivery person and punches out a party clown who has the audacity to arrive at Miles's birthday gathering drunk and belligerent. And when Buck gives a heartfelt pep talk to Tia, reminding her of her inner strength, it's another classic Hughes moment that tugs at our heartstrings and reminds us of *Uncle Buck*'s deeper message about family ties. As the poster promised, "He's crude, He's crass, He's family."

According to Hollywood screenwriter Larry Karaszewski (*Man on the Moon*, *Dolemite Is My Name*), Candy's collaborations with Hughes brought out the best in both of them. "Candy had never really been the 'cool guy' in his films," says Karaszewski. "Sure, he was very, very funny, but he was always just a little too loud. Hughes somehow made you feel sorry for him, and in a sense, that made you love him. If you go through the arc of Candy's catalogue, he'd obviously had many features that were quite successful, but Hughes just took him to another level with *Planes, Trains and Automobiles* and *Uncle Buck*. Hughes took that *too-muchness* of John Candy and made him a star."

For the first time in years, Candy appeared to have broken his losing streak. And whenever he could, he tried to appreciate his improbable life, successfully juggling fame and family, and shuttling between the cozy seclusion of the family farm in Queensville and the sunny comforts of Mandeville Canyon. Having just built a recording studio in the Frostbacks office, Candy would make good use of it in the coming year, as he continued the search for yet another perfect role.

Twenty-One

Home Alone with the Polka King

Despite the sporadic bouts of self-doubt and anxiety that had by now become a familiar, if unwelcome, part of his roller-coaster emotional life, John Candy could at least bask in the knowledge that John Hughes had once again saved the day. *Uncle Buck* was the massive hit he had needed, and, buoyed by the support of his peers and an ever-growing fanbase, Candy had, for the moment, pulled out of a downward spiral. He sat behind his desk at Frostbacks Productions, feeling enriched and artistically invigorated, as he plotted his next move.

During the *Uncle Buck* shoot, Candy's radio producer Doug Thompson had flown up to Chicago several times to record Candy's character bits for their syndicated *Radio Kandy* series. Thompson, who had by now moved to Los Angeles from Toronto, driving down Candy's Mercedes, assembled the recordings back at a new recording studio that he and two other engineers had designed and installed at Frostbacks.

The premise was that *Radio Kandy* was a "pirate radio" station, and that Candy had bought himself a powerful transmitter that could supersede any other station's transmitter, but only for two hours a week. *Radio Kandy*, launched just as *Uncle Buck* was hitting the cinema screens, quickly became one of Candy's favourite projects, providing him an outlet for his many character voices. Thompson recalls that in one of their brainstorming meetings, Candy suggested that if their imaginary station had this overpowering transmitter, it might provide a premise for a comedic "chief engineer" character. In unison, they both blurted "Scotty from *Star Trek*!'

Remarkably, James Doohan, the actor who had played Scotty in the original series, agreed to reprise his role for *Radio Kandy*.

"Jimmy [Doohan] and John would ad lib way beyond what was on the page," says Thompson, "and they were just hilarious together."

The *Radio Kandy* sessions, mostly scripted but largely improvised, often blurred into social occasions as various Second City friends, and notable rock stars, dropped in at Frostbacks.

"Our writing staff," says Thompson, "included Joe Flaherty and Dave Thomas plus around eight other writers at any given time. John wanted it to be like SCTV on radio, with parody commercials and promos, all that kind of stuff. Andrea Martin did a sketch as the new programming consultant, Edith Prickley. Martin Short brought [his character] Ed Grimley, and Joe brought Count Floyd. Valri Bromfield or Joe would make fake phone calls to the station. John never wanted to know in advance what they were going to say, because he wanted it to purely be ad libbed. Rick Moranis was over in New York, so he couldn't come over to Frostbacks, but Eugene Levy would send bits down to us from Toronto, and we'd insert them into the show."

After recording what Thompson remembers as "a whole day's worth of comedy" with Candy, Flaherty, and Thomas, Catherine O'Hara called Candy the following day to ask that her segments be removed because she felt they weren't up to standards.

"I wasn't very good at it," says O'Hara, "and I don't know, I tend to improvise a bit better within some structure, where you know where you're going or why you're doing it at all."

Candy complied without hesitation and the segments never aired.

On another session at Frostbacks, *Radio Kandy* was graced by a late-night visit from the drummer and singer Levon Helm, a founding member of the Band. Helm had previously been a musical guest on *SCTV*, and on this occasion had invited Candy to see him playing in Ringo Starr's All Starr Band. After the show, Candy brought Helm back to Frostbacks for some creative fun in a place where the bar never closed. Among the other guests were writer Michael Short, himself a musician, who asked Helm if he ever got tired of staying in hotels. Helm told him, "Nah, I don't mind, as long as they've got twenty-four-hour everything."

"Based on that idea," says Short, "I wrote a sketch called the 'Levon Helmsley Hotel,' a takeoff on [notorious Manhattan hotel magnate] Leona Helmsley, and the running tag was Levon saying, 'Stay here, 'cause we got twenty-four-hour everything.'"

Candy, himself a frustrated drummer, had installed a full drum kit in the Frostbacks vocal booth, and took advantage of the opportunity to get a few drumming tips from Helm, who even gave young Christopher Candy a turn on the kit.

"It was just remarkable who came through the front door,"

says Robert Crane Jr. "Whoever was still there at the end of the workday would go in there and the drinks would start flowing. It was a who's who of people, like Bruce McNall from the LA Kings or Dan Aykroyd."

When the late, great saxophone player Clarence Clemons was in town to play with Bruce Springsteen and the E Street Band, Candy invited Clemons to do a sketch for *Radio Kandy* after his afternoon soundcheck. Clemons had so much fun that he invited Candy to come back to join Springsteen onstage that night.

According to Thompson, as Candy's fame grew, the so-called Chongos functioned as a kind of social barrier to surround Candy whenever his social anxiety kicked in. "He trusted me," says Thompson, "and of course Frankie [Hernandez] and Bob [Crane]. John liked to surround himself with people he knew, and we seemed to have a lot of Canadians around. Whenever he'd want to go to the Century City mall or something, he'd say, 'Doug, come with me.' He didn't like to go alone because he'd get trapped. Whenever John got cornered he'd sign autographs forever, and he didn't want to let people down so he'd ask us to interrupt these encounters every fifteen minutes to say, 'Okay, come on, John, we gotta go.' He never, ever went out there alone, there was always somebody with him. He'd always say, 'Whenever we go, don't stop, just keep walking.'"

Candy's aversion to crowds likely affected his stint as a presenter at the 1988 Academy Awards in Los Angeles. Rather than sit in his designated seat in the audience at the Shrine Auditorium, Candy opted to wait backstage and generally avoided public scrutiny. Crane watched as Candy hit up Jack Nicholson for a cigarette and ended up holding court with other acting legends like Robert De Niro and Warren Beatty.

"These guys were some of the biggest stars in the world at the time," says Crane, "and John was now one of them."

After being introduced as "a very funny woman" by Chevy Chase, Candy walked out to the podium to the jaunty strains of the Sammy Davis Jr. hit "The Candy Man." After apologizing for leaving his dress at home, Candy produced some crumpled pages from inside his jacket and began reading remarks he credited to his daughter, Jennifer, an artful way of getting a laugh while acknowledging the ongoing labour action by the Writers Guild of America, of which he was a member. After presenting the award for Best Makeup to Rick Baker, Candy fled the building, preferring to watch the telecast on television at home.

Meanwhile, back at Frostbacks, Candy and his staff continued to develop new project ideas, most of which never got past the memo stage. After Candy and Joe Flaherty brainstormed about a potential *SCTV* feature film that Flaherty described as "*SCTV* in outer space," the project failed to launch and the mission was scrapped. One that did take off was an animated series called *Camp Candy*, a Saturday morning cartoon in which Candy would appear in animated form as a camp counsellor.

Camp Candy was the brainchild of Joel Andryc and Ellen Levy, who had originally intended to create an animated program based on Allan Sherman's 1963 summer camp novelty song "Hello Muddah, Hello Fadduh (A Letter from Camp)." NBC's vice president of family programming, Phyllis Tucker Vinson Jackson, would only make the series if they could convince John Candy to get involved in a major way. Family was important to Candy, and something about the premise of a children's summer camp made him think of his own kids. Candy agreed to sign on, bringing *SCTV* producer Patrick Whitley along with him as his point person with NBC.

Candy's hope for *Camp Candy* was that it would be both entertaining and educational, alerting children to the importance of protecting endangered species and respecting the environment. NBC took out a full-page print ad that promised: "The fun is as great as all outdoors in *Camp Candy*. The ideal getaway for kids of all ages!"

The series debuted on NBC on September 9, 1989, and ran for forty episodes over three seasons, during which time Candy invited a myriad of guests to voice characters, including David L. Lander, Marcia Wallace, Roddy McDowall, and good friends Valri Bromfield, Andrea Martin, Eugene Levy, Dave Thomas, and Tino Insana.

"He loved making kids laugh," Insana later told the CBC. "He liked to make everybody laugh, but kids were, kids were tough, they're not gonna laugh unless it's really funny."

Jennifer and Christopher Candy, ages nine and five, respectively, even lent their voices to the program.

"My earliest memory of *Camp Candy* was the promo swag," Chris Candy later told writer Brian VanHooker. "*Camp Candy* lunchboxes and Marvel comic books and other stuff that just showed up in the office."

After NBC decided to ditch Saturday morning cartoons, *Camp Candy* became a first-run syndicated program, and in its third and final season, Candy appeared in live-action "wraparound" segments, filmed at his Queensville ranch, promoting ecological conservation. A more sober episode of *Camp Candy*, which focused on a child with leukemia, won a Humanitas Prize for film and television writing. According to writer Joe Ramoni,

Camp Candy worked because "there was real heart at the core of the show. It treated a child audience as young adults ... It was everything we loved about John Candy, represented in a fun little show that deserves to be remembered."

Camp Candy's good-natured theme song was written and performed by Harry Nilsson, who had previously enjoyed great success with songs for television, including his own hit animated special, *The Point*. Sung by Nilsson and Candy together, Nilsson's theme was a playfully sardonic, mildly tortured organ waltz, with lyrics that encompassed the full range of camp experiences—from bee stings to "stories told by firelight"—in less than sixty seconds. Each episode closed with a variation of a traditional "camp song" with lyrics tailored to the Candy universe ("On Top of Old Smokey" became "On Top of Mount Frostback").

Otherwise, many of Candy's acting jobs around this time were either favours to old friends, such as a cameo on Dave Thomas's sci-fi sketch comedy series *The Rocket Boy*, or as an ensemble cast member with Tino Insana, Jim Belushi, David Rasche, George Wendt, David L. Lander, and Dan Aykroyd in Daniel Raskov's 1990 feature film *Masters of Menace*, a kind of *Animal House* on Harley-Davidsons that was best described by its tagline: "Hot Babes. Hot Bikes. And 500 Cops in Hot Pursuit."

From the comfort of his own Frostbacks recording studio, Candy voiced the albatross Wilbur in Disney's animated feature film *The Rescuers Down Under*. The film promised to be one of his higher-profile engagements of 1990 but was considered such a commercial disappointment upon its release that Disney's Jeffrey Katzenberg quietly suspended television advertising; it was one of the only Disney animated films to ever gross less than $100 million. That said, Candy could still be "critic-proof"; Janet Maslin, and both Roger Ebert and Gene Siskel, insisted that Wilbur was one of the best things about the picture.

Curiously, while *The Rescuers Down Under* came in fourth on its November 16 release day, the number-one film in the country that week was *Home Alone*, a Chris Columbus film, written and produced by John Hughes, which also featured a scene-stealing turn from John Candy.

As Gus Polinski, leader of the Kenosha Kickers and the self-styled Polka King of the Midwest, Candy was back in Shmenge territory. While he had no scenes with the star of the film, his *Uncle Buck* co-star Macaulay Culkin, he was happy to be back in Hughes's orbit and to be improvising once again with Catherine O'Hara.

Director Chris Columbus had emerged as a prolific writer of family films, including *Gremlins*, *The Goonies*, and *Young Sherlock Holmes*, before Hughes offered him a chance to direct *National Lampoon's Christmas Vacation*. But after disagreements with its star, Chevy Chase, Columbus backed out of the picture. Hughes understood and offered him the chance to direct *Home Alone* for Twentieth Century Fox, who saw the film as its big family release for Thanksgiving 1990, giving it an $18 million budget, with filming to commence in February and wrap up in May. Like Hughes, Columbus had been a fan of Candy's work on *SCTV* and had already cast O'Hara as Culkin's mother, Kate McCallister.

Hughes and Columbus created the role of Gus Polinski expressly for Candy, who was happy to do it, pending his agent's negotiation over the fee. Since Columbus only needed one day from Candy, Hughes, as producer, politely asked Candy if he might eschew his typical performance fee in favour of a back-end profit share from the box office take. There was some risk to this for both parties, but for Candy it meant he could reap either huge rewards, if the film was a hit, or nothing at all, if it sank like a stone. Candy instead made the magnanimous gesture of working for scale, reportedly a mere $414 at the time, and in a move that would later come to haunt him, declined to share in any future profits.

That settled, Candy was pleased to come in for one very long day in Winnetka, Illinois, to film his appearance as the Polka King, who Columbus insists had nothing to do with Yosh Shmenge, as one would imagine, but rather was based on the real-life polka king Frankie Yankovic. While Columbus was well aware that the two *SCTV* cast members would be able to wing it, he and Hughes also knew that they only had Candy for the day, so they went to the trouble of scripting pages and pages of dialogue to fall back on just in case. They fashioned a scene at an airport in which O'Hara's Kate first realizes that Kevin has been left, as the film title suggests, home alone. When she is informed that there are no more flights home that day, Gus offers to give her a ride in the back of the Kenosha Kickers' cube van all the way to her front door.

O'Hara says she was "thrilled" when she learned that Hughes and Columbus had gotten Candy to come in and do the part. "Hughes adored John," says O'Hara. "They adored each other, but Hughes could only get him for twenty-one hours or something. So he arrived early one night, and I'm not kidding, we improvised for every one of those hours."

Hughes had briefed a slightly apprehensive Columbus about what to expect on the set, but when Candy arrived, his nerves went away. "He really was one of the kindest, most gentle, nicest people I had ever met," says Columbus. "We clicked immediately. He may have sensed that I was nervous, knowing that I really wanted to impress John Hughes on my first picture, so he immediately tried to make me feel comfortable. That was just a big boost of confidence from someone who was, at that time, one of the biggest stars working in Hollywood."

It also became clear to Columbus that there would be no use for the scripted dialogue that he and Hughes had prepared. Knowing that improv was the word of the day, the director set up two cameras on each of his two lead actors and let the mayhem begin.

"This way made it easier to edit," says Columbus. "When someone improvises, it can either be magical or the unfunniest thing you've ever seen. Well, these two together were just incredible. And we probably did about twelve takes of that airport scene, and when I realized I had everything I needed for that moment, we got into the truck set and shot for hours and hours and hours."

Much of *Home Alone* was shot inside the same abandoned New Trier West High School in Winnetka that Hughes had used on *Uncle Buck*, *Ferris Bueller's Day Off*, and *Sixteen Candles*. All interiors for the McCallister home, and the airport waiting area, were filmed there, and the interior shots for Candy and O'Hara's epic truck ride were filmed inside a large wooden box built inside the school's gymnasium. To simulate the shaky ride, four crew people manipulated a series of two-by-fours under this box.

"The airport set was directly next to the truck set," says Columbus, "so we didn't have to waste any time driving John anywhere."

Kieran Culkin, Macaulay's brother, and later a star of the HBO series *Succession*, recalls being star-struck when he was introduced to Candy at New Trier while watching him and O'Hara shoot the cube van scene. In 2023, he was still raving in an *Esquire* magazine article about how impressed he had been that such a "big chunk of movie" was shot "in one like twenty-something-hour-long day ... mostly improvised. The man was brilliant."

For the most part, Hughes, the producer, had given Columbus a free hand on the picture, but on the day of Candy's visit, he couldn't resist parking himself behind Columbus and his cinematographer. "Those were the moments," says son James Hughes, "where Dad felt he *had* to be there," while adding that he also believes that his father came by simply to give Candy his full creative encouragement.

"He'd been very good for the entire shoot," says Columbus of Hughes, "and everything was going great for the first twenty-two hours of this long, long day, but in the very last forty-five minutes of the twenty-third hour, Hughes started throwing out cues to Candy from behind me."

O'Hara vividly recalls Hughes tossing out prompts for alternative dialogue to spark Candy on.

"He'd throw out anything and everything," says O'Hara. "He'd say, 'What about this, John?' or 'Talk about the funeral home,' and just feed him jokes. And John just ran with it. Never said no."

Far from feeling micromanaged by Hughes, Columbus says he was touched by the respect that Hughes showed to both Candy and himself.

"When Gus goes off on that story about being locked in the funeral parlour with the corpse," says Columbus, "that wasn't in the script. He just made that up on the spot. There was so much more they both came up with, but we couldn't fit it all into the film."

Many of O'Hara's funniest improvs had to be left on the cutting room floor, since her character was supposed to be too distraught to be having so much fun with a random polka band.

"Of course," says O'Hara, "it's edited way, way down, but you can still feel the spirit there. It was just really fun to get to improvise with John for, like, twenty-three hours, but you can't use all of it."

Columbus says he could have kept going even longer, but he began to worry about the crew.

"We had to stop," he recalls, "but John just had this incredible amount of stamina. And somehow, he still managed to be kind and gentle with everyone on the set, which was fantastic."

Candy had already boarded a private jet back to Los Angeles by the time Columbus filmed the shot of the Kenosha Kickers' van pulling up at the McCallisters' home with Hughes's driver standing in as Gus, as the day was dawning.

By the time of the preview screening of *Home Alone* for a hometown Chicago audience on November 10, 1990, Columbus was already back at work with Candy on his next Hughes production, *Only the Lonely*. A week later, *Home Alone* was the number-one film at the box office and went on to take in an estimated worldwide gross of nearly $477 million.

After Candy took both of his kids to a screening, his son Chris particularly identified with Kevin McCallister and began to adopt his precocious attitude around the house.

"John would complain to me," says Columbus, "that Chris was talking to him the same smartass way Kevin was to his parents."

Candy had taken the part in *Home Alone* as a favour to Hughes, a man who had been extremely good to him. But while he would star in a few more Hughes productions, their marathon night in the back of the Kenosha Kickers cube van set would mark the last time John Hughes would ever actually *direct* John Candy. Still, their families were now practically inseparable, and they had every intention to work together again in the near future. One of the few sources of friction was Candy's decision to wave off a profit-sharing arrangement, which meant that he was now missing out on the *Home Alone* windfall. While Columbus had no details about Candy's arrangements with Hughes, he can confirm that Candy later came to regret his decision.

"I don't know if Fox ever gave him more money later on," says Columbus, "but when we did *Only the Lonely*, I know he was still sore about it."

Hughes had been considering Candy for a part in *Home Alone 2*, and as the lead in *Dutch*, and a live-action screenplay for *Dennis the Menace* that would have put him back in *Uncle Buck* territory. But none of these projects would come to bear his name. According to James Hughes, after directing one more picture, *Curly Sue*, his father, having achieved financial independence after *Home Alone*, walked away from directing entirely. He did, however, consider directing one last project for himself and Candy.

In the summer of 1990, just months before Kevin McCallister beat Rocky Balboa at the box office, Carolco Pictures announced plans to make a new John Hughes adventure comedy, a co-starring vehicle for the unlikely team of John Candy and Sylvester Stallone entitled *Bartholomew vs. Neff*. Stallone would play Bartholomew, a disgraced former Major League Baseball pitcher living in eternal shame after the last pitch of his career gave up a grand slam in the World Series. Candy was to play his neighbour, Walter Neff, with whom an epic feud ensued.

"I am very excited about working with a director of the stature of John Hughes," Stallone said in a Carolco press release. It was no secret around Hollywood that Stallone was looking to enter the comedy market. For Candy, the pairing would bring him to the action market, working at the studio responsible for both *Rambo* and *The Terminator.* Hughes had earmarked the film for a 1992 release, but according to his son, *Bartholomew vs. Neff* became "the one that got away" after "a million things conspired against it."

When Stallone dropped out to return to strict action films, neither Candy nor Hughes returned to the idea.

"Candy and Stallone had very full schedules," says James Hughes, "plus *Home Alone* had been such a global phenomenon that they fast-tracked the sequel, so my dad had to focus on that. But it would have been a really interesting film. I was looking at the screenplay the other day, and it's incredible how much, in almost an eerie way, you can hear Candy's voice in the dialogue."

On Candy's full schedule were a number of projects designed to push him out of his comfort zone. One would cast him against type as a swashbuckling leading man, another was a favour to Dan Aykroyd, but the most significant of these would be another Columbus-directed Hughes film in which John Candy: Serious Actor could at last show off the emotional depth that only those close to him knew he was capable of.

Twenty-Two

The Actor Is Here

What you see is what you get," proclaimed travelling salesman Del in *Planes, Trains and Automobiles*, and for the most part, that was also true of Candy in real life. On the surface, he was exactly the person his friends and fans assumed he was, a beloved and charming teddy bear who had it all: a loving family and a sprawling farm in Queensville, where his horses, Peaches, Cream, Uncle Buck, and Harry Crumb lived contented lives in stables with abundant bales of hay. His comfortable movie star home in Mandeville Canyon featured a foot-high stone replica of the Statue of Liberty by the backyard pool. On film, he was celebrated in the hits and critic-proof in the misses. He could hold court at a Los Angeles Kings game or be the entertaining bartender back at the "Frostbacks Bar & Grill."

But Candy's closest friends had increasingly seen flashes of the darkness, barely visible, that had plagued him ever since he had lost his father when he was five years old. The mysteries of congenital disease hovered over every career misstep, and the spectre of mortality ridiculed his every attempt to stay on the Pritikin diet while suffering the outrageous slings and arrows of the fat jokes made either to his face or in the press. He very rarely shared the depths of his humiliation with these strangers. A born people pleaser who would generously pose for photographs and sign every autograph, Candy was first and foremost an actor, and his most convincing role was that of a happy-go-lucky movie star who had risen to the top of the Hollywood ladder without losing his folksy Canadian humility.

"Acting," Candy once told a journalist, afforded him "the ability to get lost and take up another life," and a means to hide from himself.

Noticeable cracks, however, started to appear in the facade as closer friends, such as Dave Thomas, began to witness Candy's bouts with anxiety. "John was flawed at times, but he was always a very sensitive human," says Thomas, who noted that Candy's personality changed depending on what he was drinking and when. "His daytime drink was rum and Coca-Cola, and Johnny was always jolly and jovial when he drank it. But around midnight, Johnny might switch to Courvoisier or Rémy Martin, and he would get a little darker, and he'd let you know who pissed him off. And he could go all night. You couldn't keep up with him."

Thomas remembers one especially distressing evening at the home of Martin Short and Nancy Dolman, in nearby Pacific Palisades. Toward the end of the evening, Candy slipped into a notably dark funk and had begun to spiral, and asked Thomas to drive him back to Mandeville Canyon. He had left his own car at home and, even if he hadn't, was in no shape to drive.

Thomas told him that he would be glad to, right after he drove Catherine O'Hara first. Candy grew sullen.

"John just said, 'No, forget it. Forget it,'" says Thomas. "He didn't want to go with a bunch of people. He just wanted to talk with me. So I went back to Catherine and I said, 'Look, I think John wants to talk.' She let me off the hook right away and arranged to get a ride with somebody else. But when I went back to John, somebody told me that he had already left on foot. I hopped in my car and started driving around looking for him. I spotted him walking home in the rain, so I pulled up alongside him, rolled down the window and said, 'John, come on. Get in the car.' And he said, 'No, no. No, you give your other friends a ride.' And I said, 'Jesus, John. Come on. Don't be an ass! Just get in the fucking car, will ya?' When I did get him in the car, he was like, 'You don't know, Dave. You don't know. You don't know what I go through.' And I said, 'Well, I got a little idea of it tonight, John.' He just had all these anxieties and needed somebody to talk to about it. After I got him home, I went in with him. I had stuff to do the next day, but we stayed talking until the sun came up."

Candy had always been quick to make fun of his own weight, but as Robert Crane Jr. noted, he did not take kindly to others doing the same. "On the one hand, John was Mr. Self-Deprecation," says Crane. "But I remember one time, two guys that John knew came to his office one day to try and do an intervention about his weight. I never saw those two guys again after that; they were *persona non grata*. You just didn't talk about that."

Since the general public, and many of Candy's friends, had never glimpsed his inner turmoil, most onlookers continued to see him as an indestructible movie-making machine whose career showed no signs of slowing down. In 1990, he would fulfill his commitments to make three movies, plus a cameo in John Hughes's production of *Career Opportunities*, which he shot in the final months of 1989 and into the first week of January 1990.

Candy's first starring role of the new year was in a feature directed by Tom Mankiewicz entitled *Delirious*, which began principal photography in Los Angeles in March. *Delirious* was a romantic comedy wrapped inside a hallucinatory fantasy, pitched somewhere between *It's a Wonderful Life*, *Groundhog Day*, and *The Secret Life of Walter Mitty*. Candy played Jack Gable, the head writer on a popular daytime drama called *Beyond Our Dreams*. After an automobile crash renders him unconscious, Gable awakens in a hospital bed in the soap opera's fictional town of Ashford Falls. The clever premise allowed Candy to play the romantic lead for once, if only in his character's hallucination. He led a cast that included Emma Samms and Mariel Hemingway, and Hemingway later spoke of an instant spiritual connection with him. She told writer Tracey J. Morgan that, while Candy never wallowed in his anxiety on the set, she sensed his inner "demons" as he struggled with his weight.

"I think that he knew I had a compassion for covering up pain," Hemingway told Morgan, "because I came from such a crazy family, I think he felt that understanding. He was just so generous; he couldn't have been more kind... He took care of people; he saw himself no different to anybody else."

Candy, a film buff since childhood, was thrilled to be working with Mankiewicz, a descendant from a significant Hollywood family that included his father, the Academy Award–winning writer Joseph L. Mankiewicz, who had written the screenplays for legendary films such as *All About Eve* and *Cleopatra*.

"Tom's uncle Herman co-wrote *Citizen Kane*," says Crane. "So at the end of a shooting day, Tom would start in on these Hollywood stories."

In the posthumously released CBC television documentary *To John With Love*, Tom Mankiewicz, who passed away in July 2010 after a bout with pancreatic cancer, remarked that, as lovable as Candy was, there was a "big hurt" within him. Candy, he said, had tried so hard "to be everything to his friends, to his family, to people" that he was "constantly afraid he was letting people down."

Delirious may have been fun to shoot, but post-production was hampered by studio issues and a business merger between Pathé Communications and MGM/UA that delayed the film's opening until August 1991. And in the end, says Crane, "John was unhappy with the way it was edited and how it all came together. Nonetheless, when MGM slashed its publicity budget for the release, Candy approached studio head Alan Ladd Jr. and offered to pay for some of the publicity out of his own pocket.

"That's how sad it was," says Crane. "MGM kind of dumped it out there and it was gone pretty fast."

Looking back today, Crane admits that Candy was probably spreading himself too thin, erring on the side of quantity over quality. As a case in point, he brings up Candy's involvement in *Nothing but Trouble*, which Candy did as favour to Dan Aykroyd.

As the director and star of what began as a screenplay called *Valkenvania*, *Nothing but Trouble* was very much a Dan Aykroyd production, and he had a hand in seemingly every aspect of the film, from the selection of his A-list lead actors, Chevy Chase and Demi Moore, to hiring an all-star technical crew, which included many of the same craftspeople who had made movie magic for Robert Zemeckis and Steven Spielberg.

Candy was still finishing *Delirious* when principal photography commenced on *Nothing but Trouble* in Los Angeles on May 7, 1990. Having accepted Aykroyd's invitation without even reading the script, he was surprised upon his arrival on the set that he was now playing *two* prominent roles. One was Dennis Valkenheiser, the small-town chief of police, and the other was Eldona, the extremely eligible daughter of the town's supernaturally ancient judge.

"John probably didn't think this through because he just wanted to be there for Danny," says Crane. "But once John got there it was a bit of a nightmare because he's got all the makeup and hair and wardrobe and to play both a brother *and* a sister."

Valri Bromfield, who describes *Nothing but Trouble* as "a Dan Aykroyd acid trip," played Candy's deputy, Miss Purdah, and remembers him being initially reluctant to perform in drag as Eldona but eventually finding a way to have fun with his wigs and dresses.

"Eldona was a big girl who expected men to like her," says Bromfield, "and in the end, I thought John stayed true to the reality of this girl. John made her sexy."

Aykroyd's track record for writing hits like *Ghostbusters* and *The Blues Brothers* had likely inspired Warner Bros. to entrust him with a $40 million budget to bring to the screen the fantastical freak show that he and his brother Peter Aykroyd had dreamed up.

"Danny was a first-time director," says Crane, "but this was a major production, so he's got Warner Bros. on his back because it all got way out of control. John never said a bad word about it, though, and even applauded Dan for taking on such a big challenge."

The screenplay for *Valkenvania* had been loosely based on an incident that had actually happened to Dan Aykroyd in 1977, while he was still on *Saturday Night Live*. Driving on a country road in upstate New York, he was pulled over at 3 a.m. by a rural traffic cop who wrote him a fifty-dollar speeding ticket. He was then ordered to accompany the officer, in the dead of night, to the county judge's residence, a haunted house of peeling paint and creaking floorboards. In the film version, Chevy Chase plays a Wall Street trader with Demi Moore as his corporate lawyer companion. Aykroyd, barely recognizable under layers of bubbling and oozing prosthetic makeup, plays the town's 106-year-old Judge Alvin Valkenheiser. Once Chase and Moore are taken into the judge's home of horrors, they meet his granddaughter, Eldona. In short order, it becomes clear that the town of Valkenvania is more than a speed trap; the entire town is a supernatural death trap. Somehow amid all of this madness, the hip-hop group Digital Underground, accompanied by a then-unknown Tupac Shakur, fall into the same speed trap. The final film is even crazier than it sounds on paper.

While Aykroyd says he apologized to the cast and crew when *Nothing but Trouble* wrapped in the middle of August 1991 after a harrowing and difficult shoot, he speaks fondly of his time with Candy on the project as "a fun experience."

"I thought Candy turned in just a stellar performance in it," says Aykroyd. "All the performances in that movie are buttoned up right and the picture looks great. It moves along good, and we stayed under budget."

Perhaps as a result of his experiences on the film, Chase declined to reunite with Candy for a proposed buddy picture called *Thin Ice*, in which Chase would have played a corrupt

Chicago cop assigned to work with an RCMP officer played by Candy.

Warner Bros. pushed back the release of *Nothing but Trouble* to February 15, 1991, by which time the moviegoing audience largely stayed away from the cinema. Critical reception was uniformly dismissive, with *Variety*'s anonymous staff reviewer sniffing, "It's a good bet a film is in trouble when the highlight comes from seeing John Candy in drag."

Candy didn't look back, however, mostly because he didn't have the luxury of time to do so. There was always another movie to make, another trailer, and another cast and crew to entertain. On a movie set, he could become someone else for a few weeks and keep his family fed doing it.

"Oh yes, the lamps, dirty floors with cables," Candy told the CBC. "I could be there all day. I think that's part of the reason I like to work so much; I love it."

By October 1, 1990, Candy was back in his beloved Chicago to shoot his final picture of the year, *Only the Lonely*, another John Hughes production, this time directed *and* written by Chris Columbus.

As principal photography commenced in the Chicagoland area, Columbus's career-saving *Home Alone* was in the process of becoming one of the highest-grossing films in the history of American cinema. While a palpable air of guarded optimism was evident on the set, Columbus was well aware that this time he was flying solo, without a Hughes script to fall back on. Still, with Hughes backing the proceedings, it was no surprise that Candy's co-star was Ally Sheedy, a member of the so-called Brat Pack who had risen to stardom in Hughes's teen drama *The Breakfast Club*. Candy was happy to be co-starring with Jim Belushi, and to be working with two certified Hollywood legends in Maureen O'Hara and Anthony Quinn.

Only the Lonely was a bittersweet drama with only a subtle tinge of comedy. The role of Chicago cop Danny Muldoon, a thirty-eight-year-old man-child who still lives at home with his doting and often overbearing mother, afforded Candy a chance to tone down the slapstick and reveal his vulnerability. The part had an emotional resonance for Candy, having grown up fatherless under the supervision of his mother, Evangeline.

Columbus created the role of Rose Muldoon expressly for O'Hara, the Irish-born leading lady and a frequent co-star of John Wayne; O'Hara had starred in many old Hollywood classics, including *Miracle on 34th Street* and John Ford's *The Quiet Man*. Columbus tracked down O'Hara in Ireland and sent her the script. O'Hara was said to be flattered by the invitation, but before coming out of retirement to do the picture, she first wanted to meet with Candy to see if they had any mother/son chemistry. After a hastily arranged meeting in Chicago, O'Hara was in.

"I looked into those gorgeous eyes," O'Hara told *Tonight Show* host Johnny Carson, "and I said 'Yes, I'll be his mom.' I kind of thought we looked a little bit alike ... He is a fantastic actor."

Candy, an avid fan of classic cinema, particularly O'Hara's work with John Wayne, was especially humbled by her endorsement and her belief in his potential as a serious actor.

"I used to tease him every day," O'Hara later told Tom Snyder on *The Late Late Show*, "and I used to say, 'Who came to work today, John Candy the funnyman, or John Candy *the great actor*?' And he used to sit up straight, and he'd say, 'The actor is here today.'"

Candy, in turn, tried to honour her belief in him by

summoning up every ounce of the dramatic skill he had acquired thus far.

"The relationship between Rose and Danny was one that had to be accurately portrayed," Candy told *Empire* magazine's Frank Sanello. "The tendency was to go over the top and give a real sappy, maudlin performance ... I'm capable of doing a food fight with the best of them, but I know I can do more, and I'd like to be able to show it."

According to Columbus, O'Hara and Candy "just really clicked."

"John truly loved her," says Columbus. "We got the 'real' John Candy, beyond the facade. I just knew that he could deliver a great performance, and I don't think he had ever been cast as a romantic lead in anything until that point. John told me he was very touched that I had written the script especially for him. He said, 'Nobody thinks of me in this kind of role. Thanks so much.' I was like, 'Thank you for doing my film.' And let me just say that, as a movie fan, that was quite a set to be on, to be directing John, Maureen, plus Anthony Quinn. These were some of the greatest days I've ever had on a set."

According to Robert Crane Jr., Candy became star-struck upon meeting Quinn, the Oscar-winning star of *Zorba the Greek* who played O'Hara's amorous neighbour, Nick Acropolis.

"I'd never seen John ask for an autograph from anybody until he met Anthony Quinn," says Crane. "He brought in the box set of *Lawrence of Arabia* LaserDiscs for him to sign. John was so excited. Anthony Quinn? Maureen O'Hara? Come on, are you kidding me?"

Casting Sheedy in the role of Candy's romantic co-star, Theresa, was considered a bold move at the time, considering the apparent mismatch in their size and acting styles that played against romantic comedy convention. But Sheedy had been sufficiently intrigued by this unconventionality to meet with Columbus and Candy for a table read of the script.

Columbus felt that Sheedy and Candy shared a "sweet" and genuine chemistry, and Sheedy later gushed to *Empire* magazine that Candy had a way of making her "feel like the most beautiful actress he's ever worked with."

By now, Columbus was well aware of Candy's capacity for going "off book," so he was flattered that Candy took great care to honour his dialogue exactly as written, and "stayed close to the script with just a few improvisations."

Jim Belushi was not surprised to be working with "John the actor" this time.

"That actor was always there in John," says Belushi. "To be really funny you have to commit to the emotional life of your character, and that tension is where the comedy is. I really believe that when you make somebody laugh really hard, there's an emotional trigger of endorphins, testosterone, that happens in that moment. That feeling of being present in joy, you never forget. Those laughs take you out of your body and out of your misery, out of your mind, out of this world. There's a scene in *Only the Lonely* where my character is laughing at something that John's character says. Well, that was me really laughing, not my character. I'm in the scene with this guy and he touched my heart with his compassion, his joy. His vulnerability and fearlessness about playing the fool brought that joy to people, and they never forgot it."

With all of that emotional truth swirling around, it was perhaps inevitable that Belushi would witness some of the darkness that was always lurking just below Candy's good-natured facade. Belushi once entered Candy's trailer and found him staring down his Pritikin meal, apparently committed to his diet. When Belushi complimented him on his dedication, Candy made a brief speech about how much better he felt after making healthier lifestyle choices. Then Belushi noticed a few other items on the counter, wrapped in tinfoil, including a cheeseburger, a deep-dish pizza, and an Italian beef sandwich. At one point, Candy invited Belushi to look inside the fridge in his trailer.

"There was a whole box of these almond chocolate bars in there," says Belushi. "Johnny says, 'Go on now, Jimmy, take a few.' I brought the beef sandwich over and he ripped it in half, I saved my half, he ate his half, and I told him, 'I think I like your lifestyle change, Johnny.'"

During a location shoot at an Amtrak railway station in Niles, Michigan, Columbus got a glimpse of Candy's innate loneliness.

"I don't think he liked to be alone that much," says Columbus. "We had taken the whole crew to Michigan and stayed over in a hotel. This was a night shoot, so during the day we were supposed to be sleeping. But John was wide awake, and he'd invite me and others to his room to 'discuss some stuff.' He'd be sitting there in a bathrobe, and he had a huge ice bucket filled with sodas and drinks and wine and beer and rum. I'd be like, 'John, I've got to direct tonight, and I've got to get back to sleep.' He'd tell stories for about an hour, and then boom, he'd get back on the phone and call [someone else]. He just didn't want to go to sleep. I don't want to say he lived 'a lavish lifestyle,' but he was also extraordinarily generous, and liked treating everyone around him really well."

Over the US Thanksgiving holiday of November 1990, Candy hired a semi-truck filled with turkeys and distributed them to each and every one of the over two hundred cast and crew members.

"I mean, that was incredible," says Columbus, "but I still couldn't understand how he could come to the set on two hours' sleep and just be right on top of his game. Maybe he just didn't need to sleep that much, but it was always surprising to me."

John Hughes, who was busy directing a moonlighting Belushi in *Curly Sue* at the same time, mostly stayed away from the set, but he kept tabs on what Candy and Columbus were getting up to across town. In an interview with the CBC, Hughes made no secret of how proud he was of Candy for working outside of his comfort zone.

"He did a beautiful job," said Hughes. "To put your comedy tools down and go without them is hard to do... That took a lot of guts to say 'Okay, I'm gonna do a movie that doesn't have jokes in it.' Everybody wants to do a comedy, you know, every dramatic actor wants to do a comedy, but I don't know, the amount of courage that it takes to really say, 'The things I do best, I'm gonna set them aside and try something else.'"

Like in most films made under the auspices of the Hughes Company, the city of Chicago is featured prominently in *Only the Lonely*, including a memorable "first date" sequence filmed in just one night at Comiskey Park, the former home of the Chicago White Sox, just before the aging ballpark was set for demolition. Columbus feels that the Comiskey scene was one of Candy's best performances in the entire film.

"It was a magical night of shooting," says Columbus, "with the real fireworks in the sky. And nowadays that would have been done on a computer."

There is one story from the *Only the Lonely* shoot that everyone who worked on the picture cites as an example of Candy's sense of fairness and justice.

"Maureen had this teeny little trailer," says Belushi, "whereas John had a double pop-out, twin Teton trailer, one of the biggest you can find. When John found out about Maureen's tiny trailer, he was furious and walked her right over to one of the producers and demanded they get a bigger trailer for her, yelling, 'This woman just came out of retirement to play my mother!' The producers hemmed and hawed and refused to deal with it, so John just said, 'Okay, then clean out my trailer, and put Miss O'Hara in that.'"

Crane was there and remembers Candy summoning "the Chongos" to prepare his trailer for the handover. Before they could round up all of Candy's belongings, word came down from the top that a huge trailer had magically appeared for Ms. O'Hara.

"That," says Crane, "is how you did things in the John Candy camp."

Candy managed to wrap his scenes on *Only the Lonely* in time to spend Christmas with his family. His return to Chicago had been inspiring; he had had fun with Belushi, got on well with Sheedy, and was excited to be playing it more or less straight on the screen opposite two of his screen idols.

"I know he was very proud of *Only the Lonely*," says Michael Short. "John was such a good character actor in his comedy that it just made sense that he would be able to do it dramatically."

No one was more surprised than John Candy to have made it to his fortieth birthday at the end of October 1990. His own father had died at thirty-five, and Candy now allowed himself to wonder if maybe he had beaten the actuarial tables by living longer than his old man. Despite his continuing bouts of anxiety and the occasional panic attack, he seemed to have a handle on the life he'd built for himself and his family. He was finally seeing a therapist and even confessed to one journalist his regret that he hadn't started getting help as a child.

While he sorted out his head, Candy's heart was often back in Toronto, cheering on the Argonauts. And over the coming year, Candy's direct involvement in the team would not only raise the fortunes of his beloved Argos, but also come to transform the entire Canadian Football League.

Twenty-Three

True Double Blue

Whether it was jet-setting to sunny Italy to join the stellar ensemble cast of *Once upon a Crime* or sweating in steamy New Orleans to film his dramatic cameo in Oliver Stone's controversial *JFK*, travel was very much on John Candy's agenda throughout 1991. But while acting was still his primary occupation, his major preoccupation was football. Only the former high school offensive tackle was no longer simply cheering on the Double Blue from the stands, he had become a part owner of the franchise.

Candy had by now become a fixture at Los Angeles Kings hockey games and was cultivating a robust friendship with both the team's owner, Bruce McNall, and their newly acquired star player, Wayne Gretzky. In 1990, Candy had called to congratulate McNall after hearing that he and Gretzky had approached the Toronto Argonauts owner Harry Ornest about purchasing the franchise. As Candy later recalled on *The Tonight Show* with

Johnny Carson, the call ended with McNall asking Candy to "forget the congratulations and get your chequebook out."

With some hesitation, Candy agreed to write out a cheque for no more than one million US dollars to become one-third owner of the team he had rooted for his entire life. Even for Candy, it was a lot of money to put down all at once.

"I'm not that rich," Candy insisted to CBC Radio's Peter Gzowski that year, adding that when he signed the cheque, his hands had trembled so much that his bank questioned its authenticity. According to sportswriter Paul Woods, Candy had been cautioned by his family and his business adviser Gary Kress to avoid letting his enthusiasm for the team expose him to excessive financial risk.

"I was told that Rose said to John, 'Okay, You can do this, but you're limiting it to one million bucks,'" says Woods. "'It's a toy, it's fun, but don't put anything more at risk than a million dollars.' Rose would've made sure that John didn't get dinged for anything more."

At a press conference at the SkyDome on February 25, 1991, Candy, Gretzky, and McNall, nicknamed "the Three Amigos" by some in the press corps, publicly confirmed their joint acquisition of the team and their intention to do "something big" this year. In the season leading up to the sale, the Argos had been ascendant, largely on the strength of star running back Michael "Pinball" Clemons, and the team was packing in anywhere between 27,000 and 40,000 fans for their games at the newly opened SkyDome (today known as the Rogers Centre).

"There had been a slight increase in attendance," says Woods, "because fans were curious about the new facility. Then, all of a sudden, Bruce and John and Wayne arrive, and it's like, whoa! As

Argos fans, we couldn't have asked for better owners; the greatest hockey player in the history of the world, the greatest comic actor Canada's ever produced, and Bruce, who at that time was perceived as this dealmaker with a Midas touch—everything he touched appeared to turn to gold. The thinking was that, now, celebrities are going to follow, Hollywood stars, and the like. And to some extent they did."

For Candy, owning the Argos was a chance to combine his love of football with his proven instincts for putting on a show, and he seemed giddy as he promised to bring glamour and pizzazz to the SkyDome, proudly announcing that he had secured Dan Aykroyd and Jim Belushi to appear as the Blues Brothers at the home opener.

"They're going to open up the show for us," Candy told the press. "We'll be having a lot of fun for the people. Everybody should be entertained; we'd like to get families back into the seats here and get a great show."

Shortly after the media event, Candy boarded a plane to Rome to begin filming *Once upon a Crime* for MGM under the guidance of legendary Italian film producer Dino De Laurentiis, and the first-time direction of Eugene Levy. Candy would join an international ensemble cast that also included Richard Lewis, Giancarlo Giannini, Jim Belushi, Cybill Shepherd, Sean Young, and Ornella Muti. The shoot was slated to begin the third week of February and conclude on May 3, at the Pathé studio soundstages in Rome, and various locations in and around the city, plus additional jaunts to Monte Carlo and the French Riviera town of Nice. Candy, however, almost didn't go, fearing that the 1991 Gulf War in Iraq and Kuwait might make it too dangerous to fly. After a few reassuring words from Levy, who reminded him that Italy was far from Baghdad, Candy boarded a first-class flight to join him in Rome.

"And besides," says Robert Crane Jr., "who wouldn't want to wake up every morning in Rome or Monte Carlo, and work with Giancarlo Giannini?"

And when in Rome, thought Candy, why not film a commercial for the Argos? Hiring a local camera crew, one-third of the team's new ownership stood out in front of Rome's iconic Colosseum and hawked Toronto Argonauts season tickets.

"He made this little filmed piece," says Crane, "and it got a great reception back in Toronto. He never lost track of the team, even in exotic Italy."

Belushi recalls a memorable overnight shoot in a Monte Carlo casino, which began filming at the casino's closing time, 3 a.m.

"It's this crazy scene where we're running from table to table," says Belushi. "It was done as an 'in-one,' shooting kind of wide. Then, at the end, our arms are filled with poker chips, and we throw them up in the air and we're giggling. None of that was planned, it was just real."

Co-star Richard Lewis said the three-minute casino scene was Candy at his best on the screen. "He's just running around the casino and winning every game of roulette, throwing chips on people's heads. As director, Eugene knew when to loosen the leash and let the actors play, so he would let John go wild sometimes. John didn't need a script; he always knew exactly what his intentions were in any scene. I respected him as an actor completely, and Eugene let him produce some moments of sheer comedic joy."

Levy did crack the whip a few times, such as insisting that

Candy's character, Augie Morasco, sport a tiny moustache, a nod to the one worn by a character in the 1960 Italian film *Crimen*, on which *Once upon a Crime* was based. Such was Candy's undying trust in Levy that, after first refusing, he eventually acquiesced to the facial hair after a makeup test. Off the set, Candy took to the gastronomic delicacies of the Mediterranean in what Belushi calls full "Johnny Consumer mode."

"Johnny couldn't just order *a couple* of drinks," says Belushi, "it'd be, like, multiple bottles of rum, a tray of Diet Coca-Colas, and many, many glasses of ice. I'd ask, 'Why *Diet* Coke?' He just smiled, 'Ah, Jimmy, it's a lifestyle change. I have to watch my calorie intake.'"

According to Lewis, Candy caused a commotion everywhere he went, with restaurant staff and patrons giddily craning their necks to get a better look at the beloved "American" movie star in their midst. "John was like Moses splitting the Red Sea," said Lewis. "It was crazy. He was one of the most recognizable personalities I've ever known. He had all this talent and a huge persona, but it was coupled with incredible humility, especially for a guy who was known worldwide as one of the funniest character actors and sketch comics of his generation. We became like comedic brothers in Rome. If I could make him laugh, it felt like I'd hit a home run. I loved him."

Chris Columbus briefly dropped in on Candy in Rome to have him record additional dialogue for *Only the Lonely*, and he spent an entire weekend working, dining, and trying in vain to keep up with him. "John was all about opening up these fine Italian restaurants at midnight," says Columbus, "and having these enormous meals catered. There was wine flowing all night. Those were three of the wildest nights of my life."

One night, Dino De Laurentiis threw a lavish party at an elegant restaurant in Monte Carlo as a kind of pep rally for cast and crew. "People would drink a glass of wine," said Lewis, "then throw it into a fireplace. Or they'd eat a lamb chop and throw it at somebody's head. You'd look up and see a goat walking through the restaurant, next to where John was dancing with Sean Young. It was crazy, like a Fellini movie."

In a 2005 promotional video entitled *John Candy: Comic Spirit*, Candy's long-time makeup designer Ben Nye Jr. recalled him renting a sixty-foot yacht stocked with fine foods, vintage wines, and champagne, and treating his personal team to a floating luncheon on the Mediterranean.

Immediately after wrapping his scenes on *Once upon a Crime*, Candy was back on a plane to Toronto to begin his quest to take the Toronto Argonauts all the way to the Grey Cup. Getting there would involve hours and hours of business meetings, long lunches, thousands of miles by car and plane, and more than a few dangerous financial gambles. The work was time-consuming, but by now, his blood pumped Double Blue. He began scaling back his commitments, including *Radio Kandy*, for which he and his producer Doug Thompson had managed to write and record a new show every week for the previous two years. Candy was exhausted by the pace, and with the Argos pre-season kickoff in sight, he simply didn't have the time for it.

Candy set about getting to know the players on his team. In addition to Pinball Clemons, and the strong quarterback they had in Matt Dunigan, Candy, Gretzky, and McNall agreed that if they really were hoping to win the Grey Cup, they would need to acquire a superstar player. But who? The answer was staring at them on the pages of *Sports Illustrated*. In an issue that came out on the same day as their team purchase press event, the magazine's cover story asked the question "Ready for Lift Off: Is Rocket Ismail the Next Megastar?"

Raghib Ramadian Ismail, nicknamed the "Rocket" for his evident and ample speed on the field, was at the time the biggest star in college football, gaining the attention of fans, sportswriters, and National Football League scouts alike for his three stellar seasons at Notre Dame. A runner-up for the Heisman Trophy, the most prestigious award in college football, he was widely favoured as a first-round pick in the NFL draft. While it seemed inconceivable that any Canadian Football League team could coax Ismail to cross the forty-ninth parallel to suit up in an Argonauts uniform, the Three Amigos were all showmen who dared to think big. On April 20, 1991, the three of them put their collective money where their collective mouths were and signed the Rocket for an estimated $18.2 million over four seasons.

"That worked out to about 4.5 million per season," says Woods. "For perspective, he was paid 150 percent of what the rest of the team was making combined. Nobody could believe it until it happened. After hearing John Candy was involved, Ismail allegedly said something like, 'John Candy? You mean *Uncle Buck*?' Candy's involvement sealed the deal, and that deal put the Argos on the map."

The Argos were on Candy's mind as he and Maureen O'Hara went on *The Tonight Show with Johnny Carson* to promote the May 24 release of *Only the Lonely*. At one point in the proceedings, Carson asked the legendary Irish actress if Candy had tried to sell her any football teams lately. Before O'Hara could reply to the joke, a member of the studio audience, possibly planted there by Candy, yelled "Argos!" and Carson swiftly turned to Candy to comment on the team's newest signing.

Carson: "Didn't you guys get the Rocket?"

Candy: "Yes, we signed the Rocket for $26 million [gulp] US," somewhat inflating the price, perhaps for comic effect, while adding that for that kind of money, Candy would personally go on the field and block for his expensive star. "I'm looking after him."

Apart from the football talk, Candy's brief trip to Burbank for *The Tonight Show* also triggered a bout of anxiety. Backstage at the taping, Robert Crane Jr. noted that Candy was more nervous than he'd ever seen him. In Candy's mind, the stakes were high for *Only the Lonely*, which he hoped would honour O'Hara's investment in it, but he was acutely aware that a lot was riding on audiences accepting him in a dramatic role.

"We were in his dressing room," says Crane, "and he pulls his jacket out and shows me the armpits of his shirt and there were these big sweat rings underneath. He says, 'I'm a mess; can I get out of this somehow?' I told him, 'John, no, you can't get out of it. Maureen O'Hara's here, it's Johnny Carson, you're not getting out of it.' He truly wanted to run, but Maureen really loved John, and Carson loved legends, so it was going to be alright."

Candy was more subdued than usual during his *Tonight Show* segment, blushing proudly as O'Hara announced his arrival as a serious leading man. "John Candy comes into his own as a fine, fine, dramatic actor," gushed O'Hara, comparing his screen presence to that of Hollywood legend Charles Laughton. But while Candy was awestruck by her endorsement, Crane noticed him squirming and showing signs of what we would now refer to as imposter syndrome.

"John was also getting compliments from Johnny and [his sidekick] Ed McMahon," says Crane. "I know he was thinking, 'I don't belong here.' He got through the segment just fine, but John didn't say much."

Only the Lonely went on to an estimated worldwide gross of $25 million, and the critical consensus was that O'Hara was right, John Candy "the actor" had arrived. To celebrate, Candy purchased the seventy-year-old curved mahogany bar top used in the film and, at great personal expense, had it shipped back to the Frostbacks office.

Candy, however, would have very little time to tend the bar in the months leading up to the Toronto Argonauts opening day. Since promotion was essential to what the Three Amigos hoped to achieve with the team, Toronto-based vice president Brian Cooper was given the green light to expand the size of the Argos front office. One of Cooper's first hires was Bret Gallagher, who had been working in the Toronto film business. Candy would become the public face of the Argos, appearing on every media outlet in Canada and beyond.

Over time, Candy hired Gallagher to be his point person for all of his Toronto-related business, splitting his time between promotions for the Argos and representing Frostbacks in Toronto. Promoting the team meant flying across the country with Candy as he appeared on local radio and television in every city that had a CFL franchise. Everywhere Candy and Gallagher went, mayhem ensued and headlines would follow.

"He'd been a hundred percent Argos fan since he was a boy," says Gallagher, "and now he got to return as an owner and really wanted to make it successful. He loved talking about football strategies with the players and coaches, and he appreciated what it took to play the game. In each city, he charmed the owners and team operators for the other CFL teams, and each of them felt close to him after he had taken them to dinner."

Meanwhile, back in Toronto, Candy introduced himself to every single employee in the Argonauts organization, from the front office to the locker room, shaking hands with players like Dunigan, Clemons, Ismail, and offensive lineman Kelvin Pruenster, conferring a fraction of his excitement into each of them. When one player told him that he loved to have a cappuccino after practice, Candy had an espresso machine installed in the locker room, and it was not uncommon for some of the players to find themselves invited to Candy's Queensville farm for drinks and a home-cooked meal.

While dreams of winning the Grey Gup dominated Candy's waking thoughts as the team's July 1991 home opener approached, he put his head down to prepare to film his role as the dubious and flamboyant New Orleans attorney Dean Andrews in Oliver Stone's *JFK*, with a cast headed by Kevin Costner, plus notable supporting players like Jack Lemmon, Walter Matthau, Ed Asner, and Tommy Lee Jones. Candy hit it off with another support player, Gary Oldman, who played Lee Harvey Oswald. According to Crane, Candy had been a big fan of Oldman in the film *Sid and Nancy*, which he would watch regularly on LaserDisc.

Oldman and Candy even hashed out a loose plan to stage a live theatrical production of *Henry IV*, possibly in New York's Central Park, in which Oldman would take the title role and Candy would play Falstaff. While the production never came to pass, the idea was emblematic of where Candy's dramatic intentions lay at the time.

"John was very focused about doing a good job in *JFK*," says Gallagher, who watched the actor memorizing his script "sides" in the Argos office. "John really studied for the part, learned his lines, and rehearsed hard for the role. He wanted it, and he got it."

Crane also marvelled at the amount of work Candy put into what amounted to a cameo sitting across a dining table from Costner as the Louisiana district attorney, Jim Garrison. "This was a serious acting job for him," says Crane, "so he really dedicated himself to playing this big dramatic eight-page scene with Costner. [Oliver] Stone thought John was a great actor. He had really enjoyed his work in *Only the Lonely* and *Uncle Buck*, [so] he knew John could handle this. We went down to New Orleans around the end of June, so it wasn't horribly humid yet, and stayed in some hotel within walking distance of the French Quarter."

For three solid days in the hotel, Crane helped Candy to perfect his Dean Andrews by reading Costner's part as he rehearsed the scene. "John memorized it, of course," says Crane. "That week John didn't party or mess around that whole time because he knew this was an Oliver Stone film, and it had to be perfect. He was so stressed about it that he got a huge cold sore on the day before the shoot. This thing looked like Mount Vesuvius, and while it did come down, the makeup people did some magic too."

Jennifer Candy later told *The Hollywood Reporter*'s Ryan Parker that her father's work in *JFK* was among her personal favourites, and remembered Candy studiously practising at home to perfect a convincing Cajun accent. "He is so good in it," she told Parker in 2016. "He had a dialect coach, and he worked night and day on that script ... We were having water fights with our cousin while Dad was trying to learn lines, and we did get yelled at because we were being too loud. It was a 'dad' yell. He never yelled."

The final cut of Stone's widely debated film clocked in at just over three hours, and even that was after several scenes had been cut down or out. Reportedly, one of Stone's earliest cuts removed Candy's scene entirely. After aggressive lobbying from Costner, Stone reinserted a more concise version of their exchange, which remained in the final cut. Stone later wrote an apology letter to a heartbroken Candy upon reinserting his scene and would continue to praise Candy as a "significant dramatic actor" in interviews.

Yet even while filming his big scene, Candy's mind was consumed with thoughts of the Argos. Shortly after Stone called "Cut" and released him from the set, he and Crane were on a plane back to Toronto to head right into the fray. In fact, he was still wearing his 1960s vintage cotton suit and dark Ray-Ban shades when he landed in Toronto for the Argo pep rally celebration the night before the home opener. The team had already opened their season by losing in Ottawa, but as far as Candy, Gretzky, and McNall, and all Toronto sports fans, were concerned, their home opener at the SkyDome, on July 18, 1991, was the true kickoff for the season.

"As soon as the roof opened on the SkyDome," Pinball Clemons later told one reporter, "it was showtime, baby. Every week."

Twenty-Four

Johnny Toronto

John brought Hollywood to the Argos," says Toronto sports journalist Paul Woods. "It was his idea to get Dan Aykroyd to bring the Blues Brothers, including Steve Cropper and Duck Dunn, at the cost of a million dollars, just for this one gig to their opening home game. And that continued that season whenever there were people filming up in Toronto, John would get on the phone and get them out to the games."

On game day, Aykroyd was joined by Jim Belushi, filling in for his late Blues Brother John, along with a party flown up from Los Angeles in a star-filled Boeing 727 whose passengers included Candy, Gretzky, and McNall, along with Martin Short and actress Mariel Hemingway, no doubt capitalizing on the event to promote the impending August release of *Delirious*. Likewise, Candy's *Only the Lonely* co-star Ally Sheedy was on hand, as was Bob Einstein, who was in town to film his *Super Dave Osborne* television series (and would later become known for his recurring role on HBO's *Curb Your Enthusiasm*). Forty-one thousand fans revelled in both the sideshow and the game itself.

Before the game had even begun, the entire packed SkyDome went mad upon Candy's entrance into the stadium. And Candy was loving it, obliging the hundreds and hundreds of autograph seekers throughout the game. According to Dan Aykroyd, it was one of the most exhilarating nights of Candy's life, and his own.

"John did his triumphal walk around the arena," says Aykroyd. "He was like a Roman emperor coming back into the Forum after a battle. It was a great story: 'Toronto boy makes good, Canadian and international movie star comes back and saves the Argonauts.' It rivalled the trireme races in Rome for years, and it was just a spectacular display of affection for this guy. He walked around and did the Roman salute with all his friends and neighbours, me and a few others, all of us walked with him."

"He was walking in with McNall and Gretzky," says Dave Thomas, "but they were cheering for John. Danny Aykroyd turned to me, and he went, 'Look! He's done it! He's Johnny Toronto! He owns this town.' Those of us who knew him had been able to see the evolution of John from the guy who had no money, who would order a limo just to *look like* he owned the town, and it was a wonderful thing to see. Toronto loved him, and he couldn't go anywhere where people didn't recognize him."

During the halftime show, Candy joined in on the fun, dancing and singing along with the Blues Brothers as they adapted Robert Johnson's "Sweet Home Chicago" to "Sweet Home Toronto" for the occasion.

"Candy was up there, wearing the fedora and really looking the part," says Woods, who was in attendance. "It was just a magical night. So much love washed over John in the stadium that night."

Aykroyd says that not only was Candy an "outstanding host" to the fans, but the fans picked up on his good karma. "He'd been such a true friend in times of darkness and the troubles," says Aykroyd, "and just a sweet, wonderful, loving, funny man, and a supporter of all [manner of] enterprise."

When the game ended, the hometown team had defeated the visiting Hamilton Tiger-Cats by an impressive 41–18 margin, and Candy joined Aykroyd, Belushi, and their invited guests for a celebration at the Ultrasound Lounge on Queen Street West.

"We had a massive party that went on till the wee hours," says Aykroyd. "And it was one of the greatest night parties I've ever been to."

The magical evening would set the stage for the next two years in which Toronto Argonauts games would become the place to be.

"You never knew who was going to show up," says Crane, "and John was like the little kid again in the sandbox. Talk about a dream come true. It was remarkable."

Candy's enthusiasm for the CFL was not only contagious for the fans; his financial leap of faith with the Argos most likely saved the league itself, particularly in the case of the cash-poor Ottawa Rough Riders, whose financial prospects improved just in the nick of time, largely thanks to Candy's national promotion of the league. Candy personally worked at getting local television channels to lift their so-called blackouts of local games. Candy's football revolution would be televised.

Delirious finally opened on August 9, 1991, and was widely considered an embarrassment at the box office. It had cost an estimated $18 million to make yet only earned a tenth of that in its first weekend in the US and Canada, with a worldwide gross that barely tipped $5.5 million. And while even the critics pilloried the film, Candy was too busy becoming the de facto Prime Minister of Canadian Football to even register it.

Yet, even amid the adulation Candy received as he toured the cities of the CFL, his old familiar anxieties would sometimes sneak up on him when the sheer volume of fans threatened to induce panic in him or delay his schedule. He began designating Crane or Gallagher to run interference with the autograph-seeking fans, whom he couldn't stand to refuse.

"Our routine," says Gallagher, "was that John would say, 'I want to sign some stuff, but...' and then I'd grab him, look at my watch, and say, 'Come on John, we gotta go now or we'll miss the plane.' I was the bad guy, and it was my job to get him out, but John made it clear that it was always important to be kind, and to be seen as kind, everywhere we went. He'd say, 'Treat the doorman as well as the president of the organization. Be nice to everybody.' He would always pick up the tab. The rule was 'If I can't grab the check, you grab the check and I'll pay you back. And I don't want anyone thinking they can buy us.'"

According to Gallagher, Candy made it clear that, no matter how much he enjoyed a big paycheque, he couldn't be bought, and he even turned down "a lot of money" to do a Nike Super Bowl commercial with Steve Martin recreating their motel bed scene from *Planes, Trains and Automobiles.*

While Candy was "always on" in public, Gallagher recalls him being hyperconscious of the way he was being seen and what people were saying about him. "We had our private time in the hotel room," says Gallagher, "where he'd just be watching

TV, having breakfast. But he couldn't hide when he was out in public. When the CFL teams would invite him to their sponsored dinners, John would always be at the head table, but he wouldn't eat in public. Dinner and drinks would wrap up at around eleven o'clock and John would say, 'I'm hungry. Let's go.' He told me that, because of being a big guy, he didn't want people taking a picture of him shovelling something in his mouth. He was really aware that he was a big star, so he didn't want that to be a story.

"John never did *The Howard Stern Show* because Howard would insult John on the show all the time by joking about his size. When you're rich and famous and powerful, you can do whatever you want, including not listening to people and/or doctors. John didn't. The term that John would use was 'the gallows,' as in, 'You question me, you're in my gallows.' Like Brian Cooper? Eventually he ended up in John's gallows. On the other hand, his good friend Norman Jewison, who he revered as a film director and producer, could needle John about his weight, and for some reason never wound up in the gallows. But anybody else, he didn't want to hear."

Jennifer Candy was only eleven years old at the time but later remembered how "surreal and epic" it was to see her father's glee in owning the team he'd supported his entire life. "The thing with my dad," she told the CBC's Malcolm Kelly, "was you don't just go half in, you go whole in, and he was so passionate about it—he wanted to travel through Canada, and he was not being paid for the promo stuff… That much energy, and that much love, the team had to benefit."

The entire Candy clan became part of the Argos extended family. Jennifer and Christopher were regularly shuttled down Highway 400 from the family farm in Queensville to Candy's private Skybox at the SkyDome, along with their cousins and friends, to catch Argos home games. Candy would even celebrate Rose's birthday with an annual touch football game, known as "the Rose Bowl," for family and friends and some of the Argos. Aykroyd later joked that Candy and his family had spent so much time going back and forth from Queensville that Highway 400 should be renamed "the John Candy Memorial Highway."

"At that time in his life," Chris Candy later told Paul Woods, their father had enjoyed "a cartoon show, a huge acting career, a radio show, and he was producing films. All top-level stuff, but it was pretty obvious that he really loved what he was doing with the Argos."

Candy's team paid him back that season by going all the way to the seventy-ninth annual Grey Cup game, held in Winnipeg, Manitoba, on November 24, 1991, with the Argonauts pitted against the Calgary Stampeders. The first CFL final to ever be played in Winnipeg, it was also the coldest in league history, with the temperature at Winnipeg Stadium barely touching −16°C; with the windchill, it was −18°C at kickoff.

Martin Short and his son Oliver, then five, flew up from LA with the Candy and Gretzky families on the Los Angeles Kings jet. "We flew into Winnipeg," says Short, "saw the game, and then flew right back at the end of the night. It was a big day for John."

Candy had made his presence known, and felt, all over the city of Winnipeg during the week leading up to the Grey Cup. That week, Bret Gallagher's brother Dan Gallagher hosted the nationally televised CFL awards ceremony. Late into the program, Candy made an unscheduled cameo appearance holding up a handmade sign that read "Buy Argos Season Tickets."

"The place went berserk," says Woods. "He had basically put his career on hold and had been making the rounds at radio stations at five in the morning to tell people to buy tickets. He was working it, man. He put everything into the league that year."

All through his rookie season, Rocket Ismail had lived up to the hype, and by the final whistle, the Toronto Argonauts had defeated the Calgary Stampeders by a margin of 36–21. They had done exactly what John Candy had promised all along—brought the Grey Cup to Toronto. It had been worth the money.

Sports Illustrated reporter Peter King described the atmosphere after the game in what he called a "champagne-drenched" locker room, as veteran defensive lineman Harold Hallman put Candy in bear hug and whispered in his ear, "Thanks for coming in and saving us. You guys, I love you."

"Candy," King wrote, "wiped away a tear."

The Toronto Argonauts appeared to be on the crest of a dynasty, but a series of unfortunate events and inevitable defections would see the team's fortunes falter in the following seasons. For one brief shining moment, though, John Candy was on top of the world. In many ways, the Argos' rapid rise had been a Cinderella story, but there would be no "happily ever after" to Candy's gridiron fairy tale. After that triumphant day in chilly Winnipeg, the following year would be one of roller-coaster emotions. A dark "double blue" cloud filled with his now-familiar panic attacks and the ever-present spectre of mortality would cause him to actively seek counselling for his anxiety. After what sportswriter Paul Woods dubbed "The Year of the Rocket," the sophomore slump would see the Argos crash to Earth in a way that had seemed unimaginable the previous November. After quarterback Matt Dunigan defected to the

Winnipeg Blue Bombers, Candy reached out to NFL star Joe Montana, as Montana would reveal to broadcaster Rich Eisen in 2023, confirming he had met with Candy on more than one occasion to discuss coming to the Argonauts. But this time, there was not enough money to lure another NFL star to Toronto.

In 1992 the Argos finished dead last in the CFL East, failing to make the playoffs. And while the situation on the field looked grim, it was even worse in the team's office, where the organization's precarious financial situation was in freefall. As would later be proven in a court of law, Bruce McNall's financing had been built on shaky foundations, and his accounting was even shakier; in the words of Bret Gallagher, McNall's business model was "a Ponzi scheme."

"The wheels started coming off when the bills weren't getting paid in Toronto," says Gallagher. "And news of this would get back to John, right? The creditors were lined up, not getting paid. When Bruce didn't have any money, it just really started to come apart. I think Gary Kress, who handled John's money at the time, may have advised John to not seed any more money into this endeavour."

Ticket sales plummeted, and Raghib Ismail's astronomical salary was becoming a major drain on the bottom line. Then, after the letdown of the 1992 season, the Rocket inevitably blasted off to the NFL.

Owning the team had been Candy's fantasy since childhood, but the writing was on the wall that McNall was in even deeper financial trouble than anyone knew. Candy hung in for one more year, but he had become disenchanted with the whole business side of ownership. While he still attended as many home games as he could, he mostly dispensed with travelling with the team. His anxiety had increased to the point where he was no longer out in the stands or down at the bench, preferring to remain within the comfort of his lavishly renovated family Skybox. Around this time, Candy was approached by producers Robert Lantos and Steven DeNure about starring in a film based on Toronto author Paul Quarrington's 1989 novel *Whale Music*, in which he would portray a reclusive and out-of-shape 1960s pop-music genius named Desmond Howl, loosely based on the story of the Beach Boys' Brian Wilson. Late into the negotiations, Candy would pull out of the film, in part over certain nude scenes, and the role went to the actor Maury Chaykin.

But before negotiations broke off, DeNure accompanied Quarrington to an Argonauts game for one last discussion with Candy, along with Candy's mother, Evangeline, and Wayne Gretzky's celebrated father, Walter Gretzky. According to Quarrington's friend and frequent producer David Johnston, their convivial meeting ended badly when Candy suffered a panic attack after the game.

"Paul told me that he and John were in the stands when [Candy] was confronted by the crowds leaving after the game," says Johnston. "Apparently, it was so overwhelming that he had to return to his private box and wait until the crowd cleared out of the stadium."

To a certain extent, Candy's acting life had been on the back burner while he had been putting all of his energies into the Argos. It appeared to certain Hollywood insiders that Candy might have taken his eye off the ball when it came to his film career. As the '90s commenced, significant changes were in order: Candy's agent John Gaines, at APA, was out, and Guy McElwaine, at International Creative Management (ICM), was in. One of the first announcements to come out of the new deal was Candy's intention to star in the Hollywood Pictures production of *Gone Fishing* (a.k.a. *Going Fishing*) that would have reunited him with Rick Moranis, but that project never materialized. Candy soon left ICM, while Moranis would soon retire from acting altogether.

Gallagher recalls being in the car with Candy on the way to a football game when one of his agents might call. "It would be Guy McElwaine or Ron Meyer," says Gallagher. "John would tell me, 'I'm taking time off from my career to do this right for the Argos.' The agents would ask, 'John, did you get that script? We need you to do this. Would you do that?' And he'd say, 'Guys, I want to, but I'm doing the Argos thing right now. Don't worry, I'll get back to work. I'll find something that we'll do.' And so, yeah, there was some pressure to get back to work."

While Candy's relationship with McNall had cooled, they were still on speaking terms as it became clear that the team was in financial trouble. Candy likely had no idea that McNall had discreetly instructed the club's executive vice president, Brian Cooper, to find a buyer for the team. Candy's football dreams had peaked, but his film career had stayed reasonably hot enough that he could seriously think about getting back to work. As always, the biggest challenge was finding another perfect role, and with John Hughes increasingly out of the picture, Candy found himself fielding a number of offers that, for one reason or another, failed to get off the ground.

Twenty-Five

Fumbles, Panics, and Reunions

Candy was still hot. He'd received strong notices for his cameo in *JFK*, and director Oliver Stone was telling anyone who would listen that he foresaw a "significant dramatic career" in Candy's future. "He was excellent as Dean Andrews," Stone later remarked, praising Candy's accent work and what he referred to as a "marvelous sense of timing," and affirming his stated belief that comedy actors such as Candy were "equally valid as dramatic actors, but for some reason much of the prestige goes to dramatic actors whereas comedy is overlooked."

In 2022, Eugene Levy told *Forbes* magazine's Scott King that Candy had made a logical leap from comedy to drama because, in the end, "John was a great actor. He spent his life doing comedy, but he was *acting*."

And more recently, comedian and actor Patton Oswalt praised Candy's attention to authenticity, not just in the dialect work, but in capturing the essence of the *real* Dean Andrews.

"If you go back and watch footage of the actual Andrews," says Oswalt, "Candy is doing a brilliantly researched and constructed recreation of him. That is *exactly* how that guy talked, Candy got his rhythms and his energy. There actually wasn't any warmth in Dean Andrews, so unlike most Candy characters, you're not rooting for him. Candy absolutely sinks his claws into it and goes deep."

Having proven that he could bring the appropriate gravitas to his characters in *Only the Lonely* and *JFK*, Candy went through what Bret Gallagher refers to as "piles and piles" of scripts back at the Frostbacks office in search of projects with similar dramatic heft; he was now willing not just to act, but to produce and possibly even direct. He had even begun to develop a screenplay of his own, *Our Father*, in which Candy would have played a high-living priest in a posh Beverly Hills parish who gets sent to urban Detroit to work in the inner city. Candy had always had good fortune with fish-out-of-water stories and imagined this one being a reverse of Eddie Murphy's highly successful *Beverly Hills Cop*, only this time with a priest collar and rosaries.

"It was a brilliant, character-driven piece," says Gallagher. "I know John was really proud that he had thought of it, so his brain was working overtime fleshing it out in his mind and hoping to bring in a screenwriter for it. He had all these other ideas bubbling under."

Also bubbling in the background was a script they had acquired, *Haulin' Ashes*, which would have cast Candy as a low-level employee at a Madison Avenue ad firm tasked with taking the cremated remains of his boss on a road trip across America. The premise was so John Hughes–like that it was a wonder Hughes hadn't written it. And according to Gallagher, director Quentin Tarantino had initially approached Candy to play Mr. Wolf in *Pulp Fiction*.

"I remember being in John's office," says Gallagher, "when he handed me Tarantino's bound copy of the *Pulp Fiction* script, marked 'For Your Eyes Only.' As a general rule, John didn't like to read scripts, so he just handed it to me to look at for him. I read it in half an hour, and I told him right away, 'This is fucking great.'"

Comedy producer and writer Luciano Casimiri was working with Candy's Toronto-based crew at the time and recalls Candy and his advisers taking Tarantino's offer very seriously. "John was told that this was going to change everybody's career," says Casimiri. "I mean, everybody was doing this movie, John Travolta, Samuel Jackson, Bruce Willis, and Uma Thurman. The reason I think he passed on it was the violence. He had been doing a lot of family things around this time, so he was in that zone."

Another one of Candy's unrealized visions entailed a partnership with two of Canada's most successful filmmakers and producers: Norman Jewison, and John Brunton from Insight Productions. The two had met with Candy about having him appear at their fundraising gala for the Canadian Film Centre in North York. Brunton believed that a Tribute to John Candy night could be at the heart of their charity affair, but while Candy politely bowed out of the self-aggrandizing event entirely, he and his producer at Frostbacks, Patrick Whitley (formerly of *SCTV*), seized upon the invitation to brainstorm about the possibility of creating a major Canadian film studio back home in Toronto. One idea was to partner with Jewison and Alliance Films' Robert Lantos to create what would potentially have been Canada's biggest independent film studio. While Candy had initially been very excited about the idea of putting his beloved Toronto on the world film map, enthusiasm petered out and the merger became yet another dream that never came to fruition.

The early months of 1992 saw the debuts of a few projects that Candy had shot in the previous year. *Once upon a Crime* was released on March 6, 1992, to underwhelming box office receipts and a near-unanimous chill from the critics. On April 17, the US cable channel Showtime debuted a feature-length, live-action adaptation of the animated cartoon *Boris and Natasha*, featuring two Cold War–era spy characters spun off from Jay Ward's evergreen 1959 cartoons, *The Adventures of Rocky and Bullwinkle*. Directed by Charles Martin Smith, and starring Dave Thomas and Sally Kellerman in the title roles, Candy turned in a cameo appearance as a shoeshiner named Kalishak. Two weeks later, Candy was back on Showtime in an episode of *Shelley Duvall's Bedtime Stories* in which he narrated "Blumpoe the Grumpoe Meets Arnold the Cat."

Later that year, Candy joined an ensemble cast that included many of his mutual friends from the Second City and *Godspell* days. Three years after Gilda Radner's death from cancer, a live stage event called *Friends of Gilda* was staged at Toronto's Elgin Theatre on September 26, 1992. The event, which served as both a bittersweet reunion and a fundraiser for ovarian cancer research, was directed by Martin Short, and included old friends Catherine O'Hara, Eugene Levy, Andrea Martin, Dave Thomas, Victor Garber, and Stephen Schwartz. Paul Shaffer was the musical director, and the whole show was filmed and lovingly assembled by Perry Rosemond for a ninety-minute television special broadcast on the CBC the following year.

Candy had always played up his supposed disdain for *Godspell*, but according to Short, Candy didn't really hate the show, he just knew that saying so among the crowd at 1063 Avenue Road would always get a laugh. Short and Candy had first met, in fact, backstage after a *Godspell* performance in May of 1973.

"He did his 'I hate *Godspell*' bit at the Gilda memorial," says Short; "he came onstage and said, 'I always hated *Godspell*.' But it was because he just got so exhausted by us *Godspell* people."

"You see," Candy explained in his short monologue onstage at the Elgin, "I was never in *Godspell*. And for the past twenty years I have been reminded of that at every function we go to where these people start singing 'Day by Day.'"

Backstage at the *Friends of Gilda* concert, Michael Short, one of the writers of the show, witnessed Candy having yet another anxiety attack in the wings. "John came in and says, 'I'm in a full-blown panic attack right now.' I said, 'Oh fuck, man.' Now, John knew that I had also had panic attacks in my life and we had compared experiences and what we did to cope and so on. So I said, 'Well, you don't have to get up and do anything.' He said, 'No, no. I gotta go on.' So, he and Eugene and Joe got up and did an old Second City sketch called 'Rehearsal,' just the three of them, no props, in front of a curtain, for this packed house, and he killed."

In "Rehearsal," Candy portrayed a nervous stage actor who forgets his lines, the perfect cover for his apparent distress.

"And John was just hilarious," says Michael Short. "It was like nothing had ever happened. But when he came offstage, it was clear he was still having this panic attack. Somehow, he had interrupted it to get up in front of an audience and perform. It was remarkable that he could just do that."

Joe Flaherty had also noticed Candy struggling to catch his breath backstage. "I asked him what was wrong," says Flaherty, "and John said, 'I'm having one of my panic attacks, and I'm having a real hard time dealing with it.' Now, Dave [Thomas] told me he had also seen the occasional panic attack, and we had wondered if it was something with John's heart, because I remembered that back when we were doing *SCTV*, we'd gotten word that John's brother Jim had had a heart attack. Jim was also a big guy, although not as big as John. So I don't know if he had a sense that he wasn't long for the world, but you know, he rarely shared that dark stuff with me."

Besides the Argos' declining fortunes in 1992, another Toronto-based disappointment came after Candy had accepted an invitation from the Academy of Canadian Cinema & Television to host their thirteenth annual Genie Awards ceremony, to be broadcast live from the Metro Toronto Convention Centre on November 22, 1992. Candy's own producer, Patrick Whitley, was to helm the broadcast, and Candy also brought in a few of his own writers, including Luciano Casimiri. But one week before the program, the Canadian broadcast trade magazine *Playback* ran a print ad for CBC's telecast of the Genie Awards featuring a photo of Candy under the headline: "This year we have a big host, a really *big* host. I mean, a *really, really big* host."

"It was a fat joke at John's expense," says Casimiri. "So John hit the roof and told them, 'I'm not doing your show.' We were all called in on a Sunday, and I just remember having that angst of a twenty-seven-year-old writer, asking, 'Wait, so are we fired because our boss quit?'"

"They had John's photo there with this reference to *his size*," adds Whitley, "which you just didn't do with John. I knew right then that he wasn't going to do this show. When I called him and I told him about the ad, he said, 'I'm out.' Everybody tried to convince him to do it, but it was over. I remember overhearing George Anthony, who was running [the CBC] entertainment [division] at the time, pleading with John. I said, 'You guys are wasting your time. He's made his decision. You did a bad thing. You crossed the line.'"

Back in California, Candy's film career was slowly picking up again. While the world of professional sports ownership was becoming a thorn in his side, he was happy to appear in a pair of sports-themed movies.

Candy lent his voice to the baseball movie called *Rookie of the Year,* directed by *Home Alone* star Daniel Stern. Candy's character, the announcer Cliff Murdoch, was loosely based on two legendary real-life Chicago Cubs sports announcers, Harry Caray and "Chubby Cubbie" Jack Brickhouse. It was an easy job for Candy, who by now had plenty of experience doing voice work, and he took no screen credit for his efforts. But in February 1993, Candy would get to apply some of the first-hand experience he had gained with his young Argonauts to his next major role.

He would be playing the coach of a team of underdogs with outsize dreams. Only this time, the sport wasn't football, it was Olympic bobsledding. And the underdogs were a four-man Jamaican bobsled team who had never even seen snow. For Candy, going downhill fast would prove to be an unlikely way back to the top of the mountain.

Twenty-Six

Cool Runnings

Our Father, who art in Calgary, Bobsled be thy name. Thy kingdom come, gold medals won, on Earth as it is in Turn Seven. With Liberty and Justice for Jamaica and Haile Selassie. Amen."

The above invocation, spoken by John Candy's character Irv Blitzer, a fictionalized depiction of the real-life coach of Jamaica's Olympic bobsled team, was indicative of the tongue-in-cheek tone of the many inspirational speeches in Disney's family-friendly sports dramedy *Cool Runnings*, which not only reaped gold medal receipts at the box office, but also signified a return to winning form for Candy at a time when both of his careers, as an actor and as a football team owner, had been on thin ice.

Based on the true story of the Jamaican bobsled team that charmed the 1988 Winter Olympics in Calgary, what elevated *Cool Runnings* from being the sort of one-joke high-concept sketch comedy premise that Candy and his *SCTV* castmates had invented countless times before, was Candy himself, who brought a genuine heart to the proceedings. A passion project for Disney's Dawn Steel, *Cool Runnings* had begun as *Blue Maaga*, a gritty drama about four economically challenged athletes rising up from the mean streets of Kingston, Jamaica. After Steel brought in additional writers to give the story a lighter tone, the resulting screenplay was inspirational family fare, and closer in tone to Disney's successful hockey film *The Mighty Ducks*.

Candy was the best-known member of the cast, which included one-named actor Leon as Derice Bannock, Rawle D. Lewis as Junior Bevil, Malik Yoba as Yul Brenner, and Doug E. Doug as Sanka Coffie. Candy's disgraced former Olympian, Irv Blitzer, was very loosely based on the actual coach of the Jamaican team, Howard Siler, an accomplished former American bobsled champion who had never been involved in any such scandal. Fact and fiction were blurred frequently in the film, as director Jon Turteltaub blended actual television footage from the 1988 Olympics with his own fictional action and generally didn't let historical accuracy get in the way of a good story.

"We would never get away today with the changes we made to the true story," Turteltaub later told *Entertainment Weekly*'s Samantha Highfill. "The tone is the same. The ambition is the same. The absurdity was the same. And the main key events were the same."

To take advantage of the snow in Calgary, Candy and his Chongos reported to the former site of the Winter Olympics on February 1, 1993, to begin filming the competitive bobsled sequences that happen at the end of the film. According to Robert Crane Jr., Candy had been warned that Dawn Steel had a reputation as a really fierce producer, but Candy charmed her within minutes of his arrival on the set.

"In his typical form," says Crane, "John just deflated any tense feelings by walking right up to her and making a joke about being scared to meet her, then hugging her. She was instantly in love with this guy."

According to published reports at the time, Candy was drawn to the team's underdog story and, having successfully leaned toward the dramatic end of his toolkit in his most recent roles, relished the opportunity to display some genuine humanity on the screen without the need for big laughs.

"From my character's point of view, these guys are a joke," Candy said. "They'll never succeed. We're in Jamaica. There are no sleds here, no snow. They have no idea what a bobsled is. Yet they're determined."

According to Crane, Candy took on the role of leader both on and off the camera, coaching his four young co-stars, many of whom had little or no experience acting on film or, for that matter, being in the snow. Candy's recent experiences mentoring the young players of the Toronto Argonauts had prepared him to shepherd these young actors. He was no longer John Candy, says Crane, but Coach Irv, guiding his four neophytes through the biggest project they had ever been in.

"John invited them all up to his Calgary hotel room so they could start socializing as a team," says Crane, "sharing laughs, hopes, and fears. It was just the way John could draw on his stage training to lose himself in roles. Jon Turteltaub might have had preconceptions about working with 'the movie star John Candy,' but now he was just working with this nice man who coached the bobsled team."

As a team-building exercise, Candy booked out an Olympic bobsled run, while the actors playing the team went through an intensive fourteen-day training camp, which included weight lifting and becoming reasonably proficient in handling and helming a bobsled.

"John was very kind to us," Rawle D. Lewis told *People*'s Ben Trivett. "He was very open—you didn't feel like it was John's movie, you felt like it was our movie."

Malik Yoba recalled a team dinner in which Candy presented each of the "bobsledders" with music that he thought represented each character, while Doug E. Doug, whose Sanka Coffie character sings the memorable couplet "Feel the rhythm! Feel the rhyme! Get on up, it's bobsled time," was also touched by the gesture, telling Samantha Highfill that "the long and short of it" was that Candy "was a beautiful guy."

Candy was also happy to let his young co-stars get all the biggest laughs in the film. According to Crane, he became more like "a surrogate father figure" to them, while at other times taking on the role of "team mascot, brother, and even an uncle figure. He was the *protector*, on and off the set."

In one of Candy's best moments in the film, Blitzer confesses to Derice about his shameful past and what motivated him to cheat in the first place.

"It's quite simple, really," Blitzer tells the young bobsledder. "I had to win. You see, Derice, I'd made winning my whole life. And when you make winning your whole life, you have to keep on winning, no matter what. You understand that?"

Blitzer closes his remarks with a line that could have been just as true for Candy, concluding that while winning a gold medal was a wonderful thing, "if you're not enough without one, you'll never be enough with one."

As successful as Candy had been in his show business career, there was always a sense that he need to improve some aspect of himself—lose the weight, become a better actor, manage his career better, provide for his family. That family was a lifeline when things got dark, and he liked to have them come along wherever he was shooting, and thus they were there in both Calgary and Jamaica. According to Juul Haalmeyer, the costumer from his *SCTV* family whom Candy had convinced to come work on *Cool Runnings*, having family there was "a lovely thing for John."

"He had Rosemary and the kids there for the whole shoot," says Haalmeyer, "so that was great, because then it's like real family. I played dominoes or poker with him every day in the trailer, and I'm so glad we had that time with him in Jamaica because it was so special. It turned out to be the last time I ever saw him."

Apart from the occasional anxiety attacks when location shoots were swarmed by fans, episodes that only those in the know were aware of, Haalmeyer recalls laughing with Candy as they reminisced about their times together at *The David Steinberg Show* and *SCTV*.

"He also had all kinds of entourage there," says Haalmeyer. "He had Bobby Crane, and his trainer Kelvin [Pruenster, an offensive tackle from the Toronto Argonauts], and he just wanted me there as his 'dresser' and to keep his continuity, because he was comfortable with me."

While Haalmeyer was alarmed at how much larger Candy had gotten since they had last worked together, he knew not to confront him about it. "We never spoke about things like weight gain. As far as I was concerned that was between him and his family, and I didn't want to intrude on that. Still, when I started with him, John was a 44 tall, and when we did *Cool Runnings*, he was a 58 tall."

While Candy had hired Pruenster to be his personal trainer while shooting in Calgary, he was an imposing figure who functioned as much as a bodyguard, using his immense size to eclipse Candy in a crowd. "If we walked in formation towards people, nobody could see him," Pruenster later told writer Paul Woods. "He was a big man, but with a big winter coat I could block him out. I was like a walking wall."

As big as he was, Pruenster wasn't always able to provide the kind of crowd control that Candy might need on, say, a simple trip to a Calgary shopping mall. While Candy tried to camouflage himself with sunglasses and a cap, a panic-inducing mayhem was likely to ensue if his cover was blown. This happened one afternoon when an excited store clerk shouted his name with glee, and what Pruenster later described as an "avalanche of kids" began to flood him at the shopping centre.

"There's thousands of kids and people in this mall," Pruenster told Woods, "and we're trapped in this store ... Some 14-year-old girls see him, and screaming starts. Everyone in the mall hears it and their heads all swing around. And then everyone starts screaming: 'John Candy!' Hundreds of high-school kids. We're in this little shop and they're like 20, 30, 50 feet thick ... Some of them are crying."

As Pruenster recalled, Candy became "completely panicked" as the hulking Argonaut cleared the actor's way, like an icebreaker, through the sea of young fans. Actor Peter Outerbridge, who played Josef Grool in the film, later expressed his admiration for the efficiency with which Pruenster pulled Candy away from overly aggressive fans in these situations. But he also added that being in Candy's presence showed him what it looked like to appreciate the fans.

"[John] would refuse to stop signing autographs," Outerbridge told Highfill; "he would refuse to stop shaking hands, because he really felt that the fans, his audience were who made him."

Once the snowy Calgary segments were in the can, the entire production shifted to Ocho Rios and Montego Bay, Jamaica. One published report detailed a massive party that Candy threw for the cast and crew at the luxurious Round Hill Villa resort, a favourite Montego Bay hideout for the likes of Paul McCartney and Ralph Lauren. The actor Leon frequently invited Candy and the cast over to his rented house after a long day's shooting to have his chef cook dinner for everyone, closing out the evening with songs and drinks.

"When I think about what it was like to be on the set in Calgary or in Jamaica and laughing with John," Turteltaub told Highfill, "that's as much as any person can ever expect to get out of the phrase 'a dream come true.' It was a dream of mine to one day work with John Candy and to have had that much fun and that much success with him was really exciting and really heartbreaking eventually. I think about being with [the film's lead actors] nonstop and how much they taught me about directing. The movie was not expensive, and everyone got, basically, scale to do the movie, but there was so much enthusiasm and love."

Making *Cool Runnings* had been a welcome high point in a year of Argonaut disappointments. As Candy returned to the office in the middle of April, there still appeared to be some encouraging developments in the CFL, but overall, his business dealings with McNall dwindled before breaking off completely. On the other hand, the cold war between Candy and Second City's Andrew Alexander was beginning to thaw, particularly when Alexander proposed certain new projects,

"Over time they appeared to tiptoe back to each other," says Crane. "It helped that Andrew put together that *SCTV* video compilation *The Best of John Candy*, and I remember it being one of the first times I had ever seen something like that, and John was certainly the first person from *SCTV* to get that treatment. It was a peace offering all those years later, and that was certainly a good thing."

Alexander had also been putting together a proposal for a CRTC licence for a premium cable TV channel entirely devoted to comedy, along the lines of what had recently become known as Comedy Central in the US, and a predecessor of what CTV would do with its Comedy network. When Alexander asked Candy to become a partner in the venture, he put his Frostbacks producer Patrick Whitley on the case.

"This was a big deal at the time," says Whitley, "because there were no cable channels in Canada yet. This was the first."

Eventually, Bret Gallagher stopped moonlighting for the Argonauts to work full-time for Candy, Alexander, and Whitley on the Second City comedy channel, and according to Second City's Sally Cochrane, it was a time of reconciliation for Candy, not only with Alexander but with the entire Second City organization. "I can't remember exactly," says Cochrane, "if it was John deciding to come to Andrew or how they did it, but somehow, they managed to have a very, very close, trusting relationship again.

For example, when we opened the Second City theatre in Detroit, John came down to the opening there and did all the press."

Alexander also flew down to Frostbacks' LA offices to work with a team that included *SCTV* writer Dick Blasucci on a potential film script for Candy. "He seemed very comfortable there behind his big desk," says Alexander. "He had been so emotionally invested in the Argonauts, and he had promoted the league one hundred percent, so he was deeply hurt to hear that Bruce McNall was selling the Argonauts. When he called me, I was in Detroit because we'd opened a theatre there. And we talked that morning. Bruce had always told him, 'John, I'll always let you know if I'm going to sell the Argonauts.' But I think he did it behind his back, and John was crushed by that."

Cool Runnings opened on October 1 to rave reviews and near-unanimous approval from the moviegoing public. On its first weekend in the cinemas, the endearing family film earned back just over half of Disney's estimated $14 million investment; it would go on to gross an estimated $68.8 million at the North American box office during its initial run, eventually taking in close to $155 million worldwide. Significantly, the film was particularly well received by Jamaican moviegoers for its respectful depiction of the events of 1988.

Roger Ebert, on the other hand, wasn't buying it. In his review for the *Chicago Sun-Times*, he chided Turteltaub's film and complained that Candy only had "a couple of stirring speeches that he somehow delivers as if every word were not recycled from other films. If you like underdog movies, you might like this one. Especially if you haven't seen very many."

Harsh reviews tend to sting less when a film is a hit, and *Cool Runnings* was not only that, it also heralded a return to form for Candy as a bankable star, allowing him to raise his price to $4 million per film, and putting some wind in his sails as he embarked on his next project. While Candy's role in the made-for-television movie *Hostage for a Day* amounted to nothing more than a high-profile cameo, for the first time in his career he would be calling the shots from the director's chair.

Twenty-Seven

Russian Gangsters and Canadian Bacon

John Candy's directorial debut, *Hostage for a Day*, was an inside job in more ways than one. The comedy caper, whose staged kidnapping and ransom scam plot preceded the Coen brothers' *Fargo* by more than three years, was written by one of Candy's trusted Chongos, Robert Crane Jr., with his wife, Kari Hildebrand, and developed by P. J. Torokvei, the Second City alumnus who had previously written on *Armed and Dangerous* and the hit sitcom *WKRP in Cincinnati*. The made-for-television film was the product of Candy's own Frostbacks Productions.

According to Crane, he and Hildebrand had written a first draft, entitled *Suburbia Blues*, that, although it was closer in tone to Sidney Lumet's *Dog Day Afternoon*, they thought Frostbacks might consider producing. Crane gingerly asked Candy to take a look at it, while sending another copy to his agents as a backup plan. Candy hadn't yet read the script when his agents informed him that they had found a home for *Suburbia Blues* at Fox Television, a relative newcomer to the cable market that was eager to create original movies for television. Fox brought in veteran producer Stan Brooks and commissioned Torokvei to do a script rewrite.

Sadly, Hildebrand succumbed to cancer shortly before filming commenced on the now-retitled *Hostage for a Day* on the first day of October 1993, just as *Cool Runnings* was opening at the cinemas. It was shot over the next three weeks in and around suburban Toronto and north of the city in Haliburton, toward Algonquin Park. Crane and Hildebrand had always pictured Candy in the lead role of Warren Kooey, but for various reasons, Candy declined. When Crane suggested that Candy direct the film, though, he agreed. Speaking to a press gaggle at the time, Candy announced, "I'll take the blame [if the film flops]. And if it does well, I'll take the credit. I enjoy being in that position."

To assuage his corporate benefactors at Fox, who were initially unhappy that he would not appear onscreen in *Hostage*, Candy cast George Wendt, at the time starring on the highly rated NBC sitcom *Cheers*, in the role of Kooey. Wendt, who was a fan of both Candy and Torokvei, said yes without even negotiating his deal.

"I thought, if Torokvei had written this role for John, I'm kind of flattered that they saw me in it," says Wendt. "So I just flew on up to Toronto, ready to work."

Still, to appease the suits at Fox, Candy agreed to play a minor role as a Russian gangster, Yuri Petrovitch, letting his hair grow longer and sporting a bushy beard that would cover his increasingly thickening neck for the rest of his days. According to Crane, Candy seemed happy to play director, "and that Orson Welles beard completed the image."

Wendt witnessed Candy's transition to the director's chair, which he said was totally organic. "He was unflustered," says Wendt. "His only note to me was to 'have fun.' You could tell he was ready to move big-time into directing, although I could also see how he relished playing this no-good Russian criminal; such joy he brought to that small part."

Candy's comfort and security on the set was no doubt bolstered by the hiring of so many Second City alumni to insulate him as he took on the challenge. Besides Wendt, a veteran of the Chicago cast, Candy brought in *SCTV*'s Robin Duke to play his wife, Elizabeth Kooey. Candy had last worked with her ten years earlier, when he'd hosted *Saturday Night Live*, and Duke was in the cast. He had always been a fan of her work, and according to Duke, Candy lobbied hard for Fox to agree to let him give her a co-starring role over "somebody with a bigger name or with more experience."

"He brought in a lot of friends on that show," says Duke, "and I remember feeling that there was a light around this project. It was such a gift; a time of grace."

Candy drew on many generations of the Second City, giving supporting roles to then-current Toronto mainstage cast members Kathryn Greenwood, John Hemphill, Don Lake, and Kathleen Laskey.

"It became a de facto Second City reunion," says Crane, "even Torokvei was from the Second City. And we also got lucky by having John Vernon from *Animal House* and Jack Duffy, who John had worked with on *The Silent Partner*."

Upon Wendt's arrival in Toronto, Candy proudly showed him

around the city, just as he had done with John Belushi when he first came to town. "We used to joke that he was my Toronto concierge," says Wendt. "It was 'Bonjour Monsieur Wendt, would you like centre-ice tickets at zee Maple Leaf Gardens? Oui, Monsieur Wendt.' And of course, we went to an Argos game."

On the set, Candy took the job of directing seriously, while remaining sympathetic to the needs of his on-camera talent. And just as John Hughes had done for him, Candy liked to let his own talented improvisors, such as Lake or Hemphill, off the leash after they had performed the lines as written.

"After a take," says Crane, "Lake might whisper in John's ear, 'Hey, what if I did a bit here?' And John would nod, and say 'Yeah, go for it,' and so they'd do another take."

Kathryn Greenwood, who played a SWAT Team officer in *Hostage for a Day* and had very little on-camera experience at the time, recalls Candy reassuring her by treating her "like an equal" and giving her some of the funniest dialogue in the film. "When he knew I was completely comfortable," says Greenwood, "he began improvising with me. It was almost exhausting to witness. He just didn't stop making everyone happy, and his enjoyment of it was genuine. I remember John laughing at a choice I made and pointing it out to someone on the set, and those things stick in a young actor's mind. He taught me early on that good, creative work comes from a joyful set."

By now Candy was truly at home on a film set, with a basic knowledge of what every department could bring to the project, but he mainly concentrated on his own areas of expertise, acting and comedy, and left the rest to the skilled professionals in his crew. Yet even amid such warm displays of love and mutual respect, some in the cast witnessed apparent flashes of distress in Candy. On one occasion, he found it necessary to retreat into the inner sanctum of his trailer for hours on end.

"Everyone was interpreting it as anxiety," says Duke, "but in hindsight it might have had something to do with his heart. Still, when he finally popped out of his trailer, he'd appear to be back to his usual self, giving us all his lovely big warm bear hugs."

In private, Candy had actually been making great strides in therapy and was by now more comfortable with sharing his struggles with any journalist who wanted to know. Toronto CTV reporter Sandie Rinaldo paid a visit to the set one afternoon to film what was essentially a standard "fluff piece" entertainment story. After Rinaldo opened by asking how it felt to make the leap into the director's chair, Candy assured her that he was having a blast. But when Rinaldo innocently inquired about the origins of his desire to be funny, Candy's reply was surprisingly frank.

"It was probably in high school," Candy said; "it was probably more as a defensive posture, really. I was never a 'great' student. I tried but I don't think I was a really good student. I was probably still in shock from all the tragedies that we dealt with."

Then, after a nervous giggle at the nakedness of his reply, Candy went even further, adding that, after his father's untimely passing, he had taken on "the responsibility of going to work" and had likely been "taking on the father role unconsciously. Because, you know, as a child," he continued, "when there's a loss of a parent, you go, 'Well, I'll fill in,' as children will do... I know it's only been in the last few years that I really started to deal with that, to understand why October is a really tense month for me... Because it was around the time of my birthday... So it was a bit... it's taken me a few years understanding that, you know, 'Why is October so bad?'"

During a lull in the shoot, Duke found a moment to have a serious conversation with Candy where they discussed what it was like for him, splitting his time between Queensville, where his heart was, and Hollywood, where the work was. "I remember him telling me that he would've loved to have stayed in Canada," says Duke, "but he couldn't make the same amount of money in Canada. John loved everybody and everybody loved him, but he didn't suffer fools, and he was very particular about who he was friends with and who he kept in his world. He was a smart guy, emotionally intelligent, and he had such a big heart, but it could easily be broken because he was so open with people."

As Candy raced to complete principal photography on *Hostage for a Day* throughout October, he was mindful that he needed to wrap in time to begin his next acting job, in Michael Moore's political farce *Canadian Bacon*.

The *Hostage* wrap party, held in Candy's private box at the SkyDome at the end of the month, also marked the occasion of Candy's forty-third birthday. Telefilm Canada's Bill House, who had been one of the producers of *The Canadian Conspiracy*, later remarked to journalist Martin Knelman that, in his opinion, Candy "did not look at all well" at the party. The following month, Candy and Eugene Levy co-hosted a twentieth-anniversary gala for concert promoter Michael Cohl's CPI company, featuring music from Simon & Garfunkel, Gordon Lightfoot, and Blue Rodeo.

In Knelman's account, Candy complained to close friends at the event that his now-constant anxiety had disrupted his sleep patterns, causing him to nod off some days. But it is worth noting that, his mental health notwithstanding, Candy was at that time working on two films simultaneously, while continuing to host gala events, keep an eye on the Argonauts, and find time to be with his beloved family. From November into early 1994, Candy moonlighted as a *Canadian Bacon* actor by day, portraying American sheriff Bud Boomer on location in Niagara Falls, New York, while completing post-production by night on *Hostage for a Day* back in Toronto.

"He had a full program going on at that time," says Crane. "Hey, I was tired too."

Candy again went back to his Second City family, enlisting musician Ian Thomas to compose a score for *Hostage for a Day.*

"There was almost more sweetness than comedy to the film," says Thomas. "I would come up with, say, a little string and oboe theme for a scene, then drive down to Niagara Falls, New York, and play it for John loosely synched up to a little VCR [with *Hostage* footage playing]. When I hit play, tears came streaming down John's face, and he got right on the phone to Stan Brooks, and said, 'Stan, listen to my music, listen to my music,' then he hit play again and held the phone up to the speakers. I did the whole score for him over the next two and a half weeks. John was basically stopping in at my house every night to listen to the day's cues, and we always just laughed so hard."

In December, shortly after Thomas had wrapped his score for the film, Candy dropped by his home to get his opinion on a guitar he had purchased for young Christopher.

"He'd done some Christmas shopping down in the Niagara area," says Thomas, "and he'd gotten this stubby little Fender Telecaster with a beautiful sort of robin's-egg blue finish. It was a very classic-looking old guitar, but John wanted my take on it. 'Do you think he'll like it, Ian? Do you think he can play it?' I looked at it, lowered the action, then plugged it in and told him it was a great little guitar. And John said, 'Oh, that's great, fantastic.' Johnny was so happy about that guitar; such a loving dad."

Canadian Bacon, Michael Moore's only non-documentary film, was a sardonic political satire about a hot war set off by cold brew. Moore had first written the story shortly after his 1989 automotive industry documentary, *Roger and Me*, had put him on Hollywood's radar. In its wake, Warner Bros., and every other major film studio, took a look at, then passed on, *Canadian Bacon*, mainly because at its heart the film was a farcical takeoff on the Gulf War, which was surprisingly popular with the American public in 1991. A liberal-leaning anti-war satire of the military-industrial complex was a tough sell in Hollywood. In the interim, Moore and his partner Kathleen Glynn worked for two years to get the film made while they worked on their television series, *TV Nation*, while continuing to send the *Canadian Bacon* script to influential people in Hollywood, including Candy and *M*A*S*H* star Alan Alda.

Robert Crane Jr. was in the Frostbacks offices in Los Angeles on the day Moore dropped by the big boardroom to discuss the project with Candy, who had been impressed with Moore's work on *TV Nation*, and was flattered that the director of popular documentaries was a big fan of his work. According to Crane, Candy was excited to take a smaller role in an ensemble film, and he agreed to do the film after hearing that Alda was also attached to it. Moore envisioned the tone of Stanley Kubrick's *Dr. Strangelove*, although in some ways the beer-soaked main plot owed more to *Strange Brew*. In a 1995 interview, Moore told *Film Threat*'s Dominic Griffin that, while he had initially encountered resistance from the major Hollywood studio system, the addition of John Candy to his cast changed everything. Backed with an $11 million budget, Moore began his thirty-eight-day production of *Canadian Bacon* in the winter of 1993.

"[Candy] was really a good guy ... a very funny guy," Moore told Griffin, "and I think what he liked about this film is he wanted to get back to doing something that had some substance to it. Something with an edge."

According to Crane, Candy was also impressed with the calibre of Moore's ensemble cast, which included G. D. Spradlin, from *The Godfather Part II*, Rip Torn, at the time riding high as Artie on *The Larry Sanders Show*, *Cheers* star Rhea Perlman, comic Steven Wright, and once again, Dan Aykroyd, in an amusing cameo as an Ontario Provincial Police motorcycle cop who pulls over Sheriff Boomer for neglecting to include French translations on the hostile slogans written on his van. In a riff on Canadian niceness, the officer gives Boomer a spray can and a chance to make things right. Aykroyd has bittersweet memories of shooting the scene somewhere along the Queen Elizabeth Way.

"After we had done our thing," says Aykroyd, "John came over and my family was there. I remember my two daughters were young at that time. We all sat in this hotel room and then he said he was off to finish some more work with Moore. Then he was going off to Mexico to shoot *Wagons East*. And that was it ... You just never know."

Filming in the Niagara region brought back a flood of memories for Candy. He had filmed much of *Planes, Trains and Automobiles* in the area, and in his youth he and Jonathan O'Mara had crossed the border in the White Knight during Candy's ill-fated attempt to enlist in the American military.

Having previously tackled political parody in short pieces for SCTV, and in Robert Boyd's mockumentary *The Canadian*

Conspiracy, Candy was assured by the tone of Moore's screenplay, which he felt was of a piece with some of his favourite satirical films, such as the Peter Sellers farce *The Mouse That Roared*, or Norman Jewison's 1966 Cold War comedy, *The Russians Are Coming, the Russians Are Coming.*

"It brought him back on the edge," Moore told Steve Persall of the *Tampa Bay Times*, "back to his SCTV type of humor. It's really a testimonial to what his true talent was."

It would be nearly two years before anyone would see the fruits of Moore's labour, and Candy never got to see the final cut of a film he had played such a vital role in bringing into existence. As 1994 began, Candy boarded a plane to Mexico to begin work on the wild west comedy *Wagons East*. What nobody could have known at the time was that not only would this be John Candy's final performance on film, but January and February would be the last two months of his life.

Twenty-Eight

Wagons East

The scene is somewhere along the dusty plains of the fabled American West. From atop his horse, an overweight, grizzled, alcoholic wagon master named James Harlow, recently demoted after leading the infamous Donner Party to its cannibalistic conclusion, is about to lead a wagon train of East Coast misfits to California. One of these is Dr. Phil Taylor, who informs the drunk wagon master that he and his reluctant explorers have had a change of heart. The wild west, as it turns out, isn't for them, and they would very much like to turn around and go back home. Wagons *east* it is, then.

A series of unfortunate circumstances had led Candy to Durango, Mexico, where he was to co-star with Richard Lewis in the ill-fated wild west comedy *Wagons East*. Bearded and heavy as the dishevelled wagon master, and weighed down by ponchos and hefty leather costumes in the blistering desert sun, even Candy knew he was heading in the wrong direction. While he had been a fan of Mel Brooks's western parody *Blazing Saddles, Wagons East* was a horse of another colour. Candy had made wrong turns before, but they had largely been detours along the road to better things. This time he would meet the end of the road entirely; instead of seeing him riding off into the sunset on his trusty steed as his character Jack Gable had in *Delirious, Wagons East* would be an ignoble end to a brief but illustrious life and career. He had taken the job not only for the three-million-dollar fee, but for the freedom that such a large sum might give him to finally slow down, choose his projects more carefully, and pursue his newfound passion for directing. That was the plan, anyway.

Candy had only ended up in *Wagons East* as a contractual obligation after John Hughes and Sylvester Stallone backed out of the Carolco Pictures project *Bartholomew vs. Neff.* As time ran out on his deal with the studio, Candy hoped he could simply walk away, but Carolco was eager to put him to work in another project, any project they could. When Carolco acquired Matthew Carlson's screenplay for a comedy western that had been languishing in "development hell" at MGM, *Wagons East* became John Candy's next project. According to Robert Crane Jr., the contractual obligation was merely the first of a series of red flags, and when Candy discovered that he had "no chemistry" with director Peter Markle, he knew that things on *Wagons East* were headed south.

"There was no way out," says Crane. "Three million dollars was nice money, but John really didn't want to work in the hot sun in Durango, Mexico. He was still having problems with anxiety attacks and was at the heaviest weight that I had ever seen him, my guess is that he was around three hundred and fifty pounds, maybe more. I know his neck was very thick under that beard."

Back at Frostbacks, Bret Gallagher took a number of calls from Candy in Durango where the actor conveyed his serious misgivings about his obligation to finish *Wagons East*. "John told me he was very unhappy," says Gallagher. "He said, 'I'm a whore, Bret. I'm doing this for money.' I don't think he was in love with the script. He'd say, 'I've got to do it because that's what I do. But you know what, I'm going to finish this up, then you and me, we're going to play some golf.'"

Michael Short remembers a similar phone call with Candy, who additionally shared that he hadn't been feeling well. "His doctor thought it might be [his] gallbladder or something," says Short. "I told him, 'Fuck it, John, just tell them you're sorry but you're not feeling well.' He said, 'No, I can't do that because then I'll never get hired again. I'll be a risk.' I said, 'You're *John fucking Candy*! All you've got to do is have your agents on the down low tell people the movie's a piece of shit, let's rewrite it and get it funnier or do something.' But I suppose it was true. It would have been very difficult for him to get out of it."

Most of the filming took place in Sierra de Órganos National Park in the town of Sombrerete, at an elevation of 8,200 feet, and in Durango. Candy had rented a single-storey bungalow near Sombrerete to avoid having to climb stairs in the high altitude. Crane, who stayed with the other Chongos at the El Gobernador hotel, described Candy's accommodations as a "cozy base of operations," save for the occasional sounds of gunfire cannonading from a nearby public park.

Richard Lewis, excited to be working with Candy again after having had so much fun making *Once upon a Crime*, immediately picked up on a darker mood when he arrived in Durango.

"Nobody was really in a good place," said Lewis. "We had some amazing character actors in that film, but it just smelled funny once we were doing it. There were some good moments, and everyone showed up and did their roles well, but ultimately the chemistry just wasn't right. Still, everyone gave it their best shot, including John."

Many of the crew members recall an agonized Candy appearing to be in both physical and emotional pain and having trouble breathing in the thinner air.

"The combination of the anxiety and his family background with heart issues," says Crane, "and then the sheer weight of his costume; it was not a good thing. He would slouch until Markle called 'Action,' then he snapped back into performing as though nothing was wrong."

Despite these moments of obvious struggle, Candy resisted the temptation to wallow in his misery and, as was his custom by now, did his best to raise the spirits on the set. Reportedly, Candy would throw regular parties in which he would tend a fully stocked bar, disguising himself each time as a different "mystery bartender." On Valentine's Day, Candy distributed dozens of roses and boxes of chocolates. Yet even at these high moments, crew members such as boom operator Mark Jennings would frequently glimpse cracks appearing in his upbeat facade.

"He was obviously in more and more pain," Jennings told writer Tracey J. Morgan, "and you could tell [because] he would have a way of standing that he was in a lot of discomfort, but he would never complain about it. He never let on as to how much pain he was in. Those last couple of weeks he just seemed tired, just really tired. But he never let it affect his demeanour. He was always smiling. I'm not sure I could have handled it that way."

Lewis sensed the general unease of his co-star and noticed that Candy was one of the very few members of the cast or crew "who got to leave the set to fly home to LA on the weekends, if we weren't shooting."

Candy was also allowed to return briefly to Toronto to tend to some unpleasant football business, but before he left, he asked the cast and crew if there was anything he could bring back to them from the outside world. Actor John C. McGinley, who played the flamboyant Julian Rogers in the film—as part of an ensemble cast that also included Ellen Greene, who had previously worked with Candy when she starred in *Little Shop of Horrors*—recalls the gesture as "the sweetest goddamn kind of Santa Claus thing."

"I mean, no one does that," says McGinley. "I was obsessed with the film *Raging Bull*, so he got me a tape of that and brought it back. We weren't really supposed to leave the El Gobernador for security reasons, so people were largely kept at the hotel or on the set. So John bringing that tape back for me was one of the sweetest things I could possibly imagine."

McGinley also found Durango to be an exceedingly "uncomfortable place," but concedes that the high altitude and heat there would have made it feel exponentially worse for Candy. "The oxygen is very thin there," says McGinley, "plus it was hot as shit, even when we were there, in January and February. No one is comfortable in Durango, no one."

One of Candy's flights out of Durango took him to Los Angeles, where he and Crane previewed *Hostage for a Day* for the Television Critics Association. While they were there, in the early morning of January 17, a massive 6.7 magnitude earthquake, centred in Northridge, near Burbank, resulted in numerous fatalities and injured thousands, causing over $20 billion in damages. While Candy and his family were unharmed by the event, news of the massive quake sent a wave of concern through his cast and crew back in Durango, many of whom were Los Angelinos eagerly awaiting news from their loved ones or to learn the extent of the damage to their homes. For actors like Lewis and McGinley, the seismic jolt added yet another layer of darkness to the production.

"We were seeing the pictures on CNN International of what Los Angeles looked like," says McGinley, "and if you're stranded back in Durango, the whole thing started to feel a little pointless."

Upon his return to Durango, Candy grew increasingly frustrated with Markle's direction, and according to Crane, desperately "needed to let off a little steam."

"He went on a two-day tequila bender," says Crane. "I'd never seen him drink tequila up until then. He was in pain; he literally had an ice bag on his head. I had never seen that before at all. Here's this big guy who could tolerate multiple rum and Cokes at night, but I never saw him drunk or out of control. This was tequila, though, so it was the first time I really saw him damaged. He was not happy."

As sympathetic as Crane was to Candy's predicament, he had pressing business to attend to back at Frostbacks. Leaving Candy on set in Mexico, Crane flew back to Los Angeles to take stock of a full roster of projects waiting for the boss after his return. These included a reworked screenplay for *Our Father* and an adaptation of John Kennedy Toole's densely complex 1980 satirical novel *A Confederacy of Dunces*, which chronicled the misadventures of an eccentric and obese intellectual named Ignatius J. Reilly. Set in 1960s New Orleans, *Dunces* had long been considered unfilmable, not merely for its multilevelled narrative but due to a perceived curse that began in 1982 when John Belushi passed away shortly after becoming attached to the project.

There was also a golf comedy called *Pork*, based on Tom Dulack's book about a high school teacher and amateur golfer named Pork Waller whose friends rally together to fund his second career on the PGA Tour. Candy had recently acquired the film rights for Frostbacks and was eager for Joe Flaherty to be involved. According to Flaherty, the two old friends would talk about some of these film prospects during their frequent phone calls from Durango. During one such call, Candy even shared that Christopher Guest (*Best in Show, Waiting for Guffman*) had approached him to appear in one of his ensemble comedies. Other times, Candy would bemoan the poverty and inequity he was witnessing just beyond the location in Mexico.

"John would get depressed about the miserable conditions that the people lived in, in that area of Mexico," says Flaherty. "You could smell the water. But our last phone call was just a short one. 'How's the family,' stuff like that."

One day of the shoot would remain forever etched upon Richard Lewis's memory. On the afternoon of March 3, 1994, Lewis worked with Candy in a scene with actor Robert Picardo. "Everything worked," said Lewis. "Everyone knew their lines, and there wasn't much ad libbing at all. John opened a door and the way he was delivering his lines, I was thinking to myself, 'I know this is a comedy, but this could be a drama.' I tell you it was chillingly great. He had decided to play it serious; I didn't know what movie I was in. He gave this long speech and then they cut, and we drove back to our hotel, while Frankie [Hernandez] takes John back to his bungalow. Picardo and I were so moved by this day that we called John to tell him how amazing it was to see him work that day. We thought it might make John happy to have these two fellow actors praising his brilliant acting, so we got him on the phone. It was a Thursday night, and that was the last that we spoke to him."

That night at his villa, an exhausted Candy began cooking a big pot of spaghetti while making a few calls to friends. Around 9 p.m. he made a quick check-in call with the family back at Mandeville Canyon. He had seen them recently when he flew back for Jennifer's fourteenth birthday in February, but his nightly phone calls from Durango had become a cherished part of his daily routine.

In a 2016 interview with writer Ryan Parker for *The Hollywood Reporter,* Chris and Jen Candy shared a few details of the call. "I was studying for a vocabulary test," Jennifer told Parker. "I hate this, but I was slightly distant because I was studying. So I was like, 'Yeah, OK, I love you. I will talk to you later. Have a great night.' Then I hang up, and I go back to studying."

Chris, who was nine years old at the time, told Parker that he was at least grateful that they both remembered to say "I love you, goodnight" before hanging up with their dad.

With only ten days left on the *Wagons East* shoot, Crane had returned to Los Angeles, and when Candy checked in with him that night, he seemed effusive about the great day of filming he had enjoyed with Lewis.

"It was one of the few times I heard him say 'I feel good' about something on *Wagons East,*" says Crane. "But he also sounded like a poor puppy who was still in the cage for another week or so before he got released. I could tell he was envious of me being back in LA, but I told him ten days is going to fly by, and he'd be out of there in no time and there would be plenty more stuff to do when he got back. I signed off telling him that it was nice to hear about his good day with Richard, then I said, 'Let's talk tomorrow night, I want to hear about what you do tomorrow.' So he said, 'Yeah, yeah, let's talk tomorrow night. Okay. Bye.'"

Candy made at least one other phone call that night. It was to his long-time friend and former *Second City Television* co-star Catherine O'Hara. On this particular evening, Candy was ostensibly calling O'Hara to check in, but also to wish her an early happy birthday. "It was my fortieth birthday the following day," says O'Hara, "so it was a big birthday for me, but not big important. A number you remember."

In the call, Candy told O'Hara that she was always welcome to come down to Durango and perhaps film a cameo in *Wagons East*, but the general tone of their chat was upbeat and positive, just two old friends shooting the breeze. "I think if it was an especially sad call," says O'Hara, "I would have remembered that. It might have been just one of those calls. 'Hey, what are you doing? You should come here and work.'"

It would be the last time O'Hara would ever speak to John Candy.

After sharing his spaghetti feast with some of the Chongos, Candy retired to his room. At seven o'clock on the morning of Friday, March 4, 1994, Frankie Hernandez arrived at Candy's villa to drive him out to the day's shooting location. After knocking on the door and getting no answer, he rang the bell. When he finally got security to open the door, he found Candy's lifeless body, lying on the bed. He called Crane, back in Los Angeles.

Crane's voice lowers as he repeats Hernandez's words to him early that morning. "'I don't know how to tell you, Bob. You're not going to believe this, but John's dead.' What I gathered from Frankie was that John was clothed, like he'd been getting ready. As though he had been sitting on the bed putting his shoes on and just fell backwards onto the bed."

John Franklin Candy, faithful husband to Rose and loving father to Jennifer and Chris, who had rocketed up from the Toronto theatre scene to become a world-famous and beloved comedian of film and television, was dead from apparent heart failure at the tragically young age of forty-three. In life, he had often intimated that he felt he was living on borrowed time, but when that time came, it still seemed unfair that such a gregarious person would meet his demise all alone in a rented Mexican villa.

It was too late now to do anything for him except to notify his family, and then the whole world, that John Candy was gone.

Twenty-Nine

Aftershocks

On the morning of her fortieth birthday, Catherine O'Hara's phone was ringing off the hook, as she fielded what she describes as "the weirdest mix of calls."

"Somebody would call and say, 'Oh, happy birthday' and I'd go, 'Oh, thanks,'" says O'Hara. "Then they'd get quiet and say, 'Yeah, John,' so we'd talk about John, of course. I was just horribly, horribly sad. I dreamt about him so much after he died, and I still dream about him once in a while. A couple years ago I had a dream, and we were just hanging out and doing bits, and then I said something about him being dead and he went, 'Aww, you had to say it out loud.' And I went, 'Oh, I'm sorry, I thought you knew.' [And he said] 'I did, but we didn't have to say it.' I felt like I really let him down. I was so, so sad."

Back in Durango, reaction around the *Wagons East* set ranged from dazed to devastated during what Richard Lewis remembered as "one of the most harrowing, most depressing mornings" of his life. They still had a film to finish, with the script coordinator reading Candy's lines off camera to cue Lewis and his fellow cast. "It was a horrifying thing to do," said Lewis, "but as they say, 'the show must go on,' so it did."

While Candy had filmed many of his close-ups and master shots before his passing, his body double, Bob Elmore, filled in for him one last time to cover his wide shots and horse-riding scenes. Certain footage with Candy appears twice or more in the final film, and any missing bits of key dialogue were dubbed in weeks later by the star's old Second City comrade, Tino Insana.

As Frankie Hernandez and the rest of Candy's Chongos scrambled in Durango to lock down any news of Candy's passing from getting beyond the set, Robert Crane Jr. sprang into action in Los Angeles to get to Candy's family before word leaked to the mass media.

"You've got to remember," says Crane, "this was 1994, pre-internet, with no social media. But there was CNN and all the morning shows, so my first thought was that somebody had to tell Rose, before she heard it from someone else. I got in the car with my stepdad Chuck [Sloan], who was kind of a surrogate father to John, and drove straight over to Brentwood. I'll never forget ringing her front doorbell at eight in the morning. When Rose opened the door, she saw these two guys standing there. We didn't say a word, but she immediately started screaming. She knew in her bones why we were there. We told her, then held her for a moment before we all moved into the house."

In a 2016 story in *The Hollywood Reporter*, Ryan Parker relayed an anecdote about a large piece of amethyst that Candy had sent home from Durango as a gift. The rock had inexplicably split in two on the mantelpiece on the day he died, and Rose suspected it was a kind of supernatural farewell. Rose Candy's first thought, however, was the kids. Crane drove her over to Saint Martin of Tours, their school in Brentwood, and urgently arranged to have Christopher and Jennifer pulled out of class to give them the awful news.

Crane says he will never forget the "absolutely heartbreaking" sight of Candy's children at the moment before they were about to receive the awful news, and realizing, "their lives are about to change drastically forever, in a matter of moments."

Years later Chris Candy told writer Ryan Parker that a "weird energy" had come over him that morning where he "was able to feel older. And then Father Donie walked us down to the rectory ... Our mom was there, in tears."

As could be expected, both of Candy's children also broke into tears upon hearing of their father's death. "I cried hysterically for five minutes," Jennifer Candy told Parker, "and then I stopped. And then I was done crying in public for a while. It was a whirlwind after that point. That's when we really knew about paparazzi because you had all the cameras."

While the recent seismic activity below Northridge had shaken the foundations of Los Angeles, the news of Candy's untimely passing sent shockwaves that were felt around the world. March 4 wasn't even a slow news day, as Candy's demise shared global headlines with news from Rome of the near-fatal overdose of rock's troubled prince, Kurt Cobain, who would himself be dead one month later, on April 5.

According to Crane, CNN "wasted no time" in broadcasting Candy's death, and by the time he and the family returned to Mandeville Canyon, their home was already under siege from news vultures and well-meaning fans drawn to the house as a locus for their grief. Inside the house, it was a day of fielding and making phone calls and of friends, neighbours, and family showing up. "John's mother, Evangeline, flew in from Toronto," says Crane. "And from there it was just a tsunami of emotion and people."

Chevy and Jayni Chase were among the first of their friends to arrive at the family home. Before Candy had left for Mexico, Chase and Harold Ramis had been spending long days at the Candy residence, blocking out a screenplay that never materialized.

"It was a terrible shock," says Chase, "but we hung on and stayed together. Our whole tight-knit group were these very funny people, like Marty [Short] and Steve [Martin], and of course Harold, who also died far too soon, but much later on. We all cared for each other."

Assuming that the whole town had already heard the grim news, Chase accidentally broke it to Martin Short, who took his call while he was writing a comedy series with his brother Michael, Dick Blasucci, and Paul Flaherty.

"Chevy just said, 'Can you believe how sad this is?'" says Short. "So I said, 'What?' Then he realized I didn't know, so he said, 'Oh no, I'm sorry that I have to be the one to tell you. John has died; turn on your TV.' And there it was, all over the news. We were just destroyed because it was so sudden, it wasn't like there had been a ramp-up to illness. It was just, suddenly he wasn't there. I mean, John is someone that I can still imagine walking right through this door that I'm looking at, and you'd just go, 'Hey, John.' And he always greeted me by singing because I was always singing. 'There he is, Marty Short.' He'd always be doing my version of Sinatra as he greeted me.

'He's a cool cat, that Marty *Shore*.' He'd do that, and I can just see it right now."

Joe Flaherty, who had tapped Candy to join the Second City in the first place, says the news hit him "like a ton of bricks."

"I just thought, 'Boy, there goes a piece of my life right there,'" says Flaherty. "Even though we hadn't seen much of each other the last years of his life, I had been so close with Johnny, so it was hard."

Like many of Candy's friends, fans, and acquaintances, Flaherty was well aware of Candy's struggles with his weight, and had seen him with his trainers, his Pritikin diet, and his occasional relapses into indulgence despite it all. He had long feared that Candy's magnificent heart would give out sooner than later.

"You sort of saw it coming," says Flaherty, "with his weight problems, the drinking, and cigarettes, but you just didn't want to see it. I was sitting there in my apartment, dumbstruck, and I thought, 'Oh god, what the hell's happening to my world? Johnny's gone.' It was a weird, strange time, and I just didn't know how to handle it. It was hard to face. We're both Catholics, and John was in the same parish as me, Saint Martin of Tours in Brentwood, both of our kids went to school there."

Just days earlier, Dave Thomas had spoken with Candy on the phone from Durango and found him eager to be done with *Wagons East* and already making plans for subsequent projects.

"He told me he just wished he hadn't had to do that film," says Thomas, "but we mostly just joked around the same way we always did. I remember him talking about *Confederacy of Dunces*, which he thought was a very prestigious project, but of course it was not to be."

Dan Aykroyd's roots with Candy stretched all the way back to the beginning of both of their comedy careers, when he and Valri Bromfield had first coaxed their friend into auditioning for the Second City. His brother Peter Aykroyd had also been close with Candy, and the two had been roommates back in the early days. Dan had shared countless stretches of highway with Candy, both literally and figuratively, and when his assistant Susan Patricola called him with the awful news, Aykroyd says he literally drove his car off the road.

"I was driving down in the Valley when Susie called me to tell me John was dead," says Aykroyd, "and my car left the highway and I went right up on someone's front lawn. No one was injured, but I couldn't drive after that for a few minutes."

After Aykroyd had gotten his car back on the road, one of his first calls was to Thomas, who was at the time working with Bromfield on the sitcom *Grace under Fire* across town at the CBS Radford production facility in Studio City.

"Danny called me," says Thomas, "and he said, 'John died, and I'm coming down with Donna [Dixon, Aykroyd's wife] in the car.' I told him 'Valri and I will come out and meet you,' and said to the floor director, 'We're going outside for a while.'"

Thomas then dialed Candy's home phone number, half hoping the awful news wasn't true. "This funereal-sounding guy picked up the phone," says Thomas. "He said, 'Candy residence,' and when I heard that, I knew it was true, because there was already somebody there manning the phones. I asked to speak with Rose, and of course she was crying. It was just unbelievably sad. Chris and Jen and Rose were all so wounded; seeing them all like that was heart-rending. We all loved each other, so there was a very big hole in our collective hearts when he died, because there would be no more calls at 3 a.m. where somebody would say to me, 'I will destroy you' at the beginning of the call. There was an appreciable loss that we all felt that we knew was in store for us too."

Bromfield appreciated that Aykroyd had taken such care to get the news out to Candy's closest friends before they could hear it on the news. "It was terrible," says Bromfield, "because we had to shoot our television show, but we just kept crying. I was out of my mind. I still hate to think that he died alone in a room in Mexico. I'm sure Johnny was thinking, 'I'll just do the one movie. I'll make this money. I'll go home. I won't work for a while.' Beating thirty-five had been such a marker for him, and I think we all thought he'd made it after he had exceeded his own father's age. When he didn't make it, it was awful and we *all* felt cheated. I don't even remember much about taping that episode, Dave and I were just crying in each other's arms all day. I got in my car, and I just sat there and cried. I kept hearing the news over and over."

Tom Hanks was also driving when his wife Rita Wilson called with the horrible news. "You don't want to have a health crisis on a shoot in a remote place like Durango," says Hanks. "He was doing what was probably brutal work, outdoors in the sun on the back of a horse. John had always said he would never see forty. And then, when he made it into his forties, he had this sense that he was living on borrowed time. Rita and I had dinner with John and Rose a few times over there in Mandeville Canyon, when the kids were really little. Rose was always concerned because he lived large. He enjoyed wine, he enjoyed a lot of food, and he enjoyed staying up late."

Candy's *Splash* director Ron Howard was in pre-production with Hanks on *Apollo 13* when word reached him. "It's heartbreaking because John was a fantastic guy, a great talent," says Howard. "But I remember talking to Brian [Grazer] about how John was overweight and unhealthy, so this was like our worst fear realized that his health would crumble and give way. It was such a loss because he was just this incredibly giving guy."

While Steve Martin was saddened to hear the news, he recalls it seeming to make sense at the time, given Candy's family history with heart health. Candidly, Martin admits he had always found his *Planes, Trains and Automobiles* co-star to be "a little bit reckless, health-wise" for a man living on borrowed time. "He just put on a lot of weight," says Martin. "[One] could argue that there was a kind of a rush for him. Not a death wish but, and I don't know how to phrase it, either a death wish or an uncontrollable spiral of damaging his health. I don't know if you can say that he was going for the gusto or self-medicating. I think there's a difference between living it up and trying to hide some pain. You had the feeling he was on a spiral. That he was betraying himself for some reason that I don't know."

Stripes director Ivan Reitman recalls his initial feelings of shock turning quickly to regret that the two had drifted apart in the years since Candy had walked away from *Ghostbusters*. "But I wasn't angry with him at all," says Reitman. "John was important to my life. He was a fine actor who went on to do a lot of movies and had a wonderful career, while I got lost in my own. But I was just sad that I never got to be with him in that last part of his life."

Comedian David Steinberg, who had given Candy one of his earliest breaks in television before directing Candy and Eugene Levy in *Going Berserk*, recalls feeling devastated. Knowing that Candy had been working on *Wagons East* with his friend Richard

Lewis, Steinberg tried in vain to get Lewis on the telephone. "It was just so shocking and awful," says Steinberg, "I just couldn't believe it. It was the most difficult kind of pain, the kind you would have if you lost a brother or a father. The loss of John Candy affected us all. It was impossible for all of us to not have him in our life. I was numb. We were great friends. I have to say that the community helped, though, and that was the effect of the kind of devotion that everyone found in John. It was difficult and sad, but that's the way it was. Comedians do grief very well."

On the morning of Candy's death, director Chris Columbus had stepped out of his Manhattan apartment to pick up the latest editions of the New York papers. "The *Post* and the *Daily News* both had these banner headlines that John Candy had passed away," says Columbus. "I burst into tears. I couldn't believe it. Part of me expected it, but you know, he loved life although he could be really hard on himself, I think. I remember John Hughes called me. He said, 'I had to talk to you because I know you were the only other one who would get it.' I never really knew what he meant, though, but I think he was talking about what a heavy moment it was and how tragic it was that Candy, whom we'd both worked together so closely with, had passed away at such a young age."

Howard Deutch heard the news from Hughes's attorney Jake Bloom and immediately called up Hughes to commiserate. "The entire Hughes family were devastated," says Deutch. "They were so close, which was unusual for John Hughes. He and his family were never that close to any other family in LA, that I was aware of. They kept to themselves. Nothing about John Candy was put on, there was no artifice, and he was always down-to-earth. Hughes hated phoniness, so he was drawn to Candy."

While the world had lost its Uncle Buck, Hughes's kids had lost their Uncle John. James Hughes remembers his emotionally devastated father making immediate arrangements to be in Los Angeles for Candy's funeral. Hughes had lost not only a close friend, but a frequent muse and true ally in the movie business.

"I think it was difficult for my father," says James Hughes, "to adjust during this window of time with a lot of fascinating projects that didn't quite come together. I was just in shock, fourteen years old, sitting in class at school, staring at the same page of my book for an entire hour. I was thinking of Jen and Chris. It was tough. My dad had a real bond with John Candy, and my dad was never able to replicate that with another actor, which I think contributed to Dad never directing another picture."

Shortly before Carl Reiner's own passing in 2022, he told writer Tracey J. Morgan that he had never gotten over losing Candy so young. "It was just so sad he left when he did," Reiner said. "He was the most alive person I had ever met. In [*Summer Rental*], John would find these moments ... that could only be his, he was just that creative. He had everything to live for, he had no negatives, [and] he was so in love with his wife."

In brief remarks with the CBC at the time, Wayne Gretzky praised his former Argonauts co-owner as a generous and genuine soul who was exactly the kind of good guy suggested by his public persona. "He was fun-loving," Gretzky recalled, "went out of his way to make people happy, always wanted to help the unfortunate, [and] always tried to help charitable causes."

Despite the Toronto Argonauts championship season in 1991, the team had been hemorrhaging cash ever since, and after the dismal 1992 season, with the club's debts piling up, Gretzky had implored Bruce McNall to sell the team. In the weeks preceding his death, Candy had tried in vain to rally together a consortium to purchase the team outright. During Candy's last days in Durango, McNall had made a secret deal to sell the team to the brewing company of John Labatt Ltd. According to sports biographer Paul Woods, he didn't even tell Candy.

"I think it was really a nasty thing to do," says Woods. "Some of the sources I spoke to felt that John was kind of in awe of McNall as a model businessman, and therefore slow to figure out that he was the emperor with no clothes, that there wasn't any money behind him, and that it was all sort of a scam. [Business problems] probably angered John, but even at that point his idealism about the Argonauts would've maybe overshadowed his skepticism."

But by December 1993, McNall had pleaded guilty to five counts of conspiracy and fraud and admitted to defrauding six banks out of a reported $236 million. He was sentenced to seventy months in prison. It was a sad fall from grace that was still being litigated long after Candy had passed.

"McNall turned out to be a house of cards," says Woods. "In the end, Candy, the one guy who genuinely loved the whole enterprise, died right after McNall went to prison. Every loan was used to pay down another loan and there was fake collateral used. I think if Candy had known about this, it would've really hurt him."

At the time of Candy's passing, Bret Gallagher was working for Frostbacks in partnership with Second City's Andrew Alexander to launch a cable TV channel. Gallagher was having lunch near his Frostbacks office within the Second City's Old Fire Hall complex when his wife had him paged to give him the news. After checking in with Crane in Los Angeles, he rushed back to the Lombard Street offices and saw an armada of TV news trucks outside the building. Inside, he found a sobbing Sally Cochrane standing near Andrew Alexander, who was swamped with phone calls. They locked the doors of the Old Fire Hall, then asked Gallagher to go outside and brief the press. Just then, Eugene Levy entered the building.

"John and Eugene had been thick as thieves," says Gallagher. "They were best buddies. I think that if John had a best friend from Second City, it would've been Eugene. So Eugene went out and spoke to the media. We were all crying because nobody loved his life more than John, and I believe he really wanted to live."

Gallagher's statement appears to be supported by the fact that during the final months of his life, Candy had been working with both a cardiologist and a therapist in a serious attempt to extend the life he loved. In the end, Candy's eleventh-hour rally wasn't enough to prevent what now seems to have been inevitable, but as Chris Candy later explained to *The Hollywood Reporter*'s Ryan Parker, his father's untimely death provided him and his sister with a keener awareness of both congenital disease and the importance of mindful health habits.

"He was on this planet to do a lot, and he did do a lot," Chris Candy told Parker. "He always worked on his weight and his health, and fortunately, he helped us to figure that out for ourselves. He grew up with heart disease. My sister and I are very well aware of it and take care of ourselves. His father had a heart attack, his brother had a heart attack. It was in the family. He had trainers and would work at whatever the new diet was. I know he did his best. We are fortunate to have more information than he was able to, I don't think he was aware of the genetic heart disease that was in the family. You wish he had figured it out."

In life, John Candy never did anything small, and so vast was the hole left by his absence that it would take two funerals, one on each side of the border, to mourn him properly.

Thirty

The Mourning

One of John Candy's earliest mentors, Del Close, once remarked there was "something irresistibly funny about a funeral," noting that even in the midst of the deepest tragedy, there was "always the possibility for laughter." Close was speaking about a sketch called "Funeral," which he had originally written for the Chicago Second City in 1972, and which Candy later resurrected during his own time there. While Close was not among the estimated two hundred mourners in attendance at John Candy's private funeral, held in Brentwood on March 9, 1994, at Saint Martin of Tours Catholic Church, the quote seems entirely apt given the sheer number of talented comedy practitioners on hand to pay their respects that day. Among them were Joe Flaherty, Catherine O'Hara, Eugene Levy, Steve Martin, Martin Short, Chevy Chase, Harold Ramis, Robin Duke, Tom Hanks, Bill [Murray] and his brother, the actor Joel Murray, Rick Moranis, George Wendt, Rhea Perlman, Tino Insana, Jim

Belushi, Valri Bromfield, and Dan Aykroyd. Apart from the comedians, the Candy family were joined by John and Nancy Hughes and their sons, Andrew Alexander, Sally Cochrane, Patrick Whitley, actors Jeff Bridges, Mariel Hemingway, Amy Madigan and her husband Ed Harris, Wayne and Janet Gretzky, and to the surprise of some, Bruce McNall.

"Comedians," as David Steinberg had observed earlier, "do grief very well," and as *New York Times* writer Jason Zinoman noted in 2023, "death is too good of a straight man to ignore." It was therefore no surprise that the service was both a solemn requiem for a dear departed friend and a joyful celebration of the often hilarious life he lived, eliciting equal parts laughter and tears from the assembled mourners. Insana later recalled many of the comedians in the church barely suppressing giggles as Candy's casket was wheeled down the aisle, the shrill honking of a comically squeaky wheel reverberating in the chapel like a punchline from the Great Beyond.

While the event was closed to the public, one Associated Press story remarked upon the abundant and huge floral displays placed around Saint Martin's with banners reading "Uncle," "True Friend," and "Gentleman John."

Such flamboyant flourishes at an otherwise low-key, private affair illustrated the seeming contradictions of Candy's humbly audacious nature, but the real miracle of the day was that this elaborate but tightly managed ceremony had been executed with great care and precision over a remarkably short four-day window by Bret Gallagher, Doug Thompson, and Robert Crane Jr., beginning on the Friday after Candy's passing, with Andrew Alexander joining them at the Candy home on Sunday to finalize the tightly guarded guest list. Hollywood security consultant

Gavin de Becker was brought in to manage the flow of information getting out to the press and the public. His instructions were to wait until Monday to notify the invited guests by telephone, telling them only that they should keep Wednesday open for the funeral, then await a follow-up call with further details as to where and when exactly the funeral would happen.

"All of this was to try to keep the paparazzi away," says Thompson. "Still, by the time we got to the church on Wednesday, they were all there anyway. CNN, *Entertainment Tonight*, *National Enquirer*, all of them, although we were kept pretty insulated because Saint Martin's was the Candy family church."

In one last bittersweet gesture for their boss, Crane and his fellow Chongos pressed into action to protect Candy's family and friends, working the door to ensure that "no riff-raff got inside."

Many in the Second City contingent had previously gathered in mourning for both John Belushi and Gilda Radner, and as Robin Duke surveyed the church, she remembered that Candy himself had once grieved along with them. "John had always been with us at things like Marty's parties, with Joe and Chevy, just laughing," says Duke. "Johnny had loved it all. That he wouldn't be here with us now? It just seemed unbelievable."

Having felt his relationship with Candy warming up of late, Andrew Alexander, the man who had launched *SCTV*, had been asked by the Candy family to say a few words at the service. And while he was touched by the gesture, and happy to comply, he also admits to being "so nervous" that he "probably shot down a half a bottle of vodka" before going up.

While Hanks, who came alone to the funeral because his wife, Rita Wilson, was working out of town, was touched by Alexander's respectful remarks, which covered "all the appropriate things," it was the next speaker up whose quasi-sermon stirred the congregation that day. "I will never, ever forget Danny Aykroyd giving us all a lesson in public speaking about somebody you love," says Hanks. "It was an extraordinary thing. First of all, Danny is such a bizarro genius anyway, but his fifteen-minute eulogy for John wasn't platitudes at all. It was soaring poetry about a man who had such a big heart and such a big talent that he claimed two great cities as his home. Danny saluted him as a brother. I was in tears; Danny's heartbreak came through in the words that he spoke. I've learned a lot about oratory from that one eulogy, and I'll never forget it."

When asked to recall the specifics of his heartfelt and valedictory eulogy, Aykroyd apologizes for not being able to recite it verbatim. Fortunately, a typed copy of his "Eulogy for a Golden Man," as delivered on March 9, 1994, sits in the Margaret Herrick Library of the Academy of Motion Picture Arts and Sciences, in Beverly Hills:

> I am going to give it out today in the manner in which he would have wanted it. You have been accorded a great honor. You have a job to do, you stand up, walk to the front of the room and without grief or weeping deliver loudly, clearly, short and straight to the salient points the best tribute in oratory possible from the heart of an allied professional, a creative brother and a fellow Canadian who loved this boy from the Donlands like we had the same blood.
>
> We salute first a patriot, who always professed and promoted the positive interests of the north, but who also welcomed warmly into his fold Americans and was

enfolded in turn by them. Like all on our planet they eventually came to see his indistillable value.

Some of us here are the fortunate, select few who witnessed the evolution of a man who claims two cities in his names, Johnny Chicago and Johnny Toronto.

The first name is for the trail he cut, blazed and for that swath he laid for us to glide down into Chi-town during that summer [of 1973].

Valri Bromfield and I were welcomed by a man who'd made it in America already. Charge account at Treasure Island, large Ford automobile, fully furnished apartment with color TV and anxious to share all his good fortune. Quietly and with great import he would impart the names of the teachers, the practitioners of old and new, who were part of this strange decades old free-associative, intellect driven vocation.

He was the relay runner passing the torch to us. Watch, Flaherty, Ramis, the Murrays, Tino and Jim. Del Close. Kaz. R. C. Lieberman, Joyce. Bernie, Jane. Listen and watch, he said.

It wasn't long before we were hearing from each of these very people in turn, Watch Candy! He took the school's techniques, the secrets, the skills and with these he constructed his own legacy of laughter.

The King of Second City, the Emperor of *SCTV*, with Flaherty as the acknowledged Fount, Candy, this magnetic, magnificent, magnanimous man, with his dressed-to-the-nines style and exquisite taste in life's finer things and people who revived and co-owned the Sneak Joynt back of the Old Town Ale House during the summer of '79 and was a strut in our creative triad on the *Blues Brothers* film, whose lunches, dinners, and private soirees around North and Wells became the focus of the days and nights in what was then our very own time in Old Chicago.

Johnny Toronto. Beloved by his own and by other nations. I personally witnessed an arena of seventy-thousand of his people rise to their feet and cheer him as he did nothing more than enter and walk in triumph along the forum's perimeter.

There's a word in our language we don't hear much anymore, but it applies to Candy, the word is GRAND. He was a grand man. The bold, sweeping, all embracing story of this man rivals that of Edward Arnold in the classic movie *Come and Get It*. John Franklin Candy. Devoted son, brother, nephew, altar boy, student, salesman, stage, radio, and television writer and performer, world-famous comedy ambassador, farce and dramatic actor, international feature-film star, director, businessman, connoisseur, percussionist, art collector, charitable benefactor, husband, father and the sweetest, most generous person ever known to me. I loved him from the instant I laid eyes on his first impeccable suit and will never stop.

His consideration for humankind will be recalled as a genuine current in his character and of this above all we should take note. He had time for everyone from Princesses up through to those he respected the most, the wage-earning working man. John was against the war and for the soldiers.

His respect for them resulted in many cases where he just couldn't say no. On the other hand this was a man who though he often gave them their minutes' due, did not brook sycophants nor suffer the darker fools too long. In the material matters of compensation and worth you can be sure that as he traded his talent on the block in this town, no one took creative advantage of the proprietor of Frostbacks without paying hefty premiums to make up for anything he perceived as a personal loss of convictions and principle. Usually all end up indebted to him for spinning their straw into gold. We always got much more than we paid for.

This is no meagre life we reflect on today. This is as full a life as any human can live. Joy, emotional abundance of spirit, infectious rage, a tinge of Lugosi-like madness, with his bottom reverse vampire teeth and all. A titan of a gentle, golden man.

Magnificent of visage, eyes and frame. Let none be deceived by what the less enlightened would label as girth for there are many witnesses to the clamping power of his mitts and the steel in his forearms, the delicate Oriental use of mass in nimbly repelling an oncoming physical opponent, the quickness and lightness of foot and leg. Challenge him and you will be hurled away like a toy.

For as much as his affectionate softness, warmth and sweetness endures so should recollections of his nighthawk wild boy streak remain with us, from howling, fist-hammering, good-drinking, song-singing, dawn-seeing nights apast when no one wanted to leave the room until he went home. Fun or else. Johnny Volcano.

> As seen from his side we here present are but seconds behind him as his spirit begins to thrill in the ecstatic journey through the afterplanes.
>
> Some meta-scientists say the soul weighs .00038 ounces, an actual substance made up of the person's pure spiritual essence which ultimately travels to the light of all nature's origin. For Candy, we round it off to .00040 and postulate that given his incredible breadth of heart, his positive contribution to the conscious universe plus his professionalism and commitment to duty we can assume that his essence will soon be tapped for reassignment.
>
> My bonded brother Centurion and Companion of the Road, sharer of my young dreams, I hail your work, your life, I cherish the love you poured on us, I pray for richness in your journey beyond, I vow to stand allied and protect Rose, your Mom, your family and to embrace and enjoy the living incarnations of you in Chris and Jennifer. I salute you and in many non-domestic regards, I envy your peace.

Aykroyd then pounded his chest like a Roman centurion before a brief recitation of "O Canada," which he referred to as one of Candy's favourite songs.

O'Hara was particularly touched by the centurion bit, a "call back" to a favourite Second City scene that Aykroyd and Candy had performed at the Old Fire Hall.

"There was this blackout that he always did," says O'Hara. "It was about an actor doing a play about Caesar, and Danny's character would say, 'Have you heard from Caesar?' John and Danny used to do this thing where they'd pound their chests and then put their arms out, I guess which is an old Roman soldier thing to do. So [at the funeral] I just smiled thinking of how he and John got so many laughs from that in so many years on these blackouts. I just remember crying and laughing, laughing and crying. Danny was so great that day."

Dave Thomas recalls Jim Belushi clutching his hand so tightly for the duration of the service that he began to feel uncomfortable. Within the space of twelve years since losing his brother John, Belushi was back in a church listening once again to Aykroyd mourning a fallen brother. "I knew he was grieving for both of them," says Thomas. "Danny's speech was so elegant and beautifully written, and honestly one of the most magnificent things I've ever seen. It did so many things so well and it was Danny at his absolute best, saluting his friend. It was hopeful. It was sad. It was appreciative. It was celebratory."

At noon, a procession of roughly fifty cars began the ten-mile drive south from Brentwood to Candy's final resting place at Holy Cross Cemetery in Culver City.

"We all left Brentwood down Sunset Boulevard to get on the 405," says Crane. "This freeway is typically bumper to bumper with cars at lunchtime in LA, so we had a motorcycle escort from the LAPD and the California Highway Patrol once we got to the 405 on-ramp."

In an effort to limit the number of cars on the notoriously congested 405 freeway, guests were invited to share their cars. Tom Hanks, riding with Martin Short and his wife Nancy Dolman, noticed something odd about the freeway traffic on that day; there wasn't any.

"I remember Tom just said, 'Oh my god, look,'" says Short, "and I think he was the first to notice that they had closed the 405.

We had just been thinking 'Wow, there's no traffic,' but then you looked at all the on-ramps and saw all the cops are standing there. They had closed one of the busiest freeways in the world for John. I am sure that order came from someone up above, at least in the police department; they all loved John Candy, as did every one of us."

Hanks had witnessed the rapport Candy had enjoyed with rank-and-file law enforcement officers, who treated Candy like one of their own. "When you make a movie," says Hanks, "you've got to have cops that hold traffic, and so-called rent-a-cops that run security. John had always been so convivial with them while he was filming on location in and around Los Angeles, and he'd talk with them about their motorcycles."

According to Hanks, as the omnipresent helicopters of Los Angeles TV news would famously do during O. J. Simpson's notorious "Bronco chase" a mere three months later, airborne cameras were now trained on the Candy motorcade. On this occasion, however, the notoriously invasive choppers hovered at a respectful distance, as the line of black cars made their way down a wide-open 405 at thirty-five miles an hour with their headlights on.

In another car, Thomas and Aykroyd were amazed, but not surprised, by the show of support from the law enforcement community. It seemed a token of their respect, in appreciation of the humanity Candy had brought to roles like the lovesick Chicago cop Danny Muldoon in *Only the Lonely*, the hapless LA security guard Frank Dooley in *Armed and Dangerous*, and Burton Mercer, the Orange Whip–loving parole officer from *The Blues Brothers*.

After the formalities at Holy Cross, Bret Gallagher remembers that some of the mourners returned to Saint Martin's for a small reception with sandwiches and refreshments.

"Then we took a bunch of people back to the office at Frostbacks," says Gallagher. "We had a few drinks at the big bar until about seven or eight. Then everyone left and it was just me and Bob [Crane] in the office. The place was a mess, but we were still working on some of John's unfinished business. I looked at a picture of John and thought, 'We're still taking care of you, man. We got you.' Being in that office without him was so bizarre."

The physical reminders of Candy were strewn all over Frostbacks, in bits of wardrobe, stacks of scripts, photos on the wall, his headphones hung up in the empty recording studio, and the steamer trunk from *Planes, Trains and Automobiles* by his massive desk. The only thing missing was Candy.

"It was like John had just gotten up and left everything the way it was. But he was not coming back; a light had been extinguished in the world. A lot of things were out of our hands now, because now all the lawyers and all that stuff would kick into high gear."

Even later, into the wee hours, Martin Short and Nancy Dolman invited a few of their inner circle back to their home in Pacific Palisades for what Short refers to as "a proper Irish wake," with Aykroyd playing bartender (a call back to his early days at the 505 club) and serving up Candy's favourite cocktail, rum and Coke.

"We played videos of John all night," says Short, "and it was a great, great healing thing to do with that group."

• • •

IF HOLLYWOOD HAD BEEN rocked by Candy's death, his hometown was positively bereft, and there was no question that a supplemental Toronto memorial was essential for the city to grieve its favourite son. The service, held on March 18 at Saint Basil's Church on Saint Joseph Street, was attended by an estimated 650 mourners and televised by the CBC in a manner befitting a fallen prime minister. Candy's brother, Jim, and his mother, Evangeline, were escorted to Saint Basil's by Toronto Metropolitan Police Chief William McCormack. Among those in attendance were many of the same friends and family who had witnessed the Candys' wedding in the same church fifteen years earlier. (Short and Dolman had also been wed there the following year.) Among the notable mourners on hand were Catherine, Mary Margaret and Marcus O'Hara, filmmaker Norman Jewison, Joe Flaherty, Jayne Eastwood, various current Second City cast, and a contingent from the Toronto Argonauts. Rob Salem remembers a sea of devasted faces among the mourners in the church.

"John left this large hole," says Salem, "so his absence was felt because he'd been such a public figure in Toronto and in Queensville, where he would go down the street, as famous as he was, and just be a local boy who made good. These people, from many generations, just wanted to tell him how much joy he'd given them."

Mary Margaret O'Hara's heart-rending performance of an original song called "Dark Dear Heart" brought tears to the eyes of the assembled mourners even before her sister Catherine stepped up to the podium. Catherine O'Hara had agonized over what to say at the service, given what she felt was an enormous responsibility to strike the perfect note of gravitas while remembering how the comic touches in Aykroyd's eulogy had so eased the burden of grief during the previous week's memorial in Brentwood. "I guess anybody doing a eulogy, especially for someone who was so loved by so many, you want to speak for everyone," says O'Hara. "But then I realized you just can't. I could only speak from my own heart and mind about the John I knew and loved. And with his mom there, along with his brother and the kids and Rose, you could do no wrong just talking about how much you loved John. You know, I've seen many people over the years cry when you mention John. Like the cab driver in Toronto who said, 'Did you work with John?' and just started crying, talking about John Candy. If they'd met him, they would not be disappointed."

O'Hara's remarks included proudly bragging about her friend John's police escort on the 405 freeway and Aykroyd's sermon in Brentwood. She praised Candy as a "humble, sensitive man, full of faith, who seemed forever grateful for his gifts and his time on this Earth."

Turning to Evangeline Candy in the front row, O'Hara told her, "I don't know what you did to be blessed with such a wonderful son. But all of us thank you for it. And for him."

But the main message of her eulogy was that "John Candy's life had meaning."

"John had principles," O'Hara said; "he lived by them, he worked by them. He set a good example in so many ways. He was a protector. He cared. If he felt you'd been wronged in any way, he'd risk everything to make it right. To make you know you were worth something too. In a business that indulges the weaker souls, where the insecure lend others' words far too much meaning, John was a humble, sensitive man, full of faith, who seemed forever grateful for his gifts, and his time on this Earth. Thank you, John."

After the Saint Basil's service, Marcus O'Hara hosted an impromptu wake at his hipster poolhall, the Squeeze Club, on Queen Street West, featuring a contingent that included many friends from both the 1063 Avenue Road and Old Fire Hall days. Once again, many a rum and Coke was raised in Candy's honour, late into the evening.

In the following days, Neil McNeil Catholic High School would rename part of its facility The John Candy Visual Arts Studio, and on April 4, the school held a special John Candy Memorial Mass at the nearby Saint John's Roman Catholic Church. It was attended by Evangeline and Jim Candy and Candy's childhood friend Jonathan O'Mara, along with Flaherty, Levy, and the O'Hara sisters. The *Toronto Star* published an open letter from O'Mara in which he spoke of the road trips and other meaningful events from their time together at McNeil.

"Your legacy," O'Mara wrote, "is not only your huge volume of work, but it is also your children, your friends, and the effect you have had and will continue to have on millions of people. You have given the world a large measure of happiness and that is no small thing. I will miss you terribly, but I will never forget you. And, by the way, John, say hello to Elvis for me, will you? Sleep well my friend. God bless, Jonathan O'Mara."

For those left behind in the enormous void of his loss, there would be no more late-night calls from John Candy and no more dispatches from the planes, trains, and movie trailers of his life in Hollywood. Yet in many ways, the end of John Candy's natural life was just the beginning of an enduring legacy. The big man was gone, but in the days, months, and decades to come, his legend would only grow.

Thirty-One

The Legacy

Eugene Levy had been among the Los Angeles mourners who were amazed by the miracle on the 405. Later, in public remarks for the Canadian Press, he tried to express his deep sense of loss. By his own math, Levy had worked with Candy in more films than anyone in or outside the Second City organization. He had grown to love him like a brother and considered Candy to be "one of the most gifted comedic actors that honestly has ever been in the business," who was "underrated" as an actor.

"We were very, very close friends," Levy told the CP's Victoria Ahearn, going on to describe Candy as "a lovely man" who cared deeply about people. "It always seems like John is still around. That's how much of an impact he made on your life, you know? You're still kind of waiting for a phone call."

John Candy's legacy was not greatly enhanced by the three projects that were posthumously released over the coming year. *Hostage for a Day* debuted on Fox Television on Monday, April 25,

1994, to little or no fanfare, and when *Wagons East* rode into the cinemas for its dismal first weekend on August 26, it received a critical drubbing, with Roger Ebert writing that "the loss of John Candy is made all the more poignant because *Wagons East*! (sic) is the last film he completed. It is possible he never appeared in a worse one." *Los Angeles Times* reviewer Chris Willman titled his scathing review "Snoozing Saddles," but nonetheless held out hope for the long-delayed release of *Canadian Bacon* as one of the "last chances for fearless Candy fans."

Sadly, *Canadian Bacon* failed to sizzle when it was finally released on September 22, 1995, faring no better with critics or audiences. The film that had taken Michael Moore and his partners four years to get to the screen was gone after a few miserable weeks, earning back less than $180,000 of the $11 million he had raised to make it. While Moore would thereafter stick to documentaries, he dedicated his lone comedy film in part to "Johnny LaRue—thanks to you, we got our crane shot," leaving no doubt as to how much he owed Candy for supporting his project when the major studios wouldn't.

"He backed me every time," Moore later told *Film Threat*'s Dominic Griffin. "Once he died, I didn't have that support. I went on my own to make sure the film we wanted to make would get out there."

But while the lukewarm to hostile critical reactions to Candy's parting trio of films stamped an anticlimactic asterisk on an otherwise illustrious career, hindsight has swivelled the spotlight toward the best work of his canon, elevating his SCTV work and his winning roles in *Uncle Buck*; *Planes, Trains and Automobiles*; *Cool Runnings*; and even *Spaceballs* to classic status. Sadly, the new and old Candy fans of today can only speculate on what might have been if he had been given just a little more time to complete some of the projects he had on the back burner. Would his portrayal of Ignatius J. Reilly in the "unfilmable" *Confederacy of Dunces* have made good on Oliver Stone's faith in his dramatic abilities? Would he have been the one actor to finally bring Mordecai Richler's similarly cursed *The Incomparable Atuk* to the screen? Would he have found a more dignified approach to a "Fatty" Arbuckle biopic? Carl Reiner never got to film his planned remake of *Last Holiday* with Candy in the lead role, and when Disney's *Pocahontas* finally made it to the screen in 1995, it was without Candy as the voice of Redfeather the turkey.

Among the first, and arguably least likely, tributes to Candy came from the alternative rock band Ween, whose 1994 album *Chocolate and Cheese* was "dedicated in loving memory to John Candy (1950–1994)." At the time the band explained that, after the much-publicized death of Nirvana's Kurt Cobain had dominated the alternative rock conversation that year, they felt compelled to give Candy the respect they felt he was due. Looking back on it now, Aaron Freeman, known professionally as Gene Ween, says that he and Mickey Melchiondo (Dean Ween) had particularly enjoyed Candy's work in *JFK*.

"Of course, I grew up loving Candy on SCTV and in all of his big star vehicle films," says Freeman, "but it was when I saw him in *JFK* that I truly came to appreciate the genius of the man. He was no longer the lovable buffoon we had grown to love but instead was downright menacing. When John Candy, in a perfect '60s suit and perfect '60s sunglasses, tells you that you are in too deep, you really ought to listen."

It took over a decade, but the Toronto Argonauts finally staged a large-scale tribute to Candy at the Rogers CFL Player

Awards ceremony, which became "The Grey Cup Memorial to John Candy," a blue-carpet event hosted by Dan Aykroyd at Roy Thomson Hall on November 22, 2007.

"It's been a long time in coming," Aykroyd told the *Regina Leader-Post*, "and it's just a great recognition of his massive talent [and] how significant he was, what he meant to this country, this province and to the world. We were indeed close friends and not many people in this new generation know that in addition to being an actor, a writer, an entrepreneur, a producer and a great philanthropist—he was a one-time owner of the Argonauts. So this is finally the recognition that he deserves."

Speaking at the time with Toronto weekly *Now* magazine, Rosemary Candy said that her late husband would have been humbled by the tribute, adding that "football was a love of his since early childhood. I know John's time with the Argos brought him some of his happiest memories, as did his time with Second City."

By then, Michael "Pinball" Clemons was the team's head coach. Clemons told *Now* that Candy had been "the biggest star on the team, but he never acted like it. The players were the stars to him. As a result, we felt more like entertainers than athletes."

Argonauts biographer Paul Woods notes that in the team's 150-year history, only one owner genuinely loved the team, and that was John Candy. "You know, he had always dreamed of being an Argo," says Woods, "and who knows? Had he not had that injury in high school, he might've ended up on the team. They should be making a John Candy Memorial Award, and frankly doing anything and everything they can to latch onto John Candy's name, because who wouldn't want to be attached to John Candy, right?"

Whether it was a savvy sixth sense for people-pleasing, or

just his own innate decency, Candy never lost what people refer to as "the common touch." Everyone who ever met him, or saw him on stages, movie screens, and televisions, loved him for it. Comedy historian Kliph Nesteroff says that even when Candy played an arrogant chancer like Johnny LaRue, he seemed to be in on the joke.

"Audiences can't relate to a guy who's acting superior to them," says Nesteroff, "because, deep down, we all feel like inadequate weaklings. Candy was highly relatable in the sense that he personally lacked arrogance, and his characters were never arrogant, and he never lost that self-effacing nature. Candy's characters put on a brave face and laugh it off, and when Candy smiled and laughed, you smiled and laughed. There was no antecedent to John Candy, and there hasn't been a true descendant since his passing."

In 1998, Candy was inducted into Canada's Walk of Fame and given a red-granite maple leaf star on King Street West in Toronto, which placed him in the illustrious company of stars Christopher Plummer (who headed the cast of one of Candy's first films, *The Silent Partner*), friend and filmmaker Norman Jewison, skating heroes Bobby Orr and Barbara Ann Scott, historian Pierre Berton, dancer Karen Kain, comedian Rich Little, race car driver Jacques Villeneuve, and music legends Glenn Gould, Anne Murray, Buffy Sainte-Marie, Gordon Lightfoot, and Bryan Adams. In May 2006, Candy became one of the first four entertainers—along with Lorne Greene, Fay Wray, and Mary Pickford—honoured by Canada Post with a stamp bearing their likeness as part of the "Canadians in Hollywood" series.

In 2019, Candy was the inaugural inductee into the East York Hall of Fame, and the following year, Toronto mayor John Tory officially proclaimed October 31 John Candy Day in Toronto, praising him on what would have been his seventieth birthday as "a Canadian treasure who brought great joy to so many through his humour, acting and contributions to the entertainment industry," and "a decent humble man" who brought pride to his hometown.

In the three decades since his passing, the flow of praise and remembrance has never abated from colleagues who worked with him, people who never met him, and generations of talented creators who continue to cite his work as a lodestar to their own creative journeys.

In her 2014 memoir, *Lady Parts*, Andrea Martin spoke of Candy's "deep vulnerability and authenticity" and remarked on just how well his name has travelled. "It didn't matter who you were or the status you had," Martin wrote. "John treated everyone the same. He was exactly as you would like to think he was. He was actually that guy. I'd see him with fans who had come up to him on the street and started acting out their favourite scenes with him, and he'd go along with anything. John was the first person I knew who had an entourage. There were always people in his dressing room, from all walks of life ... I'm still stopped by people, especially working-class guys, who ask me about *SCTV* and say how sad it is that John is no longer with us. Even those hulking guys let their guard down as tears fill their eyes, their grief over the death of John Candy, a man they never knew, overwhelming them ... There wasn't a cynical bone in his body ... He was not only capable of making you laugh, but he could also make you cry, which you'd know if you saw *Trains, Planes and Automobiles*. He was a singular actor and a heartbreaking clown, and the world still mourns his loss."

Catherine O'Hara echoes Martin's sentiments when speaking of the authenticity in many of Candy's characters. "When you're seeing John," says O'Hara, "you're always seeing the truth of what a lovely, open, kind, compassionate, good man he was, and how much he wanted to do for others. And I think there was just generosity, big-hearted generosity in everything he did, and you'd see that. His big heart comes across in everything."

Splash director Ron Howard says that he remains convinced that as Candy continued to evolve, he could have "knocked a serious role out of the park."

"Even though I only knew John professionally," says Howard, "he was the kind of guy where I felt like I really knew him through the work because he was just very open, and you felt like what you were seeing was the real guy. As he continued to gain confidence as a film actor, you could see more and more nuance in his quiet moments. He had this ability to recognize things like pride, ego, ignorance, and arrogance in the human psyche and align that with a kind of a vulnerability that was very winning."

Martin Short notes that even when a film suffered negative reviews, Candy's screen charisma and "that big open face people just loved" allowed him to walk away unscathed. "He was never the problem in anything," says Short, "he was just a wonderful actor and usually he was always the asset. Some people exude an aloofness, and other people exude an openness. There are certain performers through the years where it doesn't matter what they're in, or what they do, people just love them. And that was John."

In 2019, *Spaceballs* director Mel Brooks told writer Tracey J. Morgan he always appreciated how little he had to direct Candy when it came to performing the comedy. "There are a few guys in my life that could do that," said Brooks. "John Candy, Gene Wilder, and Rick Moranis ... Guys like that ... I would just say 'this is what the scene is about.'"

John Landis, who directed Candy in *The Blues Brothers*, uses the Yiddish word *haimish* when describing Candy's "warm, approachable, friendly, and sincere" demeanour. "John was a real actor and could basically do anything thrown at him," says Landis. "He could play really obnoxious people and you'd still like him, and like a lot of large funny men, such as 'Fatty' Arbuckle or Oliver Hardy or Jackie Gleason, he was extremely agile in the way that these large men were also really light on their feet."

Comedian and director Ben Stiller, himself the product of a great comedy legacy (Stiller and Meara), remembers being "pretty star-struck" when he met Candy, and says it is impossible to overstate how much he loved his work as an actor. "I started to watch SCTV with my sister Amy when I was about sixteen," says Stiller. "Candy was a big guy, but while he did physical comedy, the jokes didn't seem to have anything to do with his size. When he passed, I felt the shock personally even though I only met him that one time."

While Patton Oswalt never met Candy, the comedian and writer describes him as a bold and beautiful everyman, "like a cherub piloting a tank."

"Obviously, he could impersonate famous big guys like Orson Welles and all that," says Oswalt, "but he clearly was channelling everyday people from his hometown or from crappy jobs he had, and he saw real genuine comedy and pathos and humour in that."

When Norm Macdonald hosted the Canadian Screen Awards in Toronto on March 13, 2016, he suggested onstage that the awards be renamed "The Candys," an idea that was immediately popular with the general public and with screen awards chair Martin Katz. Katz told the *Toronto Star*'s Peter Howell that the nickname had resonance because it alluded to the word Canada "and John was obviously a giant both in film and in television both at home and abroad ... He changed the face of comedy forever, and I think this would be a fitting tribute."

At the event, Jennifer Candy asked *ET Canada*'s Cheryl Hickey, rhetorically, "What's not to love about the idea? It's always so nice to see how there is still so much love and respect for him."

In 2018, Candy's *SCTV* castmate Andrea Martin and *Whose Line Is It Anyway*? star Colin Mochrie became the inaugural recipients of the John Candy Award for Excellence at a ceremony in Ottawa that was attended by Candy's surviving family. Jen Candy told the Canadian Press that her father would likely have been thrilled that the award also promoted mental health awareness, a cause that had been near and dear to Candy, particularly in the final chapter of his life.

In more recent times Candy has continued to inspire contemporary stars such as Josh Gad, who first came to prominence in 2011 in the original Broadway cast of *The Book of Mormon* and admits that his approach to playing Elder Cunningham was "deeply inspired by a lot of John Candy's amazing roles onscreen."

"He had a gigantic influence on my childhood," says Gad. "Whatever he was in, whether it was *Uncle Buck*, *Home Alone*, or *The Great Outdoors*, there was always a performance that helped me to realize what I wanted to be as a performer. His performances were a big part of why I ultimately decided to go into this industry."

By 2022, the Toronto Second City had long since vacated the Old Fire Hall, but a part of it lives on in their current venue, a

28,700-square-foot facility located at One York Street. The venue features three performance stages, including the John Candy Box Theatre, a dedicated seventy-seat space for Second City comedy students that includes a portion of the original Old Fire Hall stage, where Candy took his own baby steps toward comedy greatness.

It was also the stage where Mike Myers learned his craft, having first heard about the Second City workshops from a tip Candy gave him at a backstage door. Myers says he sees Candy as a role model for all who practise the comedic arts today.

"In everything he did, we felt his John Candy–ness," says Myers. "Performing was an experience of getting out of his own way to get to his own self, and Second City trains you to do that and to get to your true self. Candy embodied Del Close's ideal of a theatre based on improvisation, which bypasses both the director and the playwright, and where you have to be in the moment. What makes Candy a uniquely Canadian artist is that we are often known for politeness, but there's also a toughness to the Canadian character as well, as evidenced in hockey, which has all of the grace of figure skating but all of the ferocity of football. His Second City training prepared him for movie acting, where Candy's face in close-up gave us an unfiltered sense of who he really was.

"It's funny, you know, his name was Candy and his films were like little confections that remain with us for years and years because he made a *connection* in these confections. You are happy to see him the second he appears on the screen. He was an everyman who continues to be popular because people can relate to him; they see themselves in him onscreen. Every character had a vulnerability. I have this theory that we as an audience are drawn to people who have a visible weakness, that vulnerability. Candy had the courage to show us his weakness. You can laugh at his characters, but as with Del Griffith, you should never mistake his kindness for weakness. And that contradiction is something that has always appealed to me."

To Dan Aykroyd, the quality of Candy's work will always live on, and he remains grateful that he was able to experience, first-hand, "the best of Candy." They had met before either of them was in show business, and shared time at Second City and the movies. Even in the early 1990s, sitting up in the Frostbacks office, the two were co-conspiring about projects that would never see the light of day.

"As collaborators with our different companies," says Aykroyd, "we were planning to do stuff. He had big appetites, but he was a big man, John, tall, and he had the frame, and he had the constitution to handle a big meal, and he was very strong. One night onstage at Second City, he picked Dave Thomas and I up like a pair of barrels, one over each shoulder, and spun us around and flung us against the wall. Candy had good comic chops, so I have no doubt he would've become a great actor.

"When he let people into his life and his heart, he let people *know* him, and he was universally beloved among his collaborators and then throughout the breadth of the fans worldwide, but everyone who worked with him and knew him loved him dearly. He wanted you to have fun, and he was a bon vivant, he loved life, but he was also Johnny LaRue minus the moral turpitude that the character had. He was just a joy and so funny and so talented, and one of our comrades-in-arms from that generation."

Acknowledgements

Paul Myers would like to thank the following for graciously agreeing to be interviewed for this book: Andrew Alexander, Dan Aykroyd, James Belushi, Matthew Broderick, Valri Bromfield, Luciano Casimiri, Chevy Chase, Sally Cochrane, Chris Columbus, Robert Crane Jr., Richard Crouse, Stephen DeNure, Howard Deutch, Robin Duke, Jayne Eastwood, Laurie Feig, Joe Flaherty (RIP), Paul Flaherty, Aaron Freeman (Gene Ween), Josh Gad, Bret Gallagher, Bobcat Goldthwait, Tarquin Gotch, Elliott Gould, Brian Grazer, Kathryn Greenwood, Allan Guttman, Juul Haalmeyer, Tom Hanks, Ron Howard, James Hughes, David Johnston, David Kamp, Larry Karaszewski, John Landis, Richard Lewis (RIP), Steve Martin, Kevin McDonald, John C. McGinley, Deb McGrath, Michael McKean, Tracey J. Morgan, Terry David Mulligan, Joel Murray, Mike Myers, Briane Nasimok, Kliph Nesteroff, Catherine O'Hara, Jonathan O'Mara, Patton Oswalt, Prairie Prince, Ivan Reitman (RIP), Rob Salem, Martin Short, Michael Short, David Steinberg, Ziggy Steinberg,

Ben Stiller, Dave Thomas, Ian Thomas, Doug Thompson, Robyn Todd, George Wendt, Susan Whitall, Patrick Whitley, Rita Wilson, and Paul Woods.

Thank you also to Douglas Richmond at Anansi and David Johnston at Factotum for making this book happen, and to Jody Beth LaFosse for your superb transcription of hours and hours of often meandering (on my part) interviews. Special thanks to Tracey J. Morgan, James Hughes, Jason Bailey, Judd Apatow, Susan Whitall, Paul Woods, and David Kamp for your scholarship, and for guiding me to sources and suggesting others. Thanks to Scott Dobson for the Second City background. Thanks also to my brothers Peter and Mike, for our built-in childhood symposium on the history and appreciation of the art of comedy, which continues to this day.

Sources

Books

Judd Apatow, *Sicker in the Head: More Conversations About Life and Comedy* (Random House, 2022).

Mel Brooks, *All About Me!: My Remarkable Life in Show Business* (Ballantine, 2021).

Nick de Semlyen, *Wild and Crazy Guys: How the Comedy Mavericks of the '80s Changed Hollywood Forever* (Crown Archetype, 2019).

Kirk Honeycutt, *John Hughes: A Life in Film* (Race Point, 2015).

Martin Knelman, *Laughing on the Outside: The Life of John Candy* (Penguin Books Canada, 1996).

Andrea Martin, *Andrea Martin's Lady Parts* (Harper Collins, 2014).

Bruce McNall, *Fun While It Lasted: My Rise and Fall in the Land of Fame and Fortune* (Hyperion, 2003).

Paul Mooney, *Black Is the New White* (Gallery, 2009).

Tracey J. Morgan, *Searching for Candy: John Candy: A Biography* (self-published, 2019).

Sheldon Patinkin, *The Second City: Backstage at the World's Greatest Comedy Theater* (Sourcebooks, 2000).

Martin Short, with David Kamp, *I Must Say: My Life as a Humble Comedy Legend* (Harper Collins, 2014).

Dave Thomas, with Robert Crane and Susan Carney, *SCTV: Behind the Scenes* (McClelland and Stewart, 1996).

Sam Wasson, *Improv Nation: How We Made a Great American Art* (Houghton Mifflin Harcourt, 2017).

Paul Woods, *Year of the Rocket: John Candy, Wayne Gretzky, a Crooked Tycoon, and the Craziest Season in Football History* (Sutherland House Books, 2021).

Articles

Victoria Ahearn, "'Still Very Loved': Jen Candy, Chris Candy and Others Remembering John Candy," The Canadian Press, March 3, 2019.

Dan Aykroyd, "Eulogy for a Golden Man," transcribed from original document displayed at the Margaret Herrick Museum (AMPAS), Beverly Hills, CA.

Dan Aykroyd, "On a Mission from John," *Ottawa Citizen*, August 14, 1991.

Jason Bailey, "A Forgotten Chapter in the Rowdy History of Bad-Movie Lovers," *Vulture*, November 24, 2022.

Jason Bailey, "*Planes, Trains and Automobiles* at 35: An Oral History of One of the Most Beloved Road Movies Ever Made," *Vanity Fair*, November 22, 2022.

Kathryn Baker, "HBO Live from Montreal Comedy Festival," The Associated Press, July 19, 1988.

James Barber, "6 Amazing Facts About the Army Comedy 'Stripes,'" Military.com, February 14, 2022.

James Bates and Lisa Dillman, "McNall to Sell CFL's Argonauts," *Los Angeles Times*, May 5, 1994.

Andy Breckman, "Anatomy of a Bomb: *Hot to Trot*," WFMU website.

Duane Byrge, "*Spaceballs* (review)," *The Hollywood Reporter*, June 22, 1987.

Simon Brew, "*Bartholomew vs Neff*: The Lost John Candy–Sylvester Stallone Comedy," *Film Stories*, May 15, 2020.

Joshua Chong, "The Second City to Unveil New Home in Toronto," *Toronto Star*, October 31, 2022.

Lawrence Christon, "A Python in Hermosa Beach: And Now for Something Completely Warmed Over," *Los Angeles Times*, July 29, 1987.

Robert Crane Jr., "John Candy Goes Hollywood," *Penthouse*, March 1984.

Robert Crane Jr., "Sweetmeat," *Oui*, August 1982.

Robert Crane Jr., "20 Questions: John Candy," *Playboy*, August 1989.

Kieran Culkin, "Kieran Culkin Remembering John Candy on the *Home Alone* Set Is Incredibly Sweet," *Esquire*, March 27, 2023.

Logan Culwell-Block, "Frank Oz Reveals Who Ad-Libbed and Who Stuck to the Script When Filming *Little Shop of Horrors*," Playbill .com, October 19, 2017.

Mark Di Franco, "Just for Laughs Festival Takes the Stage," *Fringe Arts*, May 3, 2017.

Jason Diamond, "Why *Planes, Trains and Automobiles* Is the Ultimate Thanksgiving Movie," *Rolling Stone*, November 23, 2019.

Lisa Dillman, "McNall Gets 70 Months in Prison for Fraud," *Los Angeles Times*, January 10, 1997.

Cutler Durkee, "John Candy Surfaces in the Big Pond," *People Weekly*, July 13, 1984.

Roger Ebert, "*Cool Runnings* (review)," *Chicago Sun-Times*, October 1, 1993.

Roger Ebert, "*Planes, Trains and Automobiles* (review)," RogerEbert.com, November 12, 2000.

Roger Ebert, "*Spaceballs* (review)," *Chicago Sun-Times*, June 24, 1987.

Roger Ebert, "*Splash* (review)," *Chicago Sun-Times*, January 1, 1984.

Roger Ebert, "*Uncle Buck* (review)," *Chicago Sun-Times*, August 16, 1989.

Roger Ebert, "*Wagons East!* (review)," *Chicago Sun-Times*, August 26, 1994.

James Endrst, "Real-Life Sadness Behind Fox's Comic 'Hostage,'" *Hartford Courant*, April 22, 1994.

Ian Freer, "*Splash* (review)," *Empire*, September 22, 2006.

"Great One Avoids Great Fall," *The Washington Post*, September 1, 1994.

Patrick Goldstein, "John Candy's Ready to Take Control," *Los Angeles Times*, August 28, 1986.

Dominic Griffin, "Moore the Merrier," *Film Threat*, December 1995.

Jason Guerrasio, "*Home Alone* at 30," *The Insider*, December 24, 2020.

Charles Hallman, "Bill Murray Reflects on His Storied Career," *Minnesota Spokesman Recorder*, October 1, 2016.

David Handelman, "Candy Goes to Harvard," *Vanity Fair*, February 1985.

Samantha Highfill, "*Cool Runnings*: An Oral History," *Entertainment Weekly*, February 9, 2018.

"Highlights of a Meeting with Paramount Studios, re: *Summer Rentals* [*sic*], Feb. 12, 1985," The Margaret Herrick Library (AMPAS).

Hal Hinson, "*Spaceballs* (review)," *The Washington Post*, June 24, 1987.

Hal Hinson, "*The Great Outdoors* (review)," *The Washington Post*, June 17, 1988.

Mike Hogan, "Sold: The Birth of the McNall, Candy, and Gretzky Era," Argonauts.ca, February 22, 2021.

Stephen Holden, "Starring John Candy and Various Crude Jokes" (*Wagons East* review), *The New York Times*, August 26, 1994.

James Hughes, "Holy Cow, *Home Alone* Is 25!," *Chicago Magazine*, November 10, 2015.

James Hughes, "John Hughes's Day Off," *Grantland*, May 1, 2013.

John Hughes, "Vacation '58," *National Lampoon*, 1979, republished in *Zoetrope: All-Story*, 2008.

Jessica Dee Humphreys, "John Candy Was Exactly Who Everybody Hoped He Was," *Toronto Star*, January 31, 2021.

"John Candy: 'Your Character Is Formed Here ...,'" *Spiritan*, May 2008.

"John Candy Finally Gets His Grey Cup," *Now* (Toronto), November 22, 2007.

"John Candy Laid to Rest," *Calgary Herald*, March 10, 1994.

Pauline Kael, "*Splash* (review)," *The New Yorker*, March 1984.

David Kamp, "Sweet Bard of Youth," *Vanity Fair*, February 10, 2010.

James Kaplan, "Stay Up Late," *The New Yorker*, January 16, 1989.

Dave Kehr, "John Candy Is Back in a Role Just His Size," *Chicago Tribune*, August 16, 1989.

John T. D. Keyes, "Margaret Trudeau Tries TV Comedy," *TV Guide*, September 27, 1980.

Jordan King, "Director Frank Oz Discusses 'Little Shop of Horrors' 35 Years On," *Filmhounds*, December 19, 2021.

Scott King, "Eugene Levy on Nissan Super Bowl Commercial, 'Schitt's Creek,' and More," *Forbes*, February 10, 2022.

Gayle MacDonald, "Duking it out in Canadian drama," *The Globe and Mail*, October 8, 2003.

Janet Maslin, "Country Life for Aykroyd and Candy" (review of *The Great Outdoors*), *The New York Times*, June 17, 1988.

Janet Maslin, "*Heavy Metal*, Adult Cartoon," *The New York Times*, August 7, 1981.

Janet Maslin, "John Candy in 'Berserk'" (review of *Going Berserk*), *The New York Times*, October 29, 1983.

Janet Maslin, "Mickey Plays the Palace, and Rescuers Go Walkabout" (incl. review of *The Rescuers Down Under*), *The New York Times*, November 16, 1990.

Janet Maslin, "Missteps of a Gumshoe: 'Who's Harry Crumb?' (review)," *The New York Times*, February 3, 1989.

Janet Maslin, "'Splash,' a Mermaid's Love (review)," *The New York Times*, March 9, 1984.

Alison Mayes, "Calgarians Remember Candy with Affection," *Calgary Herald*, March 5, 1994.

Patrick McGilligan, "*Playgirl*'s Seventh Annual 10 Sexiest Men," *Playgirl*, September 1985.

Julie Miller, "*Uncle Buck* Stars Remember John Candy: 'He Was Just That Guy You Wanted Him to Be,'" *Vanity Fair*, June 14, 2016.

Karen Murray, "Candy Too Big for Genies," *Daily Variety*, November 18, 1992.

Jonathan O'Mara, "I Remember John," *Toronto Star*, April 6, 1994.

Dylan Parker, "The True Origin of John Candy's *Cool Runnings*," *The Things*, February 8, 2021.

Ryan Parker, "John Candy Remembered: His Children Share New Stories About Their Late Father on the Eve of His Birthday," *The Hollywood Reporter*, October 24, 2016.

Steve Persall, "The Heat Is On!," *Tampa Bay Times*, May 26, 1995.

Zachary Pincus-Roth, "They All Starred in 'Godspell': Then They Became Comedy Legends," *The Washington Post*, May 19, 2022.

Bill Pullman, "The First Time a Fellow Actor Had My Back," *The New York Times*, July 25, 2017.

Nathan Rabin, "Control Nathan Rabin 4.0 #165 *Brewster's Millions* (1985)," *Nathan Rabin's Happy Place*, January 20, 2021.

Nathan Rabin, "This Looks Terrible!: *Who's Harry Crumb?* (1989)," *Nathan Rabin's Happy Place*, April 6, 2020.

Don Redmond, "When the Late John Candy Came to Niagara Falls for His Final Film," *In Niagara*, April 24, 2023.

Rob Salem, "John Candy Feature," unpublished, November 1980.

Frank Sanello, "*Only the Lonely*: John Candy Interview," *Empire*, October 1991.

Sandy Schaefer, "*Uncle Buck* Was a Playground for John Candy and the Cast," Slashfilm.com, May 16, 2022.

Karen S. Schneider, Joseph Harves, Natasha Stoynoff, Fannie Weinstein, and Vicki Sheff-Cahan, "Exit Laughing," *People*, March 21, 1994.

Shauna Snow, "Stars Say Goodbye," *Los Angeles Times*, March 10, 1994.

Susan Swan, "Cashing In," *Marquee Magazine*, April/May 1985.

Ben Trivett, "*Cool Runnings* Cast Reunites 30 Years Later to Reflect on Movie, Cheer on Jamaican Bobsledders," *People*, February 17, 2022.

Brian VanHooker, "An Oral History of 'Camp Candy,' John Candy's Saturday Morning Cartoon," Cracked.com, December 27, 2022.

Courtney Wagner, "Aykroyd pays tribute to Candy," *Regina Leader-Post*, November 23, 2007

Rachel West, "The Academy Awards Has the 'Oscar,' Now the Canadian Screen Awards Has the 'Candy,'" ETCanada.com, March 17, 2016.

Susan Whitall, "*SCTV* Takes Off, Eh? (Thank You Canada)," *Creem*, March 1982.

Chris Willman, "Movie Review: 'Wagons East!'—Candy's Final Film—Just Pokes Along," *Los Angeles Times*, August 26, 1994.

Jeff Wilson, "Last Rites for Comic Actor John Candy," The Associated Press, March 9, 1994.

Amy Kuperinsky, "Macaulay Culkin talks *Home Alone*, Joe Pesci, Fallout and what he really thinks of that sequel," NJ Advance Media for NJ.com, December 15, 2024.

Variety Staff, "*Nothing But Trouble* (review)," *Variety*, December 30, 1990.

Video/Broadcast

"*Camp Candy*—A Look Back at John Candy's Saturday Morning Show," video by Joe Ramoni, Hats Off Entertainment, YouTube, May 22, 2021.

"Chris Candy and Jennifer Candy," interviewed by Carol Off, *As It Happens*, CBC Radio, October 31, 2016.

"Brendan Fraser," *Fly On the Wall with Dana Carvey and David Spade* podcast, January 18, 2023.

"Colin Hanks," *Conan O'Brien Needs a Friend* podcast, October 30, 2022.

"Eugene Levy," interviewed by Jennifer Candy, *Couch Candy with Jennifer Candy*, YouTube, February 25, 2015.

"Jean Louisa Kelly: Anything Can Happen," interviewed by Marc Tumminelli, *Little Me* podcast, January 5, 2023.

"John Candy," interviewed by Brian Linehan, *City Lights*, syndicated, 1986.

"John Candy," interviewed by Brian Linehan, *City Lights*, syndicated, 1989.

"John Candy," *Later with Bob Costas*, NBC TV, August 17, 1989.

"John Candy," *Morningside with Peter Gzowski*, CBC Radio, February 2, 1991.

"John Candy: Everybody's Uncle Buck; A Docu-Mini," video by Joe Ramoni, Hats Off Entertainment, YouTube, April 19, 2020.

"John Candy: Comic Spirit," MGM/UA Home Entertainment, 2005.

"The Making of *Spaceballs*," MGM/UA Home Video, 1987.

"John Candy," interviewed by Charles Gibson, *Good Morning America*, ABC TV, March 23, 1989.

"John Candy's Stunt Man Bob Elmore," *The Valley Indy* podcast with Eugene Driscoll, August 23, 2021.

Late Night with David Letterman, NBC TV, February 4, 1982; December 29, 1982; August 18, 1983; February 23, 1984; February 26, 1985; August 1, 1985; August 13, 1986.

Sandie Rinaldo, video report in Aurora, Ontario, on the set of *Hostage for a Day*—CTV News feature, 1993.

"The Lost Version of *Uncle Buck*," video by Joe Ramoni, Hats Off Entertainment, YouTube, January 4, 2021.

"The Unknown History of John Candy and the CFL's Ill-Fated Expansion into the US," CBC Sports, December 2022.

To John with Love: A Tribute to John Candy, CBC TV program with various interviews, debut air date, July 17, 1995.

"*Uncle Buck:* Behind the Scenes," Universal Pictures EPK, August 1989.

"Laurie Metcalf Remembers Her Hilarious Dance with John Candy on *Uncle Buck*," *Chicago Today*, NBC5 Chicago, May 8, 2020.

"We Need to Talk about How Weird 'Nothing but Trouble' Is," Meg Shields, Film School Rejects, YouTube, September 21, 2022.

"Bill Murray," *The Tonight Show Starring Jimmy Fallon*, NBC TV, March 15, 2024.

"Maureen O'Hara," *The Late Late Show with Tom Snyder*, CBS TV, December 24, 1996.

"John Candy and Maureen O'Hara, Shirley Horn, Jim Valvano," *The Tonight Show Starring Johnny Carson*, NBC TV, May 17, 1991.

Index

FILMS AND TV SHOWS

PAUL MYERS is a Canadian writer and musician living in Berkeley, California. His previous books include *The Kids in the Hall: One Dumb Guy*, which was the source for the Canadian Screen Award–winning documentary *The Kids in the Hall: Comedy Punks* from Amazon Studios, on which he served as executive producer; the critically acclaimed *A Wizard a True Star: Todd Rundgren in the Studio*; *It Ain't Easy: Long John Baldry and the Birth of the British Blues*; and *Barenaked Ladies: Public Stunts, Private Stories*.